"Valery Ponomarev's story is electrifying and inspiring. Most of all, it's living proof that dedication to truth and beauty can and must triumph over artificially imposed impediments."

**Bob Bernotas** (Jazz journalist, author, and radio host)

"I thought I knew this man -- a great friend and colleague with whom I've often toured over the past 15 or so years -- pretty well, but after reading this memoire, my eyes were really opened! Fascinating! Valery Ponomarev's skill with storytelling nearly matches his prowess with the trumpet, and the content of his remarkable stories -- and of course his outstanding playing -- is rich, intelligent, humorous, and naturally, always swinging. Enjoy this book, then go listen to his music!"-

**Don Braden**
Jazz Musician/Composer/EducatorMusic Director, Wachovia Jazz
For Teens, the Litchfield Jazz Camp
Visiting Professor, Prins Claus Conservatoire

...I learned of the people's of the USSR passionate love of jazz brought to them by the Voice of America's jazz radio programs hosted by the inimitable Willis Conover. What would their impressions be, thought I? My answer came in Valery Ponomarev's wonderful book "On the Flip Side of Sound". Written with the same zest and inventiveness that Valery brings to his trumpet solos, this is an amazing saga of a musician's journey, marvelous adventures and unbelievable dream. As Valery's feet are firmly planted in both America and Russia, he brings the fabric and intricacies of both societies into sharp focus.

**Maria Ciliberti**
Retired VOA Russian-language broadcaster
Special Assistant, VOA USSR Division
Co-host of VOA jazz program "Conversations with Conover"
Coordinator, Worldwide VOA Listeners' Clubs

Finally, the world gets to read Valery Ponomarev's story! The main points are that in addition to being a fine trumpet player, Valery is a skilled storyteller and that his story never fails to enchant, inform and inspire my students and that now the world will get to hear it.

*Nina d'Alessandro* (Professor, Faculty of Arts and Science, New York University)

My old friend Valery Ponomarev is the only non-American trumpeter that I know to fill the (big) shoes left by the likes of Clifford Brown, Kenny Durham, Freddie Hubbard, Lee Morgan and Donald Byrd in Art Blakey's legendary Jazz Messengers. Like Miles Davis, Artie Shaw, Camille Saint Sns, Richard Sudhalter, Nicolas Slonimsky, Oscar Peterson and a few others,"Paramon" as his Russian peers affectionately call him belongs to that select group of musicians who also possess the ability to communicate through the written word. In this book he tells us, with humor and wisdom, about his interesting life and career.

*Paquito D'Rivera*

It's a fascinating, and unique story. I have had the privilege of producing seven of Valery's recordings since 1985. Not only is he a great trumpet player and composer, but also an inspirational bandleader who gets the very best out of anyone who plays with him. Just listen to Joe Henderson on his Profile CD, and you will see what I mean.

*Dr. Mark Feldman* (Reservoir Music.)

After reading two chapters out of the book:"If all of the chapters are like these two, you should definitely have the book published"

*Ira Gitler* (Jazz Journalist, author, Jazz Historian)

I have unilaterally pronounced Valery's version of Benny Golson's tune, *I Remember Clifford* as the most beautiful, the most spiritual song ever recorded. Valery Ponomarev's story and his music are about dreams and spirit. He did it!! It is a thrilling story of determination, vision and the love of music. This is a must read!!

*Reverend Clinton C. Glenn. Presbyterian Church of USA.*

Valery Ponomarev's life story is a phenomenon brought to life as an almost fairy tale scenario. His life has been one affected by a votive determination to eventually and permanently touch the spectrum of success. His eventual success has not been unwarranted because his talent was up to every challenge, big and small. His talent is as a stentorian voice that will continue to consequentially speak, invading the medium of the air, reaching not only ears, but also down into the deepest grotto of awaiting hearts. Though the future will always have an indistinguishable face, Valery is giving it a face of his own unique making.

*Benny Golson* (Legend in his own life time. Jazz superstar. The first musical director of the Jazz Messengers)

As a virtuoso hard bop trumpeter, Russian-born Valery Ponomarev creates beautiful, expressive solos that crackle with visceral, right-to-the-point, memorable musical narratives.

As a writer recounting his own fascinating life Ponomarev is also a riveting storyteller. As with his music, his words wring with candor and direct, unaffected emotion.

Packed with enough dramatic juice to fuel a Hollywood biopic, the Russian émigré's autobiography is an invaluable contribution to jazz literature. Beyond that, the trumpeter/composer's verbally deft memoir, for all its deep roots in jazz, makes for a good read for a wide general public both as a winning human interest story and as an invaluable slice of contemporary cultural history.

*Owen McNally* (A longtime jazz and arts features writer for The Hartford Courant)

"There is no better example of the internationalization of jazz than Valery Ponomarev. A musician's musician, his story defines the spirit of jazz, which truly has no birthplace, no central location and no owners. He proves that the music lives inside great musicians from throughout the planet. And thank God it does, for in the case of Valery, the trumpet heavens have one more light in the sky with which to guide our weary souls. Valery is the bonafide real deal and if you don't believe me, believe the great Art Blakey who invited Valery to take his place in the jazz messengers alongside the greatest players of our time. What more can one ask for?"

*Arturo O'Farrill* (Leader of the legendary Arturo "Chico" O'Farrill Afro-Cuban Jazz Big Band.)

I understand Valery very well, because I know what he had to go through to learn and play Jazz in his native country. I hope many people read his book and appreciate the effort to keep this beautiful music alive. Congratulations Valery! Your book is very helpful and very well written with real passion and love for Jazz. I hope that many, many people will learn a lot from it. God bless America, and God bless Jazz.

*Arturo Sandoval* ( Jazz super star)

One of my earliest recollections of the wonderful trumpet player Valery Ponomarev was at the famed Five Spot in New York City 1975-76. I had recently just joined the Jazz Messengers and Valery was sitting in. The scene is beautifully described in the book. Needless to say the rest is history. In my opinion Valery is the living embodiment of the "American Dream".

*David Schnitter* (Jazz Messenger, Tenor Saxophone, composer faculty /New School University)

This book is an incredible story of an incredible life. Reading this is fascinating.

I'm so glad that it is documented, because it's part of the history of jazz!

I can really feel what happened in these stories, because I have been touring Russia since before the wall came down and I also came to America in search of possibilities to be working with great jazz musicians.

*Joris Teepe* (Bassist-Composer-Educator, Director of Jazz Studies, Prince Claus Conservatory)

"Coming from Kansas City to New York and meeting Valery in 1977 showed me how far Jazz had spread throughout the world. Now, after reading his story, I learned something else. I never knew how much Valery had to go through to play the music he loves. His love and devotion to Jazz should be an inspiration to all aspiring Jazz musicians in this country and around the world." "I only said that because it's true."

*Bobby Watson* ( Jazz Messenger, Musical director of the Messengers in the Seventies, Director of Jazz Studies at the University of Kansas)

"Valery Ponomarev, in addition to being a great trumpeter, is a colorful storyteller with an impressive memory and a memorable and unique life story. From his days growing up in the Soviet Union through his tours as a member of Art Blakey's Jazz Messengers up to the current day, Ponomarev has experienced quite a bit. His frank memoirs balance wit with drama and contain many fresh tales that add to the history of jazz. Get this book!

*Scott Yanow* (Author of ten jazz books including Trumpet Kings, Jazz On Film, The Jazz Singers and Jazz On Record 1917-76)

# "On the flip side of sound"

## by Valery Ponomarev

authorHOUSE®

AuthorHouse™
1663 Liberty Drive, Suite 200
Bloomington, IN 47403
www.authorhouse.com
Phone: 1-800-839-8640

First published by AuthorHouse  8/19/2009

ISBN: 978-1-4389-7046-2 (sc)
ISBN: 978-1-4389-7047-9 (hc)

Printed in the United States of America

Bloomington, Indiana
This book is printed on acid-free paper.

"Truth is stranger than fiction." "If you know the truth, don't be afraid to say it."

"Buy our records. God knows we need the money."

Art Blakey

If I had collected only one cent for each time I had to answer the questions: "How did you join Art Blakey and the Jazz Messengers?" "How did you escape from Russia?" and "How did you learn to play jazz like that in Moscow?" I would be a billionaire by now. So I have decided to answer these questions once and for all.

Valery Ponomarev

DEDICATED TO MY SONS SERGEY AND PAUL

# Instead of a prologue...

The trumpet. What is it in the mysterious nature of its sound? How does it touch the soul of a warrior, making him brave and fearless in front of a mortal enemy and lead him to a hard-fought victory? How does it make a grown man cry, and young ladies in the audience feel amorous. How do you figure this magic?

I will always remember an Italian mechanic in work overalls, covered in grease and oil, wiping tears off his face. A few days earlier his son had asked me: "Val, the day after tomorrow, on the way to the gig, we will stop by my father's garage. Can you play for him a little bit? He loves the trumpet. Every time he hears it he cries."

What made a teacher lose her regal demeanor and come running around the corridor where I was entertaining my classmates with my newly acquired rotary trumpet, while waiting for class at the Moscow Architectural College to begin? Her knees were shaking and she was blabbering: "That's you!? Is this the trumpet? Do you play the trumpet? I didn't know you play the trumpet so well!" The Math teacher totally lost it.

What made me, a six-year-old in a summer camp, drop a ball I was playing with and run towards a bugle sound when I heard it for the first time? I ran from the far side of the camp to the first barracks, where the official bugler, an older boy by the name of Sergey Shivkoplias, was proudly standing with the horn raised in the air and blowing those enchanting sounds.

And, of course, I will always remember Art Blakey saying: "When Valery plays a ballad, girls in the audience feel amorous." He said it many times.

# Chapter 1

# Messenger from Russia

I was born and raised in Moscow, Russia, long before Perestroika and Glasnost, when the brainwashing of Communist propaganda, secrecy and disinformation raged at their highest peak. Everywhere, from school to street advertisements, the soviet government ideology was injected into the life of every citizen. Whatever one learned at school or heard on the radio or TV always had the bitter taste of brutal law, trying to disguise "Dead Utopia" as a beauty in a wedding gown.

*On the way to Red Square May 1st Procession*

*On my first tricycle.*

None of the branches of the arts, history, science, medicine, you name it - nothing could escape it. All of the creativity, inspiration, and talent of the country, which is so blessed with it, was under the ever-watchful eye of "Dear Father Communism." Suspicion, mistrust, and paranoia were the reality of the unreal world created and artificially maintained by the merciless rulers.

All of the natural resources, including human, were misused and wasted. Only the wild woods, although attacked from everywhere, retained their glory. I am lucky I had a chance to share in on one of the greatest Russian treasures – woods and nature.

As a boy, I used to go to a pioneer summer camp near Moscow every year. That was paradise on earth. The campsite was in the country about 50 miles from the capital in a hamlet called "Karalovo." There were dusty roads through rich woods, leading to collective farms and villages, which kept their appearance from prehistoric times. A 10-minute walk from the camp and you were in a pristine forest. To go on your own to the river, which looked more like a stream, was strictly prohibited, but I do not remember a single pioneer who took that law seriously.

We called the stream "Spitover." All day long, we were busy playing all sorts of games: volleyball, basketball, ping-pong (I was the reigning supreme ping-pong champion), chess, or hanging out in the forest nearby, collecting mushrooms, berries, cherries, wild nuts, chasing animals. Our job was to have fun and we were good at it.

*1st yr summer camp singing my heart out.*

*Smallest in line.*

*Smallest in the camp.*

To get to the soccer field we had to walk off the premises through the woods towards the river. If you left the camp through the arch and followed the road to the left, you would climb down the slope and up the hill. There, on top was a summer resort for the employees of the official TASS news agency, where my mother worked from the age of nineteen until the age of 65, when she retired.

If you followed the road further, it would lead you away from the resort and the road turned into a dark birch alley stretching from the mansion house to the woods, where the alley turned into a bumpy path over old roots of gigantic spruce and pine trees. At that spot the camp counselor would always point to the left, between the trees, and say: "Children, this is Levitan's [the Russian genius landscape painter] 'window', he used to sit here with his palette and paint this very view."

No matter how far from the camp we walked, the bugle or fanfare signals would reach us. I was drawn to those sounds from the very first time I heard them. I still remember myself, the only six-year-old in the camp – the rest of the kids ranged from seven through 15 – looking up at Sergey and begging him to let me play that beautiful horn.

He paid no attention at first, being used to other kids nagging him, but then he had a mercy on me, after everybody around us joined in on my behalf: "Let him try, let him try. That's not your horn. He has come to the camp for the first time. He is the smallest one." Sergey handed it to me with the air of democratic royalty mingling with commoners. I took the horn in my hands as if it had always belonged to me, raised it in the air just like Sergey did, and blew out of it exactly the same sounds. That is when I had my first taste of applause. The audience went berserk, screaming and cheering.

*7 year old offical signal giver.*

From that point on it was even more difficult to get the horn, because its official caretaker guarded his no longer unchallenged royal status of bugler with his life. Kids, they are always in a world of their own. When Sergey grew too old a boy for the camp and stopped coming, the responsibility of waking up the camp with revelry – calling everybody to dinner and playing taps at the end of the day – was handed to me by the camp's elders.

All of the signals had words to them, known to all pioneers and inhabitants of nearby villages, who could sing along with them if they wanted to, in Russian of course. The rough translation would be like this: Revelry – "Get up, get up my little friend, out of bed and right to the pot;" Dinner – "Take your spoon and take your bread and sit down for the dinner," Taps – "Sleep, sleep, to your wards, pioneers and the counselors."

For a while the horn existed to me only in connection with summer camp. During the autumn, winter and spring months I had no access to bugles or fanfares. There were none in the regular school or the art school, which I attended after my regular classes.

One winter evening my mother brought home a magazine. That was a very special magazine: it was printed on very good and shiny paper. On top of it in bright letters was written "America." That was a new precedent – for the first time in the recent history of the Soviet Union an American magazine was being sold to the public from Moscow newsstands.

*Making sketches.*

The whole magazine was in Russian and featured articles on life in the United States. Some advertised the standard of living of its citizens. There was a picture of a boy rolling down a trail on his bicycle with his legs dangling over the handlebars. The caption under the picture announced: "My mother hasn't seen that one yet."

There was an article about the American poor, from which I learned that they were the richest in the world. There were a lot of pictures, but except for the boy on the bicycle I remember only the pictures of jazz musicians, especially the one of Louis Armstrong. It was such an expressive picture. It must have been taken while Louis Armstrong was playing. Red color dominated; bulging eyes expressed delight and excitement, which moved in one motion towards the bell in the foreground.

I could hear the sound coming out of it loud and clear. What a picture! To express sound by visual art! That was a masterpiece of a picture! I loved it.

The next day I took out a thick piece of paper and copied the photo in watercolors without a single pencil stroke. The picture captivated me. The more I looked at it – the more I imagined myself playing trumpet. The portrait occupied only the left half of the sheet of paper. That kind of paper was the best for watercolors and hard to find, so in order not to waste the other half I drew a picture of myself, in pencil this time, utilizing the remaining space. I was thirteen years of age at the time and had never seen a trumpet up close before. One can easily tell that, because it shows in the drawing that I did not know how to hold a trumpet. Otherwise the sketch came out all right.

*L. Armstrong in water-colour*

A couple of days later, I was hanging out with my buddies around the sheds in the back yard, where residents of the nearby houses kept stacks of wood and some other necessities. A neighbor was fussing in front of the open door of his shed, so we went up out of curiosity. There, among the logs of stacked wood I saw a bell of a horn.

"What is that?" I pointed at it not believing my eyes.

"That's a trumpet; I played it in a brass band when I was in the army," the old man said and pulled it out of the pile. That was a real trumpet!

"I heard that you blow bugle in the summer camp. Here, you can have it," he said and handed it to me.

"Really? You really mean it?"

"Yeah, yeah, take it. It's been here for long time, I don't need it anymore. Too bad, there is no mouthpiece to it."

I grabbed the beaten-up and rusty treasure, hardly believing that he was serious. Forgetting about my buddies I ran home. My mother was still at work, so there was nobody to tell me what to do and what not to do. I cleaned the trumpet as well as I could and then took my mother's reel of thread and cleared it off the wood. Then with a penknife I cut off the rim of the reel on one end, cut out the pulp on the other and what I got was very reminiscent of a mouthpiece. I had only to smooth the edges with a file, clear off the dust, put it in the mouthpiece receiver and blow. The sound came out pretty clear, which surprised me.

When my mother saw the horn, she did not make any comment, other than ask me how it had made its way into our house. I told her how I found it. All the next day in school I could not help but think of the horn. When I came home, the horn was in front of our door, as if it were a wet umbrella or dirty galoshes.

"Mother, why is the trumpet outside the door?"

"You can't keep it in the room; it's too dirty. Besides anybody could've been blowing into it before. Who knows what kind of germs are living in this thing?" was the answer.

The next day my prized possession disappeared altogether.

"Mother, where is the trumpet?" I confronted her when she walked in.

"I don't know. I am busy."

"Where is my trumpet?"

"Synok [a Russian term of endearment, from the word "son"], I don't know. I am busy right now; I gotta prepare food."

"Mother, were is my trumpet?"

"I told you, I don't know. Somebody must've taken it outside."

I never cried, not even as a baby, so my mother and neighbors used to tell me, but this was too much. Tears just streamed down my cheeks. That was an unbearable pain. I still remember myself sitting on the sofa and looking at my mother who was sitting by the table and facing me. What happened next shocked me – she started to cry.

"What happened to you?"

"I realized you will be a musician," she answered through sobbing.

Art Blakey loved that story. He would ask me again and again, always laughing: "What did your mother say when your trumpet disappeared?"

In Karalovo, where my mother had no authority, I could still blow the horn. My supreme position in the camp was unchallenged until I, too, grew too old for the camp and passed the throne to my successor. Actually I never met my successor. The next year and the one after

*With Mom at summer camp.*

that, when I went back to the camp for a weekend as a visitor, they played the signals over the camp's loudspeakers and after that I don't know. I never had a chance to go back.

Now, when I tell my friends in America that I used to spend every summer, from the beginning of June through the end of August, in the country, they assume that my parents were very wealthy. My mother was not rich by anybody's standard, but it was the tradition in the capital that every kid was supposed to go to the country during the summer months. I don't know if it's still the same, but in those years Moscow was devoid of children during the warmest months of the year.

Lately I visit Moscow rather regularly – two or three times a year. Every time I visit my mother we end up talking about Karalovo. She says that the hamlet is almost gone, replaced by newly built cottages, but the woods are intact in their original glory. This year, for the first time in a long while, I am going to Russia for a couple of weeks during the summer months. Man! I will be in "Karalovo."

At the age of 18 I was a student at the First Moscow Regional Music College and playing my first professional gigs. The gigs were in dance bands with a repertoire of popular Soviet songs and melodies. One of the attractions of the gigs to us musicians was the fact that we could sneak some American standards into the program, always "off the record." It seemed like the more American tunes we played, the more pretty girls showed up on the dance floor.

On one of those gigs my friend, the tenor-player Tolia Boiko, announced: "Val, I recorded something off the short-wave radio yesterday – it sounds incredible! You should come tomorrow and listen to it. Knowing you, I am sure you will love it." The next morning, I took the Moscow Metro from "Mayakovckaia" station to "Sokol", walked around the station, through the courtyard to the building in the back, walked up the stairs and knocked on the door.

When I walked in, Tolia was sitting on the bed, having just gotten up from under the blanket. He didn't say a word. He just stretched his hand out, pushed the button on his tape recorder. Out came the sound of Clifford Brown's "Blues Walk" …

I was absolutely swept away by the sound of the music. It was not only exciting, but the pinpoint accuracy and purity of every note struck me – so perfect, it was like total truth coming out of there.

Until that morning I was only vaguely aware of jazz. I was literally bug-bitten from that point on. I raced around Moscow looking for tapes of jazz musicians – records were impossible to find – and the first one that I acquired was by Art Blakey and the Jazz Messengers. The record called "Moanin'" was on the tape. It had an incredible effect on me.

Now, like my friend Tolia I would stretch my hand to the button on the tape recorder first thing after waking up. I listened to "Moanin'" all day long. Soon I could sing all of the solos, not only Lee Morgan's and Benny Golson's, but Bobby Timmons' Jimmy Merrit's and Art Blakey's too. Tapes of many other artists followed. Art Blakey's "Night at Birdland" was too much.

Before I knew it, I was standing in the middle of the room, music on, eyes closed, horn in my hands, and pretending it was me playing with Art Blakey behind me. For a minute, I was just like my school friend Seva, who had seen a bass-player at a gig, and now he was always going through the motions of a bassist, plucking an imaginary bass in his hands. Seva was helpless and pitiful. No, no, no, that was not good enough! I had to learn to play for real.

Some guys more experienced than I told me to write out the solos to see what I could get out of them, comparing the melody line to the chord underneath it. Very soon I stumbled upon patterns: this phrase repeated exactly like Lee Morgan's, Clifford Brown played a phrase I had heard Charlie Parker play. Blue Mitchell played the identical phrase in a different key in a different tune. It was like finding a mountain of gold.

I sat there, digging the mountain day in and day out, checking out chords on the piano, transposing patterns to all the keys, applying phrases to different keys and tunes. Before I knew it, I was picking up the language of jazz.

College, soccer playing, hanging with my friends on the street, everything was now forgotten. I was in another world altogether with my heroes. There was no way to meet them, no way. Only the Soviet elite could travel to the West, and they were not interested in meeting Art Blakey. All they brought back with them was cheap clothes, and stories of how the working class was exploited in the capitalistic world. My musical heroes existed to me only through music, in the dimension of sound, which for an ordinary citizen was impossible to enter. I thought I was stuck in the wrong sphere for good.

## Chapter 2

# Escape from Gorky Park

The Youth Café, the hippest place in all of Moscow, was the place to be. Everybody wanted to get in. But as the most bohemian site in the Soviet capital, its doors were open almost exclusively to foreign tourists. However mere mortals, the Moscovites, sometimes found ways to sneak in too. Good-looking girls were more successful on average.

The whole idea for the café was to impress the guests from the West with the existing freedoms in the Communist Heaven and demonstrate to them that life in the headquarters of the modern day Utopia was not much different from that of the West.

Instead, what the authorities managed was to establish and maintain a little island with an atmosphere resembling that of anywhere west of the western frontier of that huge and once prosperous empire, now called the Union of Soviet Socialist Republics. The Youth Café was an oasis of Western culture in the heart of a violently anti-Western society.

Everything inside the café was supposed to be just like the West: a bar with a wide assortment of alcoholic and non alcoholic beverages, a relaxed atmosphere, good manners and an excellent grand piano on stage. Even in the kitchen, everybody from chef to busboy would say please and thank you to each other, not to mention to the customers.

What a far cry from, say, the Ostankino restaurant where I played after the café was converted into a fast food joint serving Siberian dumplings. I don't know if foreigners or good-looking girls patronized the dumpling joint, but there was no jazz there any more, that's for sure.

At Ostankino waitresses acted as if it was their god-given right to curse and scream at the customers. There was one waitress, Lena, who was a favorite of Valentin Bagerian, our drummer from Baku. Lena was a big, stately woman bearing the traces of a great beauty, which had started to fade not that long ago. The 5' 1" toothpick Valia (short for Valentin) and Lena, a northern splendor who seemed bigger in diameter only than her admirer in height, would have made a very attractive couple.

Valentin was considerably older than any of us. He was born and raised in the Caucasus mountains, where the men, according to legend, were all mustachioed and always in pursuit of women. According to the same sources they were very ferocious, hot-tempered and short-fused. Valentin himself used to tell and retell a story of being present at a terrible scandal which broke out at a wedding reception in a distant mountain village.

Two Caucasus natives, flushed with liberal libations, quarreled over something right at the head table. The dispute quickly escalated into an exchange of the worst possible insults and then into a brutal, ruthless fistfight. They don't even fight like that on Pay Per View's "Ultimate Fighting". It all came to a savage end when one of the rivals unsheathed his saber, which was supposed to be no more than an obligatory costume decoration, with lightning speed, and smacked his offender with a full swing on the neck.

I still remember how Bagerian posed as a decapitated body, digging its spread legs into the ground with the hands alongside the body. On the spot where a second before rested the head, according to Bagerian, was a gaping hole with a fountain of blood gushing out of it. The head rolled and came to a rest in the dusty grass next to the body and its dying lips were still moving in the last insults. Bagerian delivered his story so convincingly that we all believed everything he said, and only wondered: "What is it they drink there in the Caucasus mountains?"

I don't know about all of the tribes and nations packed into that maze of beautiful snowy mountain tops – some ranking among the world's highest peaks – with their blue skies, sharp cliffs, mountain lakes, streams and rivers, rich vegetation, prehistoric caves and ancient castles, but it sure was the case with our drummer. Outbursts of screaming, cursing, death threats and the most dramatic gesticulations would erupt at any time of day or night and always at the worst possible moment. Yet he was a great guy and everybody loved him anyway.

But only Lena had a magic power over him. Around her he was like a quiet little kitten. After all, in her heyday, Lena had worked for an animal trainer making announcements at the Moscow circus arena.

One day when we were about to start our first set, Bagerian was offstage still sitting on a bench next to Lena, sandwiched between her and our cook. I think it was the first time he had gotten that close to her. Despite many signals from the stage that it was time to get behind the drum set, Bagirian remained motionless, showing no intention of playing music. Eyes staring out into the vastness of space, he looked like he was having an out of body experience, stretching out a blissful moment.

Our band leader, Vladimir Antoshin, who went by the nickname of "Bear's Lair," got off the bandstand and moved closer to the trio making all sorts of signs that we were supposed to have started at least fifteen minutes ago. Bagirian still remained frozen as if in amber. Lena and the cook, oblivious of everything, kept on talking.

"Bagirian, what's wrong this time? I haven't seen you drinking vodka yet today. We have to start the first set before the boss says something. There have been enough warnings already just this month alone. You want us to get into trouble?" Antoshin's voice grew more and more impatient. Even the chef stood up from the bench to clear the path for our drummer who still sat motionless, totally merged to the side of his Dulcinea, glassy eyes staring at the dirty ceiling.

"Valia, enough already."

Bear's Lair stretched out his hand to pull Bagirian out of his stupor. There was not any transition. As if activated by some invisible switch, Bagirian jumped up from his seat, pulling his right hand out from under Lena's behind, screaming and yelling.

His routine rantings were flying left and right. "I hate this job," "Fuck this restaurant," "Meat is always rotten," "Drinks are always diluted," "Can't have any time for myself," "I

Bagirian.

could've held my hand on that behind for as long as I wanted to," "I speak fluent French." The last was the absolute truth. Bagirian was an honors graduate of the Institute of Foreign Languages at Baku, the capital of the former Soviet republic Azerbaijan. But his career as an interpreter was short-lived as he remained true to his first love – jazz. (Once we had a chance to hear and see how Bagerian laid the very same damnations, in perfect French, on the heads of French tourists.)

"Bair's Lair, you can't swing." That one was the worst! Bagirian didn't really mean that; he just wanted to get Bear's Lair back for interfering in his personal life. When Valentin was not completely drunk, he and Antoshin made a pretty good team. Everybody knew that.

"You musicians always have only one thing on your mind," said Lena, getting up from the bench and straightening out her skirt. Only now did our princess on the pea realize what had set off Bagirian this time. Later that evening, when Lena was gliding royally through the kitchen doors with a big tray of hors d'oeuvres and main courses, she bumped into a customer, who was the first obstacle on her course, hitting him on the head with the tray.

*Fred Grigorovitch, Bagirian in his normal every day appearance and Igor Vysotski.*

"Dumb asshole! Couldn't you find a better place to sit than right next to the kitchen exit?" She yelled at the casualty. "Jerk," was all she added and continued on her appointed rounds to deliver the precious cargo, not even offering an apology.

None of that could possibly have happened at the Youth Café where there was always perfect order. Not too many things should have gone wrong under the watchful eye of the big brother, represented by Dmiterko, Vinogradoff and their staff of rosy cheeked, wide-eyed, naive, relaxed Komsomol (Communist Party youth organization) youths, ranking from sergeant to KGB captain.

None of that was any of my concern. All I cared about was the jazz band which was featured in that exhibit of freedom and prosperity. The band consisted of Valerii Bulanoff, Andrei Egoroff, Vadim Sakun, Alexei Kozloff, Nikolai Gromin and Andrei Tolmasian. They ranked among the absolute best in the whole country. Even Georgi Garanian, a brilliant alto sax player and a conductor of the Moscow Radio State Orchestra, would come to the café, despite his very busy schedule, to sit in with them.

This band had just returned from an International Jazz Festival in Warsaw, the very first one ever attended by Soviet musicians. In the program of jazz classics were included Alexey Kozloff's ballad and Andrei Tolmosian's "Gospodin Velikii Novgorod". The following year Nat Adderley's quintet recorded Andrei's composition.

At the same time a rumor sprung up around the café that the recording was mainly inspired by the CIA. Whether it was a political stunt devised by the CIA or not, I don't know, but I liked the tune very much. Although the tune was based on the sound of American Negro spirituals, one could still hear a multitude of church bells ringing around the ancient city of Novgorod. It was a very expressive tune.

There were many more rumors. Another one had it that the Westerners at the Warsaw festival were amazed and gave the band a thunderous round of applause. According to another rumor, there was a group of people, much larger than the sextet, who also came to the jazz festival from Moscow. This group attended in order to help look after and care for the Russian musicians on foreign soil, thrown into the midst of those capitalist sharks with their musical instruments.

Vinogradoff and Boltashev, his subordinate, were in charge of the group. Boltashev established himself as the real star of the band, making all sorts of announcements and speeches regarding his role in promoting and perpetuating Soviet jazz. Although he could not play any instrument, he spent more time on the bandstand talking than the musicians played.

Back in Moscow he was telling everybody how well he was received and how important it was that in the future he accompany musicians to their performances so he could ensure that they would get their due.

At that time, every trip abroad had to be authorized by the government. Tourism was virtually non-existent, even to fellow socialist countries in the Eastern Block. Applying for an exit visa to a capitalist country meant risking a jail term.

Whether the Moscow jazz stars got their due or not didn't matter to me. I had a great respect for those guys. They were older and further ahead than me. I was catching up fast, though, learning a lot from transcribing the solos of my favorite musicians: Charlie Parker, Clifford Brown, Lee Morgan, Blue Mitchell and Dizzy Gillespie. I was making more and more discoveries with each day.

Although by then I was already accustomed to attending the club on a regular basis, thanks to Sakun, Bulanoff and Egoroff, who would always put me on the guest list, I had never had a chance to sit in with the most celebrated trio in all of Russia.

One day Vadim Sakun called me. "You wanna play with us tonight?"

"Yes, sure," I said without deliberation.

I had been forewarned by my friend, Vitalii Kleinot, that the trio was looking for a horn player. The only problem was that I had a terrible hangover from drinking too much vodka the night before. The whole summer, which had just ended, I had been hanging out in the resort town of Sudak on the Black Sea with my Moscow friends from Mazutnii Drive – Kolia, nicknamed of "Luna" because of his round face; Yuri Repenko, a.k.a. "Goga"; Boris Rossin; and some other guys.

Luna and Goga were drinking uncontrollably, celebrating their freedom from the Geodesic and Economics Colleges. As for Rossin, he was celebrating unruly graduation from his first prison term. I could drink too – let's not be too modest here – but not in the Mazutnii style. To have that ability one had to be born on Mazutnii Drive. Well, I caught up quickly.

Thanks to my friends' expert tutoring, I learned how to drink the national beverage all day long, with full glasses each time. As soon as you woke up, somebody would be sticking a full glass in your face. At the age of 20, you learn everything fast and extremely well.

Along with drinking bouts I was teaching my alcohol consumption professors the basics of solfeggio. Goga could play saxophone a little and Rossin could play "When the Saints, Go Marching In" on trumpet from beginning to end. Kolia not only played no musical instrument, he couldn't even sing a drinking song straight. None of them had ever heard of anything as sophisticated as solfeggio.

That was a scene: all of us drunk out of our minds braying degrees and intervals within a diatonic scale. The tritone was the favorite with my pupils. Somebody would fall asleep right on the floor not having finished an interval and then the rest of us would sign off. To my great surprise all of them got the idea of resolutions and intervals very well. Drink to that!

Only Goga got kind of weird and gave a new girl several slaps in the face for not going with him to the adjoining room, most of which was occupied by a king size sofa. "You teasing bitch," he kept on screaming as the poor girl ran away. She never tried to rejoin our class.

That was then, but now I was back in Moscow where business was waiting to be taken care of. It was already time to go to the gig, which was practically an audition, but I still had a terrible splitting headache and nausea. One single shot would have fixed me right up.

"Surgeon General warns: Drinking more vodka to feel better is a sure way to Hell." I knew that. Since my childhood I had seen too many people turn into hopeless alcoholics. The other way was to suffer through martyrdom to the bitter end, to return back to normal the next day. Well, make your choice.

I don't know how I did it, but I got a steady job at the most prestigious place in town, "The Youth Café". Vadim said that my playing that night busted him up. Also, from that point on, I didn't even drink dry wine for several years.

It did not take too much time for me to get used to my new status as an employee. It included, among other privileges, not having to stand in line to get in or to spend painful eternities proving to bouncers that I was on the guest list, or had been invited by one of the members of the band, and then another eternity explaining to the red-cheeked degenerate who Vadim Sakun, Bulanoff or Egoroff were. Now I just could march to the front of a huge stunned queue of hopefuls, and continue right through the first door, past a couple of bouncers, then through a second door, where I squeezed past two more good-natured Komsomol youths.

Now I was on the other side: everything was brightly lit, festive. Once inside, there was no need to show any credentials or any kind of passport. I just turned left and went down the stairs to the dimly lit basement, where I could drop my coat in a small enclosure and warm up. The basement stretched through the whole length of the café, with two entrances at both ends. There was room for everything: auxiliary services and a storage room stocked from floor to ceiling with colorful bottles and a freezer. If for some reason the stage was not available we could rehearse there too.

The basement could also serve, on occasion, some other functions. Under the pretext of giving a tour of the café to a guest, some naive looking Komsomol youths would lure a female muscovite there and then it would be difficult for a good looking patron of the establishment to get safely out of a fix. Once, the good-natured bouncers noticed a hustler trying to bug a foreigner about exchanging some Soviet novelties for an LP. They snuck him into the basement so fast, that on the festive surface of the café nobody even noticed the disappearance of the free trade enthusiast.

Later, some were saying that in his bag was found a whole bunch of LPs, which he had obviously traded some time previously. Needless to say, all of it was confiscated and the guy was pushed through the doors with a black eye and a bump on his head, and passed on to somebody already waiting outside just as fast as he was snuck in. Just imagine how low these self-made Western style merchants must have fallen – to conduct their vile business right on Big Brother's territory!

Boy, weren't my buddies from Mazutnii Drive proud when I put them on the guest list for the first time. All dressed up in their Sunday best rags, shoes shining like northern lights and Ninka with them. I had seen her before, a very good-natured girl always dressed in foreign clothes, which she would get somehow from tourists. Waitresses set up an extra table on the side for them, because when it came to the guests from Mazutnii Drive all the seats were already occupied by the guests from abroad.

During the break, I went over. There were so many people everywhere, I didn't even intend to ask the waitresses to bring me a chair, knowing full well that their resources had been exhausted a long time ago, so I just stood by the table.

"Ninka, move a little bit." Goga issued an order to his dame for that night.

"Where can I move? There's no room," said Nina trying to keep the composure of a lady on a big night out. Right away Goga slapped her lightly. "Move your ass, dumb bitch, don't you see Val wants to sit down?"

"Hey Val, I heard in your solo those lines you were practicing in

Sudak. They must've been Clifford Brown's," Kolia stated, confident as he always was, that he had passed the graduation test.

"I heard some too," jumped in Goga.

"Which ones?" I wondered.

"This one," said Goga and sang a phrase very clearly.

"Oh, that one. That one is from Blue Mitchell's solo on 'I Wish I Knew.' We just played it as the last tune of the set."

"I thought you liked only Clifford Brown," murmured Luna, looking kind of disappointed. "You talk about him most of the time."

"He talks about Art Blakey, too." Rossin couldn't wait to show that he had learned a thing or two that past summer.

"That's a drummer and the leader of the 'Jazz Messengers,' Rossin. How could Paramon play his phrases on a trumpet?" Paramon, my nickname, was the hero of an ancient Russian folk tale.

"Luna, you think I don't know what Art Blakey plays?" Rossin stood his ground and a whole discussion broke out over who played what instrument, and so on. Each time they couldn't agree on something their eyes would turn to me as a referee. Nina in the meantime fluttered off to dance with some Italian guy.

There was a space in front of the stage, free of tables, where everybody danced between sets. In the crowd of dancers I noticed a guy from Iceland who didn't miss a single night that week. Every time he would come with the same Russian girl, who was resolutely hugging him in a dancing embrace, head on his shoulder, eyes closed in a radiant rapture. From a distance they looked like Romeo and Juliet, struck by love.

Vinogradoff came up to our table. "Valer, can you take your horn and blow one of your high C's at them?"

"She is luring him into marriage, so she can split to the West," Goga summed up.

A few years later I bumped into her at the "Sverdlov" metro station.

Moscow's Juliet had flown in from Reykjavik to visit her mother. She was already divorced from the guy and their child was in somebody else's custody. She didn't look very happy.

The Youth Café was always packed, mostly with tourists from Europe including the English, French, and Italians – hardcore capitalists.

One day, before we started our first set, Vadim pointed at the group of 15 to16 year-old kids and said, "Those are Americans." (The hardest core.)

A short black man with them looked like he was in charge of the group. After our first set, as I was stepping down the three stairs from the stage, he came up to me. He was very excited and kept saying something to me; from his enthusiasm and smile I figured he liked the way we played very much.

Immediately somebody jumped in right next to me and translated: "He is a teacher from America with his class of junior high students on a tour of Eastern Europe. He loved your playing."

I said, "Thank you." The teacher's face lit up even more and he kept talking to me.

In those days I didn't speak any English at all, with the exception of a couple of words and names of musicians and tunes like "Blues Walk," "Blues March," "Moanin," "Are You Real," "Come Rain or Come Shine," "Quick Silver," "What's New," "Now's the Time," "A Night in Tunisia," and so on.

The guest from overseas kept on talking; this time I heard him saying "Clifford Brown." When he stopped, I said "Thank you." Then he said something else and stopped. Again I said "thank you." It kept on going like that for a while: he would say something and stop, waiting. I would say "thank you," he would resume and wait and I would say "thank you" again until the interpreter jumped in: "He says you play like Clifford Brown and is asking for your address so he can send you Clifford's records."

The Russian language is incredibly rich and expressive; they say that Russian obscenities are the most expressive in the world. A lot of them were flying through my head as I listened to this interpreter. The subtext of the Komsomol interpreter guy was that this red-headed trumpet player was crossing the line by getting into close contact with a foreigner from an enemy state, potentially an illegal activity against the Soviet Union.

"Thank you, it's OK," I said. The interpreter translated. The foreigner from an "enemy state" looked at me in disbelief and addressed the rosy-cheeked asshole again.

"Thank you, it's alright, really," I said, not waiting for the translation, trying to sound like I could get those records at a local supermarket any time I wanted. The teacher tried again, thinking that something had been lost in the translation, and I thanked him again, convinced that I would never be able to explain to my American friend what was going on here.

God only knows what he was thinking as he walked back to join his kids. Back in their school, I wondered what would they write in their essays on "Our Trip to Moscow, Russia," or "A Visit to The Youth Café". "Russians were unfriendly, the trumpet player was arrogant and didn't even want to talk to our teacher"? "That rusty head should know that our teacher plays very good saxophone himself and his brother plays trumpet in a professional jazz band. He is friends with Dizzy Gillespie"! Get that! Oh boy!

\*\*\*\*\*\*\*\*\*\*\*\*\*\*\*\*\*\*\*\*\*\*\*\*\*\*\*

Musicians from other Russian cities would pass through the club often and jam. They came from Baku, Leningrad (now identified by its real name, St.Petersburg), Erevan, Tbilisi, Sochi, etc. Their hometowns were so far from Moscow that at the club our fellow citizens looked like they were foreigners themselves. They couldn't fool me though; everybody was under the same law.

Kostia Nosoff, Roman Kunsman, Gennadii Golstein, David Goloschokin, Vladimir Feyertag, Vagif Mustafa Zade, Petrosoff,

Vladimir Tkalich and many others – all were extremely talented and enthusiastic. The guys from Leningrad were on the sophisticated side, those from the Caucasus mountains more on the raw, emotional side.

Kostia had a beautiful tone on trumpet, Feyertag didn't play any instrument but knew everything under the sun about jazz. I guess he was what you would call a musicologist.

One day, Earl "Fatha" Hines and his orchestra with Budd Johnson on tenor-sax were in Moscow on tour. All of a sudden everybody was talking about this legendary pianist/band leader and his men coming to the club. I don't even remember how it started; I think Vinogradoff brought the news. Did this mean that Bud Johnson would come too?

Earl "Fatha" Hines! Coming to the club! Tonight! That was inconceivable.

Nevertheless, Vitally Kleinot, my buddy and a very talented tenor player, was already downstairs rehearsing a Bud Johnson tune with some other guys. "Hey Val, join in." Kleinot always knew all the tunes and the right changes to them. Although the tune was a simple riff, we went through it a couple of times anyway.

Then the rumor was modified a little – Earl "Fatha" Hines had come down with the 'flu and was not leaving his hotel room but the other band members were coming: Bud Johnson, Bob Donovan, Michael Zwerin (an American of Russian descent), Oliver Jackson and Milt Hinton.

It was already 8pm, time for the house band to play, but nobody special had arrived and it was still business as usual at the café: Komsomol guys ushering guests to their seats, Vinogradoff and Dmiterko directing the traffic, waitresses running back and forth, bouncers checking IDs, a huge queue outside.

As far as I was concerned it would take a miracle for these travelers from a dimension of record albums, articles in Down Beat, Willis Conover's jazz hour on The Voice of America, the mythical Manhattan

Island and 52nd Street and voices on tapes passed from friend to a friend, to materialize in flesh and blood at The Youth Café.

The first tune we played was Vadim's composition, "Those Who Move". I always liked blowing on that tune. It was based on rhythm changes and that gave me an opportunity to check out in a playing situation some of the material I had transcribed and practiced at home. Our rhythm section was kicking, it was always a lot of fun playing with these guys. Vadim Sakun's trio was not called the best in all of Russia for nothing. I was blowing chorus after chorus like I was caught in a volcanic undertow and the lava was rolling and tumbling me, rolling and tumbling me, ever hotter and hotter until it surpassed even the melting point for diamonds.

When I finished my solo, they were all there, sitting across the room from the stage at a long table, almost like a jury, Oliver Jackson was pointing at me using silverware as a baton. The aging, out-of-shape man in a bright yellow sweater with a tenor sax was Budd Johnson. Right away, he took his instrument out of its case and came up to the high stage, where he hesitated: the three steps leading to it were clogged with people.

Kleinot and I got the idea right away and grabbed the patriarch from both sides by the elbows, helping him to the pedestal. «In a Mellow Tone» he asked. «What key?" somebody tried to show off his English. Who needed it, we all knew the original key was $A^b$. One- Two, One... here we go.

For Kleinot, myself, and most other Moscow musicians, it was the first jam session with Americans. We were all so inspired, our best licks never sounded better. It was an incredible feeling to play this music with the people who came from the time and place of its origin and had even participated in its creation! After the first tune the rest of Earl "Fatha" Hines' men beamed themselves onto the stage.

Then it really started, we were just calling tune after tune and our guests from the other dimension played everything. No matter what we came up with they just stamped it out. It kept on going and going on like that until it was time to close the establishment. Not even Vinogradoff could argue with that. We all poured out into the street to watch our guests leave.

In those days I used to call almost everybody "Crocodile" for some reason. I don't even remember how it started. It must have been some kind of slang around town. I would even call good-looking girls "Crocodilchiki," the diminutive of crocodiles. As the cars took off, I just screamed for a chaser: "Good-bye Crocodiles!" in Russian of course. Vinogradoff's car with the Americans tightly packed into it drove off and vanished.

"Hey Val, do you know there is an almost identical expression in English?" Valera Kotelnikoff, another buddy of mine and a namesake, asked when there was no one left to scream good bye to.

"No," I said. How could I know that, I didn't speak any English then.

"It translates as 'See you later, Alligator.' I'll teach you how to say it, repeat after me: 'See you later, Alligator.'" That sounded good, so I repeated after him a couple more times, "See you later Alligator."

The names Michael Zwerin, a very good bass trumpet player, and Bob Donovan, a young musician from NYC who played a mean alto sax, were new to me. Zwerin was also a writer and his article describing that evening in Moscow was published in the Village Voice a month or so later. A copy of the article was in The Youth Café a day after that, or maybe even a day before it hit the news stands in New York City.

The article said that Valery Ponomarev played like Kenny Dorham. I was very hurt; nobody had ever called me anything but Clifford Brown, my absolute and supreme idol.

"Come on Val," said Kleinot tired of seeing me so depressed, "Kenny Dorham is not that bad. He didn't confuse you with Ruby Braff or something. Besides you did play some Kenny Dorham lines that night."

28

He knew what he was talking about. Around that time I had just finished transcribing Kenny Dorham's solos from his record "Solid" featuring Sonny Rollins. Vitalii had gotten the LP on the black market, of course, and had let me copy it on my tape recorder. That's what it was! Credit to Michael Zwerin for identifying the lines!

Between 1966 and 1972, other inhabitants of the Jazz dimension showed up in Moscow. This almost always meant that there would be a jam session at The Youth Café or some place else. Charles Lloyd with Keith Jarrett, Jack DeJohnette and Ron McClure. Gerry Mulligan accompanied his wife, the actress Sandy Duncan, to the Moscow International Movie Festival and ended up playing standards with us at the club on alto. He had come to Russia without his instruments and we could not find a decent baritone for him, so Valia Ushakoff, a fellow musician, brought his selmer alto. Duke Ellington and his Orchestra, Toots Thielemans with Milt Hinton and Ben Riley, the Thad Jones-Mel Lewis big band.

*Duke Ellington in Moscow (VP is 2nd from the left)*

With Paul Gonzalves.

*Asking Pepper Adams (member of the Thad Jones - Mell Lewis orchestra) to sit in.*

*Jamming with Pepper Adams in Gorki Park.*

A meeting with the Thad Jones-Mel Lewis band was organized at a big lounge in Gorky Park. It seemed like all the Moscow musicians and their friends were trying to get through the cordon of the capital's militia guarding the entrance leading up to the second floor, where musicians were already unpacking their instruments. Not everyone was lucky.

Ever since my move to New York, Billy Harper, a Jazz Messenger of previous editions and a member of the reed section of Thad-Mel's big band at the time, has invited me many times to see a videotape he made that day in Gorky Park. The tape was made as he and other band members were approaching the entrance to this prospective cordial interaction between East and West. I'll take Billy up on his invitation one day, but I know what is on that tape anyway and I've watched scenes just like that documentary many times in real life.

The footage depicts militia beating the living shit out of a guy with a musical instrument who tried to get through the border patrol. Maybe his name wasn't on the guest list, or maybe the poor guy was too anxious to get in and didn't wait for the militia morons to check his identity and grant him legal entry – who knows. One way or another the musician in question ended up not jamming with the Americans.

Each close encounter of the Jazz kind was more or less the same as that night with Earl "Fatha" Hines and his band. They would materialize out of thin air for a brief moment and then dissolve into space, leaving us exactly where we were – in the whirlpool of Soviet paranoid ideology where a political stunt resembling a spring thaw could turn into a tidal wave at any time, wiping out any tendencies inharmonious with communist brainwashing.

Each time after rubbing shoulders with the jazz stars from the West we would walk the streets until dawn, too excited to sleep. The sun would be already in the skies, but my friends and I would still be afoot and talking.

"Where do you see yourself in the future?" Kleinot asked me once at the end of one of those outings. "There isn't any kind of money involved, being a jazz musician isn't even recognized as a profession in this country, and it doesn't look like things will change any time soon. What do you say Valery?"

"I don't know," I told my friend. "I do wake up almost every morning with a feeling that the previous day had been lost in vain, but I don't linger on it at all. I just want to learn to play as well as I can and stay with this music, no matter what the future has in store for me."

There was no kind of instructional material available, not to mention jazz education courses or LPs in Russia, a country nonetheless with such a rich musical heritage. There were occasional breakthroughs on the black market though. If I got a new record, all of my musician friends would have a chance to copy it, and vice versa.

Willis Conover's jazz hour on the Voice of America provided a lot of music. My short-wave radio dial was always tuned to the station, with the tape recorder wired up. So I ended up having a huge collection of jazz recordings, mostly on tapes. They filled up the entire middle section of my mother's enormous wardrobe, which she had inherited from her mother.

It was a monstrosity, but was gorgeous, made of solid oak, decorated with stained glass. It reached up to the ceiling and extended almost the entire length of the room from the door to the window, four to five meters in length. On the left side, on the top shelf, above the finest china, porcelain dinner sets, crystal goblets and drinking glasses were stacked my grandmother's volumes of printed music – opera scores, arias, exercises.

I think my mother donated those volumes somewhere before she sold the wardrobe when it was time for her to move to a new apartment. I had already grown up by then and been living on my own.

Long before, when I was still a little boy, she sold a huge oil painting in a gilded wooden frame. That frame itself was a piece of art, with all sorts of fruit in a most intricate design carved out of solid red wood. Papers of authenticity for the painting itself attested to the artistry of Chardin. The painting was also sold with the frame.

After the opportunist hustlers disappeared with their newly acquired treasure, my mother socked 800 rubles in a big jar. The jar never left the top shelf, but I don't think the rubles stayed in it for too long. It hurt me so much to see an empty wall instead of the beautiful pastoral, which had been hanging there for as long as I could remember. I ran away that day and stayed on the street until the darkness fell.

A few years later I would permanently fix on that wall pictures of my favorite musicians: Clifford Brown, Charlie Parker, Miles Davis, Ornette Coleman, Max Roach, Sonny Rollins, Horace Silver . . . Art Blakey.

*Igor Kondakoff, Boris Midny, Villia Yaveroff and Igor Beruktshtits*

\*\*\*\*\*\*\*\*\*\*\*\*\*\*\*\*\*\*\*\*\*\*\*\*\*

Just as sensational as the appearance in Moscow of residents from the other dimension was the disappearance of Soviet citizens from the face of the Earth. The very first time I heard of something like that was the case of two Moscow musicians, Boris Midnii, a saxophonist, and Igor Berukshtits, a bass player.

Rumor had it that after their disappearance, they materialized in full flesh and blood in America. After "Literaturnaia Gazeta" (literally "Literature Newspaper") pronounced them anathema, the story became more or less official. While on a tour of Japan as members of the Moscow Circus Orchestra, they devised a plan of escape from the circus residence right into the American embassy.

The plan worked so well that even the thoroughly-trained extra personnel, which came with the regular company to capitalist territory to help and care for the artists, did not notice anything wrong until it was too late. According to the law, for running away to the West and betraying Communist ideals, you had to go to jail for seven years if you were to return to the Communist Motherland. Seven years in a Soviet jail!!!

Where was Kunsman? What happened to the legendary alto player from Leningrad? One day he was coming to The Youth Cafe with other touring musicians to jam, the next he was just not there. Vanished, nowhere to be found!

"He didn't vanish, he went to Israel to join his relatives who are millionaires. Otherwise he could never afford to leave Leningrad where he had as much work as he wanted." I think it was Andrei Yegoroff who spelled out a rumor which was already buzzing around the Cafe. "Once in Israel he can go anywhere in the West, to New York for example."

Little did I know that the "millionaire relatives" part of that rumor was deliberately circulated by the KGB to discourage other Soviet Jews from joining the exodus from Russia which had already begun. The KGB didn't only stick to the "millionaire relatives" tale.

During my first month in New York a fellow immigrant came to my new apartment in Astoria to show me a letter he had received from his ex-wife. The scene is still in front of my eyes: my friend is sitting on the sofa, the letter is in his hand. His ex's handwriting is pretty good. I read: "I feel so bad that Paramon was killed in a car crash". When I spoke with my mother on the phone after that, she cried uncontrollably upon realizing it was me on the line.

A couple of years later there was no secret anymore; everybody was talking about it: Jews were officially allowed to leave for their historical homeland, Israel. Although it was not as easy as going to a travel agency and simply purchasing a ticket, people were leaving all the time. The catch was that one had to receive an invitation from a relative in Israel. The invitation needed to be presented at the Visa and Immigration Office in Moscow (in Russian it sounds like OVIR – a special branch of the KGB) and then one could only wait and hope. If the permission was granted, one went to heaven; if permission was denied, the authorities would create for the helpless hostage a living hell on earth.

By the end of that year I was attending farewell parties at the rate of two or three a week. It seemed like every Jewish friend of mine had relatives in the Promised Land. Some of the guests at those parties looked like they were at a wedding ceremony, others like at a celebration of children coming of age, some like they were at a christening of a baby, others like at a drunken debauch, some like at a funeral.

There was a devoted communist father of a friend of mine who to the bitter end refused to agree to his son's departure. To the very end he was trying to talk his son out of taking the flight on El-Al. None of the conniving, bullying, scheming or pleading helped. My friend was determined to take his life into his own hands. They say that the old man broke down in the Sheremetievo airport and cried uncontrollably as he was embracing his child for the last time, blessing him for the new life in the land of his ancestors.

\*\*\*\*\*\*\*\*\*\*\*\*\*\*\*\*\*\*\*\*\*\*\*\*\*\*

One day my high school buddy Igor Visotsotskii called. "Val, come as soon as you can. My wife and I have something important to tell you."

That was the reality of life; nobody would trust telephone lines. People were afraid to say even person-to-person what they really thought, let alone to confide into a receiver connected to the widest net of wires with the Big Brother eavesdropping.

What could it be? Igor, drunk at a rehearsal again, or fired from his radio gig? Or maybe it would be his wife Irka again, complaining about everything from the wrong size shoes she'd bought from a friend who had acquired them from an Italian tourist, to the rotten eggs she'd brought from a supermarket.

"I'll try to come by tomorrow," I said.

"Can't you come now? It's really important."

Oh boy! Igor really did it this time. Why the hell did he have to drink so much at work; couldn't he get wasted on his time off? After all he wanted that job so much and it took Irka's mother considerable effort using her most valuable connections to put him on the payroll of the Moscow Radio Orchestra.

All right, I thought, I should take a break anyway from practicing trumpet before my chops get swollen again.

"See you in a minute,"

*With school buddy (Igor Vysotsky) Moscow Jazz 68.*

My friends lived just a short walk from my house in an area called "Old Arbat," a labyrinth of ancient little streets and dead ends, residential houses and fashionable buildings erected before the Revolution.

It was a beautiful day. The sun was bright and warm, shining through the big windows of their room. Irka took a break from ironing her outfit for the night. It looked like it wasn't Igor's fault this time that she messed up a crease on her skirt, or maybe she hadn't messed up anything on this occasion. They were both subdued and amicably sitting on the sofa.

"What's up?"

"Valery, what we are going to tell you should not go any further."

"What's going on?"

"A few months ago we tucked in an invitation; it came with today's mail."

"What!?"

"As a result, a couple of days from now, they will fire me from my radio gig. For the next two to three months we'll be living on our savings and whatever occasional jobs we'll be lucky enough to find. Then we are out of here."

"To tuck in an invitation" in the latest slang meant to ask relatives in Israel to send official papers with a government seal to their Moscow folks with the request that they should join them in their original motherland.

"You've never mentioned any relatives outside of Moscow, let alone in Israel; besides you are not even Jewish."

"Irka's Father was Jewish."

"I thought he was a big Communist Party boss. How could he have anybody in Israel?"

"He didn't."

"What are you talking about then? Where did you tuck in your invitation, to the Gulag Archipelago or something?"

"Ee—gar." Irka would always stretch both syllables of her high school sweetheart's name. They had only recently acquired the new status of husband and wife. "You are only confusing Paramon. You have to explain to him how it works."

*Irene (Irka) & Igor on their wedding day.*

"Here it is: the international community has worked out a deal with the Soviet Government – I think it has something to do with grain – according to which all Jews who want to go to Israel should be allowed to leave, and this deal is very strictly observed. The Israelis have established an agency in Tel Aviv, which is taking care of invitation letters with the government seal. For those who have close relatives the procedure is very simple – potential applicants contact their close kin in Israel and ask them to go to the agency and take care of the paperwork. If one doesn't have anybody there, then he just seeks help from those who have already received permission to leave or Jewish activists from the Moscow synagogue.

"What happens next actually is very simple also. New immigrants gladly take along the name and address of the person in need and, in most cases, his family, and once in Tel Aviv they just deliver it by hand to the agency with the appropriate explanations. There is a huge waiting list of foster parents, brothers and sisters, uncles and aunts who are ready to step up at any time and claim new hopefuls as members of his or her family. It's like the whole country is swept up into one patriotic idea of helping their own to leave the Soviet Union.

"There are several reasons for this: for the Russian Jews obviously it's a chance to join their own nation, contribute to the building of their own country, escape possible reprisals which could break out at any time, and just simply go to the West to live by the standards of a free and modern society where one doesn't have to bow to any dogmas or endure constant shortages – even of bare necessities, let alone luxuries.

"For the Israelis, it's a chance to increase their population and strengthen their army in the face of the Arab threat. The population of Israel is six million people, half of whom are Jews and the other half, or almost half, believe it or not, Arabs and catching up fast. In a Jewish State! You know what that means? Golda Meir recently said that she is afraid to wake up one morning in a country with an Arab majority. So for her it's a chance to tilt the balance in her own favor. Anyway, the postal services of both countries have gotten very busy lately delivering a chance for a lot of people to live as they please. Once the application is submitted to the OVIR..."

"Igor always calls it Tel- OVIR." This had been the first time I ever heard Igor talk in the presence of his better half for so long uninterrupted. I just thought myself that OVIR sounded like Aviv.

"May I continue?…"

Uh-Oh, here comes the messed-up crease on the skirt. I was fully prepared for the logical escalation in the exchange between the sweethearts, but this time it didn't follow; the storm passed by on its way to deliver its damage somewhere else.

"…Once in the OVIR, the papers are processed within a couple of months and the applicants depart. Almost everybody ends up getting an exit visa, but there are exceptions. Prominent scientists, big party bosses or Army personnel are not allowed to leave. As soon as something like that happens, the international community launches a huge campaign in the Western media against human rights violations. You don't hear much about it in Moscow, but in the West it's all over the radio, television, newspapers.

"The deal is so important to the Kremlin that it had to give in to the pressure from the West and let some of these people go. You've heard of dissidents and refuzniks. Irka and I don't fall into this category. I figure in two to three months from now we will be out of here."

"You are so lucky. I am very happy and proud for you." I was stunned – my friends would disappear from here just like so many other Muscovites.

"Paramon, you are the first we broke out the news to, we were absolutely sure that you would support our decision."

"Listen, I may have some relatives in the West myself, maybe in France. My grandmother's side of the family had to flee after the Revolution; their name was Lavroff. For most of the nobility it was either leave Mother Russia or face execution by the Bolsheviks. What about other nationalities?"

"There is very little immigration to West Germany, only for those who have really close relatives. Also I've heard of some Ukrainians going to their fathers and mothers in Canada and that's it. If everybody were eligible for this immigration law, then there wouldn't be anybody left in the Soviet Union to work for the communist cause.

"Here is the latest story: Kosygin talks to Brezchnev, 'Leonid Ilyich, people are leaving all the time; if it continues like this, soon there will be only you and I left in the whole country.' 'I won't stay here with you, comrade Kosygin.'"

The joke made me laugh. Try to imagine senile Breznev, who was supposed to be an omnipotent communist god ruling over all of the nationalities trapped in the boundaries of the Soviet Union stretching the length of twelve time zones, escaping to the miniature country of Israel to shoot Arabs.

"That's a joke. The gloomy reality is that I am stuck to rot here without a chance to live the life of a jazz musician."

"Maybe not. First you should forget about your relatives who might turn up somewhere in the West. Even if we find somebody with the same name, after so many years they would be very distant relatives; furthermore, it is very unlikely that they would be willing to go through so much trouble as to bring someone they've never heard of to their home. A much more realistic way is to claim that you are Jewish."

"I can't do that; they'll put me into jail for that."

"Not necessarily. Jakhot says it's absolutely all right."

"Who is Jakhot?"

"You've seen Victor Jakhot in the Youth Cafe many times. You just didn't realize who he was. He is a big jazz fan and loves your playing."

"I think I know who you are talking about, a thin guy with ascetic features, always dressed in shabby clothes, right?"

"Yeah, that's him. He is a Jewish activist helping potential immigrants to split as smoothly as possible. He's the one who helped us. Jakhot is a real hero, you know; he is walking on thin ice here. The KGB knows exactly who he is and what he is doing, but are not interfering yet since the quota has to be fulfilled. The doors may close at any time and if he is still on this side, then he will be in big trouble.

"Believe it or not, we've talked about you many times. He says since your father disappeared when you were only a few months old, you can safely claim that he was Jewish and his relatives live in Israel. Once in Tel Aviv, I guarantee you, Irka and I will take your name and address to the agency and you will get the papers in due time. Write this story in your application and submit it. Although the KGB knows very well who your father was, that you are a Russian national and that this story is fake, they will let you go anyway. For them it's much more convenient to fulfill the quota with musicians instead of scientists.

"Yakhot knows all the nooks and crannies of this business; he says its one hundred per cent safe. If you are not given an exit visa, for example, your name routinely goes into the papers and causes a big scandal again, with the USSR blamed for violating human rights. The agency in Tel Aviv goes to extreme lengths to bring every potential emigrant to Israel."

"I understand. Brezchnev and Kosygin don't want this trouble because of some trumpet player."

"That's right, you will be out of here without delay. In the meantime, stay in touch with the departing and applicant community, particularly with Yakhot. They will help you to deal with OVIR and to fill out the papers. We'll be writing. Once you are in the West you are in the free world where you can tell local immigration authorities the whole truth and they will let you go anywhere you want to. Irka and I decided to go to Israel first for a year, to get used to the life outside of the big cage and then we will be ready to join you in New York. Isn't that where you are going?"

Yes, Igor knew exactly what was on my mind.

From that point on, events followed each other like slides in a projector. A couple of days later, Igor was duly fired from the Moscow

Radio Orchestra, then, after a couple of gigs here and there, it was already time to go to the airport to see my high school buddy off to his new frontier.

Next set of slides: an envelope in my mailbox with a red wax seal and a return address in Pettakh Tikva, Izrael. Slide two: I am submitting an application for an exit visa. Frame three: I am fired from the Moscow Organization of Musical Ensembles. Next slide: letters arrive from a new frontier, then a blur of small gigs in an out-of-the-way restaurant where I was lucky to play for tips as a non-employee on a day-to-day basis.

As it turned out, the leader of that band had tucked in an invitation himself and was fired later from his job, too. I was already in the smoke and fire of the take off: getting the visa, paying for identification papers which confirmed that I had relinquished Soviet citizenship, picking up tickets, packing. I am sure that somebody helped that bandleader also as much as possible under the circumstances.

To pay for forfeiting my citizenship, I was forced to sell my "Conn Director" trumpet, a shining, beautiful, right off the black market instrument with a "Made in USA" inscription. Its round polyplastic – or some such fabric – case alone was an absolute novelty in Moscow. I couldn't take it with me across the border anyway since American products were not officially sold in the Soviet Union and therefore were on the list of objects along with antiques, icons, works of art, rare books, etc., which were not to be taken out of the country.

OK, soon I'll be able to buy myself a "Bach" or a "Martin Committee," or maybe even a "Conn Connstellation," so for the time being I bought a "Veltclang," a product of brotherly East Germany. As far as quality was concerned, those trumpets were only slightly better than their Soviet counterparts, crafted on a conveyer belt in a furniture factory. Goods made in the Eastern Block countries were not that easy to buy either, but at least permission was not required to carry them out of the country.

Submitting the application provided some excitement. Though after getting my education from Jakhot and others I slipped into a feeling of safety, entering KGB territory for any reason was always treacherous. Following Jakhot's instructions I filled out the application, several pages long. On the last page I had to write an explanation of how "my relative" who had sent the invitation turned out to be an Israeli citizen.

I had to really strain my imagination, which was pretty developed by then, to make all loose ends meet. My counselor looked it over and, after a couple of minor adaptations, said that the story was good.

They say that the human mind retains only positive experience, but I doubt I'll ever forget how that KGB officer – whose name by the strangest of coincidences was Izrailova – a big stout woman in a captain's uniform with shoulders twice as broad as mine, removed her spectacles after leafing through a couple of pages of my presentation and turned to me.

"How is it that you, a Russian national, write here that you have Jewish relatives in Israel?"

The question made me feel like I was falling through the floor; at the same time I felt like my teeth were separating from their roots. The only time I would ever again feel this way, years later, was while driving at night, after a sharp turn from Ocean Parkway onto the BQE, I came upon a stalled car with two guys changing its tires. Whatever my first reaction was, I managed to maneuver the car past those lunatics, avoiding an impact at 55mph. The pressure in my teeth roots subsided only many miles down the road.

"It's all explained on the last page," I somehow answered in a steady voice, staring into the glass eyes on the round, emotionless face.

As the officer turned back to the pages, engrossed in reading, I kept falling through the floor, knowing full well that the other door at the far end of the office would open at any time now and two guys would appear, just like in the movies, commanding me to follow them. My life as it was until now was about to end. There would be no America, no jazz, no Art Blakey.

Izrailova moved, now she would press the button. Slowly and deliberately she turned towards me, epaulets in a straight line.

"This is good," she said pointing to the last page. "Your application will be passed along for examination, and the answer will arrive through the mail in a couple of months."

I thought I noticed some sign of respect. Was it in her voice or her countenance, which was no longer that of a frozen mask, or in the eyes which ceased to be a pair of glass buttons on a dummy's face. Now there was something mortal about them.

A few days later, my mother's hysterical voice on the phone summoned me to come immediately to her apartment.

"How could you write such a thing about your own mother? How could your hand possibly even write those horrible lies? What Israel are you talking about? There is always war over there; I've had enough of wars already," my mother screamed as I walked in. "You are not going anywhere; I won't allow it. They requested that I should come to the office. I had to go there – you know what place I am talking about. Those people made me read your "confession." How could you do this?! You are not going anywhere! The officer said that the visa is issued with the parents' consent only."

"They will tell you a lot of things. The fact is that I am of legal age and don't need any parents' consent."

"They will put you in jail for trying to get an exit visa illegally, you will be in Butirka [a famous Moscow prison] instead of hanging out in Manhattan with Art Blakey and Miles Davis. What about Freddie Hubbard, is he waiting for you there too?"

So I had to enlighten my mother about the business of getting the invitation from my "relatives" in Pettakh Tikva, and the political situation, which she was very familiar with.

"Ludmila," broke in Mark Stepanovitch, my mother's husband, a decorated war hero. "You know better than anybody once this kind of business has been started you'd better go through with it. Valery should emigrate while it's still possible."

My mother slowly calmed down. A couple of days later she said that I should bring the papers for her to sign. That's when she broke down crying. "Do you remember how in the fifth grade you stole cables to the reel-to-reel projector in school, so you and your buddies could sneak in to watch movies, and you got caught? Someone must have heard me when I was screaming and yelling at you in a fury threatening that you would never stand by my grave. Lord, forgive my trespasses!"

The right thing to do, according to Jakhot, was to stay away from friends so nobody would suspect them of leaving too and to keep as low a profile as possible, which I did. Nevertheless, there was already a persistent rumor that Paramon was leaving. Some people believed it, some thought it was a joke, some just dismissed it altogether.

One day Goga, Kolia-Luna, Rossin, Liova Karabitsin – another prominent member of our clique – and some other guys showed up in my living quarters.

"Have you disappeared from the face of the Earth or something?" Goga was drunk and depressed. "What is this rumor Val, how could it be true?" I didn't say anything.

"I know when it all started," said Liova, "when last year you quit drinking again and started shaving every day."

"And enrolled in an intensive English language course, memorizing all those words daily" added Goga "How is life on the other side?"

The newlyweds wrote regularly, mostly one letter for everybody, sent to the mother-in-law's address. Every time a letter arrived, Irene's mother would have a little get-together. From the letters we learned that the life on "the other side" was good. The very first day, Igor and his honey moved into a beautiful apartment, care of a government program, which welcomed new arrivals. The same with work – almost right away he joined a jazz group at a nightclub for a few gigs a week and played concerts with a popular local singer.

At the first concert in front of a huge audience Igor accidentally said "ass" in Russian into a microphone. At first he got very embarrassed, but the audience made fun of it, picking up the word and chanting it. Igor became an instant celebrity. A description of a high living standard followed. In the last letter Igor and Irene wrote that they were not requiring any loans, so they could move to America before the first twelve months were up, the mandatory period of time before becoming a citizen of a country surrounded by Arab nations, with all possible consequences. One of the pages of that letter was entitled: "For Paramon."

"Paramon, when you get off the plane in Vienna, there will be an Israeli representative, a nice old Russian jew, waiting for you and other emigrants en route to Tel Aviv. When he approaches you, tell him to fuck off. His function is to collect everybody's documents and transport them to Castle Shenau, a short ride from the airport. It's a transfer point. You have to understand the barbed wire and guards with machine guns around the Castle – a terrorist threat is always there. As soon as there are enough people to fill up a jumbo jet, after a few days, passengers in total secrecy at night are driven back to the airport from where, under cover of darkness, they take off for Israel.

"If you are going directly to America, DO NOT give the old man your credentials. Insist on meeting with the Austrian immigration authorities and tell them your story. They will transfer you to another camp for refugees from which you can go anywhere you want to. Otherwise you will end up in the Promised Land and waste a lot of time. You may even get stuck here. Good luck."

Among the guests that evening there were a couple of musicians – a piano player and a drummer – as well as a friend of the hostess (half her age), and Uri Kushnir (who used to get me LP's from the black market) with some drunken beauty on his arm. The piano player also had submitted an application to OVIR and was expecting a decision any day. Irka's Mom came up with an idea of making a little jam-session.

I didn't have my horn with me so I decided to sing. A couple of days before that I had memorized the lyrics to "What's New" in English. I liked that song anyway, but in the rendition of my idol Clifford Brown with a string orchestra it was a sheer masterpiece. I would never shy away from singing. In the music college it was even suggested that I should attend choir as well as trumpet classes.

The piano player sat behind the set of beat-up keys, spread a dominant chord and the song sailed off. The lyrics to the song were also beautiful: a man and a woman, after a long break-up, meet by accident and try to engage in small talk, barely able to conceal their feelings for each other, which threaten to burst from undercover at any moment. In other words – Love.

All that Love again! Can't somebody come up with some kind of restraining order for it? I was singing lyrics which some poet from a far away capitalist land dedicated to who the hell knows who, but was thinking of blue-eyed Komarukhina, whom I had to leave behind in Moscow – all things considered – forever.

"Oh! Paramon, it came out so good, you should sing more often," the lonely mother-in-law clasped her hands in delight, having put her empty wine glass on the night desk. It was not easy for her. She was really losing it.

"Why are you not giving me the line?" A little later that evening she was trying to get some sense out of an anonymous long distance operator. "We are not some fools here, I will find out the name of your supervisor. I am a Mother! I need to talk to my daughter!"

When everybody was leaving she tried to force her friend to stay, but, after being chased around apartment for a while and being cornered several times, he managed to break free from her embraces and snuck through the door out into the street. That was the last time I saw Igor's mother-in-law.

Before I knew it, I was at the point of final countdown – ten, nine, eight, sitting in a taxi on the way to Sheremetievo International Airport.

"Stop! I gotta make a call," Goga's phone was disconnected. I dialed Kolia-Luna.

"Valerka [the informal form of Valery] is that you? Kolia is not home," Tiotia Katia, his mother answered.

"Tiotia Katia, I am calling to say good bye. Please tell Kolia, Goga and everybody..."

"We know, we know. When are you leaving?"

"Right now, I am on the way to the airport."

"Oi Valerka, Kolia is not home. God bless you. May God spare you the pain of missing Russia."

"Thank you Tiotia Katia. May God bless you all, too. I have to run, the taxi is waiting. Farewell."

...five, four, checking through customs, "Wait a minute, not so fast," a boarder patrol officer said, withholding my trumpet.

"Why can't I take it with me?"

"It's a foreign-made instrument; we need a release form from the bureau of appraisals and evaluations."

"The bureau told me that there is no need for any release form for an instrument made in a socialist country."

"They told you wrong."

"How can I go without a trumpet?"

"Do you choose to miss the plane and stay here?"

...three, two, one, engines roaring, take off.

Most of the seats on the TU104, a mid-size Aeroflot plane, were occupied by emigrants to Israel with a transfer in Vienna. For most of the passengers it was their first international flight, for some their first flight, period.

Two or so hours into the flight there was an announcement: "We are flying over the Soviet border." Several celebrations broke out right away. They then quieted down and there a complete silence descended over the passenger compartment...

One-sixth of all of the earth's land mass, Mother Russia – loved, hated, richest, poorest, the most ingenious, stupidest, generous, miserly, master, slave, forgiving, vindictive, the strongest, the weakest, God-fearing, atheistic, beautiful, ugly, loving parent, Cinderella's stepmother, drunk, sober, insane, sensible, sick, healthy, heroic, cowardly, treacherous, loyal, violent, peaceful, cruel, kind, vulnerable, secure, saint, sinner, criminal, lawful, transparent, mysterious, naive, sophisticated, backwards, in the space age, polluted, pure, vile, honorable, ruined, forever young and beautiful, its turbulent history, all 12 time zones of it, no longer yours, left behind.

An audible sound of sobbing interrupted the dead silence, then somebody began celebrating once again as the TU104, at a speed of 900 kilometers per hour, kept on flying westward away from the border.

Just as Igor described in his letter, there was a nice little old man collecting everybody's papers.

"You are the last one in line. You must be Valery Ponomarev. Welcome," said the old man in clear Russian as he checked his clipboard. "Please give me your travel document."

"I can't," I told him, and explained why.

"Please don't make a scene. The Austrian Government very reluctantly allows us to conduct our business here. If we create any kind of a problem, we'll be asked to leave. Please come with everybody else and there we will figure everything out to your satisfaction."

I realized that I was creating a big problem for the old man. He was begging and pleading as I kept thinking that I had never wanted to go anywhere but the jazz headquarters of the world. Why should I give away my freedom of choice, after all I had just gone through.

The letter specifically said DO NOT give this very person your travel documents, otherwise you will end up far away from where you were going.

"I am sorry, I can't." It was hard, but I had to disappoint the old man.

"Then you have to go to the second floor and wait in the lounge for transit passengers." My welcoming committee to the West didn't have any other choice either.

The lounge was full of people waiting for their planes to take them to their appointed destinations. A huge board illuminated the timetable of flights to Calcutta, Ankara, Madrid, Paris, Rio de Janeiro, Bombay, Rome, Berlin, London, Santiago, Addis Ababa, Sidney, Boston, Delhi, Tokyo, Copenhagen, Montreal ...New York. Only I didn't have any place to go to. One thing I could be certain of – I wouldn't be sent back to the Soviet Union.

In about ten minutes I heard a multitude of footsteps coming up the stairs. First a big head appeared above the handrail, then enormous shoulders, probably two to three times wider than Izrailova's, then a chest the size of two to three barrels, then a huge belly. After a few more steps, a wholesome giant in a bright greenish-yellow jersey appeared. With him was a short wiry man and my old friend from the welcoming committee. The jersey must have been the size of XXXL at least, but still too tight a fit and threatening to burst open at any time. I got up before the eyes of the old man spotted me.

"I am with the Airport's security forces," said the giant, and he stretched out his hand.

"Give me your documents." I opened my mouth to tell him that I was a refugee not an emigrant, but didn't have a chance to finish.

"I don't need to hear any of it, I just need your documents," interrupted the security officer, his hand still stretched out.

I didn't intend to argue with the guy. I just thought that this was the time to recite in English my well-prepared speech. After all, wasn't he the Austrian authority?

"Give me your documents," repeated the giant. This time there was a little annoyance in his voice. I pulled the document out of my breast pocket and handed it to him. "That's good," said the officer, and right there in one motion he passed it along to the Israeli representative.

"Everything will be just fine," my man assured me as we walked down the stairs.

Indeed, at the Castle Shenau I was treated very well. I forgot what was served for dinner, I just remember that it was very delicious. I was given a seat away from the main pack of emigrants. Some of them came over to my side to find out what was going on, so I told them. Almost every one of them told me that he didn't intend to stay in Israel for more than a year, but move to America. Some mentioned Canada or Australia and wished me good luck. After dinner I was invited to the supervisor's office.

"Why don't you want to go to Israel?" the supervisor, a man in his mid-thirties in plain clothes, asked me. His Russian was very good with only a slight accent.

"I am not Jewish," I told him, and then explained to him the whole scoop.

"One doesn't have to be Jewish to live in Israel. Very many different nationalities live in our country. Besides we love jazz. One of your countrymen, jazz artist Emil Gorovets, just moved to Israel. His first concert attracted thousands of people. Maybe you will play in his band."

Obviously my interviewer didn't know much about jazz, so I explained to him that, although Emil Gorovets was a very good and popular Soviet artist, he was not a jazz musician. I told how important it was for me to get to the Jazz headquarters of the world.

"So you used our country to get out of the Soviet Union."

"I guess you can put it that way, but what else could I do? That was the only chance for me to escape. I thought I was in the West now and could tell the whole truth. I didn't think anybody would judge me for it."

"That's good. I respect that. Of course nobody will judge you for that. Let me call the local branch of the International Rescue Committee. Maybe it's still open."

An hour later I was in a car with my bag being driven through the gates, past guards with machine guns, into Vienna.

Years later, in 1996, I did go to Israel to play at the Tel Aviv International Jazz Festival. I absolutely loved the experience and can't wait to go there again, maybe this year. As for now I am in my apartment in New York City writing the next chapter.

March 20, 1999

## Chapter 3

# On the flip side of sound

From Vienna, the International Rescue Committee moved me to Rome, Italy, where I applied for an entrance visa to the United States. A big surprise waited for me there: some local musicians already knew me from the record that had been made at the Moscow Jazz Festival a few years before. On that record, every band that participated in the festival had a track.

Italian guys liked my playing very much and offered me a lot of gigs while I was waiting for the word from the U.S. embassy. They even tried to talk me into staying in Italy permanently. They used to tell me how difficult it was for jazz musicians to make it in America, how many musicians were out of work. They even introduced me to some of the American musicians living in Europe, who would say the same thing.

"You could have everything here a human being could dream of. Even citizenship is no problem – we will help you with that. In a couple of years you won't have to worry about anything. Look how much work we have," my new "amici" used to tell me.

Yes, there were plenty of gigs all over Italy. Driving to gigs with beautiful Marina and Roberto up and down the "Boot" was a lot of fun in itself: one incredible view replaced the other at a speed of one hundred and forty kilometers per hour. Quaint villages, statues, churches – the whole country was like one incredible museum of antiquity. What a country! After the gloomy atmosphere of the Soviet regime, Italy, at the peak of vacation season, seemed like paradise: sun, sea, mountains, multitude of colors, happy-carefree people all dressed like they had just stepped off pages of fashion magazines, highways, resorts, restaurants, food! I couldn't even dream of all of that!

Finally, the long awaited word from the U.S. embassy arrived: I had been granted a visa and residency in America. "Dear Romano, Picci, Orso, Carlo, Luciano, Roberto, Marina, please understand," I said, "I have to go to America to meet Art Blakey." Romano said he always knew I would never stay.

The day has arrived. I am one of a group of refugees being cared for by the Italian Division of the International Rescue Committee with Dr. Korach as the head of the office. I am on the way to the Leonardo da Vinci airport in Rome, leaving behind Italy, the place of my first transfer after a successful escape from the Soviet Union. It is a beautiful October day: 25 degrees Celsius, bright sun, and not a single cloud in the blue skies, just like any day, it seems, anywhere over the Apennine Peninsula.

Although most tourists and vacationers were not showing up on the beaches any more, the weather was still gorgeous by anybody's standard. But for me, a Muscovite, Italian atmospheric conditions in October were perfect.

"Goodbye, Italy and my new Italian friends." A huge party had been thrown the night before, which lasted well into the morning and left us with hardly any sleep. In the back of my mind there was a nagging conviction that I'd be missing all of them and their country, but the foreground was totally occupied by the immediate future, only a few hours away, across the ocean.

Destination – America: Land of the Free, Prosperity, New York, the Brooklyn Bridge, skyscrapers, sounds of jazz pouring out of every open door and window. Customers in barbershops strumming standard chord changes on banjoes while waiting for haircuts, housewives practicing saxophones while dinner simmers and washing machines hum, kids trotting off to school in the morning carrying lunch boxes along with Selmer and Bach instruments. Art Blakey, Horace Silver, Sonny Rollins, Max Roach – the world's greatest jazz superstars, and my idols. A lot of things existed in the realm of my imagination. Some of them proved to be exactly as I expected them to be; the reality of the others is still hard for me to get used to.

Dr. Korach gave every one of us IRC dependents a present on behalf of his organization: elegant shoulder bags with the IRC inscription on them. Only a moment before, passengers with those shoulder bags were a noisy and excited pack, moving through a crowd of people in the terminal. Now we were devoured by the Boeing 747 in its monstrous belly. I had never been on a plane of that size before. The only thing left to do was to make myself comfortable in the chair next to the window. That was my first of what would be innumerable flights across the Atlantic.

But I had seen such a big plane once before, if not a larger one. My friends and I were practically kids when a whole bunch of us aspiring musicians went on our first gig outside of Moscow. It was at a summer resort on the Black Sea. We had rented the second floor of a house on top of a hill which overlooked an old, out-of-the-way airport. That airport had never had any security around it and we all had gotten used to running across the field back and forth whenever we wanted to, having discovered it was a shortcut to the seaside town where the vacationers stayed. Every evening there, we played dance music for these vacationers at the hippest discotheque in town – a stretch of unpaved ground surrounded by a wooden fence.

One morning Vitali Kleinot – our tenor player and musical leader – Sasha Terekhoff, three glistening memories of girls, myself and Boris Rossin were on our way to the beach. Sasha was only slightly older, but already had a lot of experience living under guard in forced labor camps. Nobody was exempt from them, whether in actuality or in fear. We all knew it could happen to any one of us at any time. That was the reality of life in the Soviet State, which could support itself only by making its citizens work for free, particularly in places where nobody would even think of going, no matter what the salary.

Vitali's turn came some years later, when I was already in the West. But this day, we were helping Sasha have as carefree a time as possible in between his misfortunes. Needless to say we couldn't wait to show off in front of the girls and headed along the short cut, down the slope to the airfield, where we made a right.

"Halt right there!" We heard a barking command coming from a diminutive looking man carrying a shotgun. He was Kalmik, from a small sub-nation of the Soviet Union. It was common then that army personnel were drawn from other republics to serve in Russia. Behind him was a huge plane, which looked as big as the hill we had just climbed down.

"Come on, man, what are you talking about?" I said and took two more paces.

"Tiorn back," the Kalmik barked as he took the rifle off his shoulder. This time I definitely heard the accent.

"What kind of a joke is this?" I asked making one more step. The guard said nothing but took aim at me. He looked like a bronze statue, one of those stereotype statues of a Soviet hero, created and reproduced through the years in great quantity by socialist-communist sculptors. I wanted to explain that we had taken this path many times each day since the beginning of the tourist season, that everybody knew us there, that we were professional musicians playing at the most glamorous place in town for comrade vacationers – drunken bums – so they could spend an evening in style.

Before I had a chance to utter a word, Sasha's strong hand grabbed me from behind and pulled me back. I tried to protest but Sasha turned me around and pushed me in the direction of our house. He kept pushing me until I started moving on my own. "Run," he screamed, and took off in pursuit of the girls and Vitali, who were already climbing up the hill. Seeing big and strong Sasha Terekhoff run had a "get set, get ready, go" effect on me and I gave chase.

"Are you crazy?" he yelled as I caught up with him. "This guy with the gun doesn't have any brains; you can't talk any sense to him. There is frozen shit inside his scull. Authorities always use degenerates like him on jobs where compassion or thinking may get in the way of firing a weapon. Morons like that one shoot inmates in the Gulag just for being unauthorized near the barbed wire, and that's in Siberia with hundreds of square miles of glacial tundra around the labor camp. One would be frozen to death in no time even if he managed to escape!

"Do you know how close to serious trouble you were? That piece of shit was ready to use his gun. You would've been messed up for life at best and he would've gotten a citation for it and felt proud of himself too, if he were capable of any feelings at all."

I felt humiliated in front of the three Dulcineas in shorts and beat-up sneakers. They went to the beach without me, I stayed in the house listening to "Moaning" by Art Blakey, my newly discovered idol, and his Jazz Messengers.

\*\*\*\*\*\*\*\*\*\*\*\*\*\*\*\*\*\*\*\*\*\*\*\*\*\*

By sunset everybody was back in the house with the latest news brought back from town. Rumor had it that the biggest party official had flown in complete secrecy to the south for vacation. In the meantime his buddies in the government had conspired against him and ousted him from office. Truly don't leave the store unattended.

That's whose plane was on the field! God Almighty!

In Russia everything is classified material and yet nothing is a secret. With so much secrecy everywhere about everything, how these rumors originate is a mystery. Sure enough, the morning papers reported that he who had been the greatest leader of all time only yesterday was now the worst scum imaginable and had been relieved from his duties by the will of the people, blah-blah-blah-blah-blah.

"Fasten your seat belts, we are descending into JFK International Airport." I heard a pleasant voice waking me up. The trip is already over?!

"Welcome to America," said the border control officer, a big broad shouldered guy about my age, who smiled as he handed back my papers. It was not one of those routine stretches of mouth corners either, but an honest, well meaning smile. "Thank you," I said, and crossed the line.

Only minutes later, I was already in a car moving towards Manhattan. The skyline on the horizon was fast approaching. One more turn, what a view! Water below, evening skies above, and buildings, buildings, buildings in between!

What a profound and harmonious symphony of gigantic cubical forms, vertical and horizontal lines and countless brightly lit stories! Getting bigger and bigger still, I could no longer see the ground or the sky, only a tangle of concrete, glass and steel. I wanted to laugh and scream at the same time. I am not sure I didn't. I was beside myself.

This was the real New York: lights everywhere, flooding everything in sight, left and right, above and below. Right there, beyond the car windows were jazz clubs, musicians, trumpet-players, saxophone-players, drummers, composers. Who is that black guy walking so rhythmically down the street? He must be a jazz star. Let me out of the car!

Yes, I understand, we have to go to the hotel (the Latham on 28th Street between Madison and Park), check in, and show up the next morning at the headquarters of the International Rescue Committee, a worldwide organization which was taking care of countless other refugees and me.

I was like a spirit locked up in a bottle, which was just about to pop open; a little bit longer and I would spew outside into the streets, looking for jazz. I needed to hold out just a little longer.

"Being a jazz musician is not a full-time profession in America," Ms. Barankovitch, my counselor at the headquarters, told me. "The organization can't keep on paying for your food and lodgings forever. We will have to find you a job, that of a salesman, for example. The holiday season is almost upon us; help will be needed everywhere. You understand?"

Of course I did. I didn't want to live at anybody's expense. Although I'd never imagined myself as a salesman, I would accept anything just to be on my own as soon as possible.

"Since you already speak English well, I can send you to B. Altman's. It is a beautiful department store. I have good friends there in the personnel department. They will find you something. I am doing you a favor really; those who don't speak or speak very little English are sent to manual labor jobs: handing out leaflets on the streets, packing cartons, loading and unloading trucks, and so forth. I have a math teacher delivering milk containers at a supermarket!" (That was true. Some time later I saw an immigrant from the headquarters on the street handing out leaflets advertising whorehouses around town).

I had to go regularly to the IRC headquarters for the next couple of months. One day, while waiting in the corridor for my appointment, I was sitting next to a delicate young Russian lady. She was very upset.

"Ms. Barankovitch sent me to a factory. Grease and dirt is everywhere. She says I need to speak English if I want to work according to my education. I am a dental technician, you know. How could I learn to speak English in this factory environment with only uneducated people from Latin America around? Nobody even tries to speak English; Spanish is the state language at that factory. There is no need for me to speak English well as a dental technician at all, or any language for that matter, because I never even see the patient in the laboratory; it's a doctor's job in the office. I can understand instructions very well, they are all technical terms anyway. An interpreter told me that the manager at the factory was very surprised to see me there. He didn't think it was a place for me. 'Isn't there a position for her in dentistry somewhere?' That's what he said."

"Don't worry. You are in America. Nobody has to do anything he doesn't want to. It's only for now, for the first few months. You will find your way around soon." I tried to console her. "You will own your own dental laboratory one day. Cheer up." She waved me off with her pretty little hand, dismissing everything I said and tried to force a smile. She wanted to believe me, but kept on sobbing anyway.

Free, Free! Nothing could stand in my way any more. The Village, Harlem, West Side, East Side, uptown, downtown, jazz clubs everywhere in the city, or so it seemed to me, after a near starvation level diet of only one authorized jazz club in the entire capital of the Soviet Union. Despite the fact that the authorities kept it functioning only to impress foreigners with the "freedoms" which existed in the "Communist Heaven," in many respects it was, in fact, a real jazz club.

Right after my workday at B. Altman's ended, I would run home, blow long tones, eat and then take off, looking for jazz. I would never tire of traveling by subway or walking through the streets from club to club into the very late or rather very early hours of the following day.

After just two months in the jazz headquarters of the world, so many musicians, who had existed for me only in the realm of sound, whose tone or articulation I had grown accustomed to and could recognize from the very first couple of notes, merged with their visual image. I heard so many great jazz artists perform live, not missing the slightest opportunity to sit in or at least to socialize with any of them!

Check the schedules of New York City jazz clubs in October-November 1973: the Sonny Rollins quartet with Walter Davis on piano at the now defunct "Half-Note" on 54th street, Horace Silver opposite Art Farmer at the same club the following week. Within a couple of years the club became a strip joint.

That reminded me of the fate of our own Youth Café on Gorky Street in Moscow, just about the only place in a huge city where musicians and fans, starving for jazz, could congregate. It was turned not into a sex shrine but a fast food joint, offering Siberian dumplings. Naked girls are better, if I had to make a choice.

On the other side of the street "Under the Clock," "Eddie Condon's," and "Jimmy Ryan's" where Roy Eldridge had a steady gig in town for many years. Howard McGee was with Joe Carroll at the bottom of a Skyscraper on 52nd street and Broadway playing "Stormy Weather," Tommy Flanagan at the "Village Gate," a legendary New York tourist attraction, now a huge prescription drugs outlet. I wonder if it provides the girls with some necessary medicine.

Charley Rouse at some small club in the Village, George Coleman and Frank Strosier at a club on 72nd Street. (Frank said after my first sitting in with them, " I am sure I will hear your name again.") Chet Baker at "Struggles" across the Street, Harold Camperbatch on baritone, Ed Lewis on trumpet and Mathew Gee on trombone at Churchill's on East 83rd Street. Boy, were they swinging!

On my second or third time after jamming with them for the first time at that smoky little bar I was sitting near the stage and listening. Harold asked me: "Why are you not playing?"

"Well, I kind of didn't have a chance to ask for permission to sit in yet," I said.

"You don't need to ask for permission, Val; you are one of the guys."

I hadn't heard that expression before, only sensed that it was something real good.

"What's 'One of the guys?'" I asked.

"You know, one of the guys, one of us," Harold said. "You will figure it out soon."

A myriad of musicians inhabited the jazz Mecca. Some of them were playing on the streets and sounding just right. On the Moscow jazz scene as well as anywhere East of the Iron Curtain there were a few "giants of jazz" – in their own minds – who could get a pretty sobering lesson on the streets and subway stations of New York City. A lot of jazz enthusiasts dwelling in the closed society in the Soviet Block, due to complete isolation, had adopted wrong perceptions of the genre.

Once on the way to the "West End Café," I passed by a flute player. He was sitting right on the asphalt a couple of doors from the club and improvising on some changes. I couldn't figure out which ones.

Inside, the room was full of students from nearby Columbia University. Half an hour later I was already on the stage sitting in with the band featured for that night. I thought I spotted the flute player from the street in the crowd.

In the break a very tall guy, perhaps as tall as seven feet, came up to me and started a conversation about communism, how good it is for the working class, and so on. It would always amuse me when Americans try to tell me how good communism is for the common people in Russia, not even taking into consideration the fact that there must have been a reason why I went through so much trouble to break out from there.

Despite his height John looked like a baby, only a very tall baby, rosy cheeks, wide naïve eyes. He sounded like he was delivering a well-rehearsed speech rather then holding a conversation. Maybe he was working on some kind of thesis at the university and practicing it on anybody who was willing to listen. All right, I thought, I'll listen for a minute; after all it is interesting to know what people in the West are thinking about something they have never experienced for themselves.

"Have you ever lived in Russia, like a private citizen, not like a tourist?" I finally managed to squeeze in.

"No, I've never been there period, but I would love to go."

His "I would love to go" sounded like he was thanking me for something in advance; maybe he thought that I could help him to get a free ticket on Aeroflot or put him in touch with some kind of Young Soviet Communists Exchange League or something.

Actually I would have been happy to help him if I could. Only please don't end up like your namesake – John Read – bricked up in the wall.

"Don't take him seriously, Valery. John will be talking 'til the night is over if you let him," broke in Phil Schapp, the manager of the room and a student at Columbia whom I'd met a couple of days before.

He looked pretty much like John himself only not as tall. Very soon I realized that Phil is a very special person – his encyclopedic brain holds information concerning everything he has ever encountered: events, names, dates, records, titles and repertoires. You name it; it is all stored in his head.

This phenomenal talent serves him very well in his other job as a disc jockey at the Columbia University jazz radio station. Sometimes his immense knowledge of facts and details gets in the way of the music, I must admit, but it is still a great musical program, particularly when he is paying tribute to Clifford Brown.

For the twenty-four hours of October 30th, the day of Clifford's birth, Phil Schapp plays music by the trumpet genius only. I just love it.

One day on the eve of such a tribute I called Phil to find out if he was going to play anything I might never have heard before.

"Be prepared at noon," was the answer.

Until "Electra Musician" and Philology S.I.A.E. (Italy) released it on CD, it seemed to me that I was the sole owner of a treasure – a recording of a broadcast, which I had taped off the radio. This broadcast featured a tape made by the radiantly beautiful LaRue some 30 years previously in the sanctuary of her and her husband's house – a recording of Clifford Brown practicing.

To this day, every time I see Phil, he greets me the same way: "Valery Ponomarjoff, arrived in NY on October 29th 1973."

On the way back from the West End Café, I passed by the flute-player again. He was still sitting on the same spot. "Hey-Hey, trumpet player," I heard him call out. "You sound like you know 'The Jazz Messengers' music very well. What was your name again?" I introduced myself.

"David Grice, I am Gee Gee Grice's distant relative," said my new acquaintance as he folded his flute. Somehow I didn't think David was really related to the renowned alto saxophonist. He gave me the impression of a person who adds a mythical title to his name like a professor or baron or ambassador, to impress guests at a social gathering.

"How do you know me?"

"I was inside the club for a minute while you were on the stage. You say you are from Russia, playing like that? You should meet Art Blakey. He will hire you. Bu [short for Buheina, Art's Muslim adopted name] lets everybody play, no matter where the guy is from, as long as he can play the music."

I had never thought of being hired; I just wanted to play with Art Blakey. Treating it as work never had occurred to me.

Another night I was sitting in at Under the Clock on my new large bore 72 bell Bach Stradivarius. That horn was so beautiful, so sparkling new, it played all by itself. A music fan came up to me, asking, "Did you escape from the Half Note to sit in here during the break?" "No," I answered, not quite understanding his New York accent, "I escaped from Russia two months ago."

Yes, I met a lot of people and a lot of people, to my surprise, already knew of me. One night I wanted to sit in with a band in the village. During the break I came up to the drummer, who seemed to be the leader of the organization and asked him about joining the band for a couple of tunes. He asked me right away, just like most Americans do, where I was from. My accent in those days, of course, was very different from what it is today.

In the City almost everybody is from somewhere else originally. If not he, then his parents or grandparents most likely had been born in some other part of our big wide world. That's why New Yorkers are so inquisitive about other people's origin and are also so polite and patient when it comes to figuring out what it is that this particular immigrant wants.

No matter how much a foreigner might be trying to murder the rules of the English language, not to mention pronunciation, a New Yorker will be very attentive and will figure out the meaning of any mangle-garble-jumble even if this murderer is afflicted with a speech impediment. Not the same in Paris, for example, where a Parisian won't tolerate even a slightest deviation from the norm.

Anyway, "From Russia," I said.

"Do you know Valery Ponomarev?"

"What?! I am Valery Ponomarev, I am from Moscow."

"Oh sure you can sit in, as soon as the second set starts. I heard about you, everybody says you can play your ass off."

A scene from that period is flashing in my mind: I am sitting in with

Walter Davis somewhere in the Village playing "I Remember Clifford." Walter is quite impressed.

Can you imagine that I was still not quite happy? Yet, it is true that my jazz Heaven was still not complete. Art Blakey and the Jazz Messengers were missing.

Almost every jazz musician and fan I met claimed he knew Mr. Blakey personally and very often even called him by his nickname, Bu. Blakey, as I learned later, was on the road. Whether he was in Japan or driving, as was his custom, along some thruway en route to a distant gig in one of the states of the Union, I don't know. But he was not in New York City.

Slowly but surely I was learning to understand the tape produced by the Jazz Interaction Service advertising jazz clubs in the City. At first I couldn't understand the New York pronunciation at all. While I could speak a bit of English and was very good at imitating a British accent, which had been featured in the short course I took before escaping from my motherland, dealing with the New York accent was an entirely different proposition.

One incident stands out in my mind, a scene at B. Altman's. I was looking for something in the Pots and Pans department. A coworker came out from the storage room, so I explained to him, in what I knew was very proper English, what I needed and he answered. His answer sounded like a cross between a cat's meow and a dog's bark, albeit a very friendly meow-bark. I repeated my question and heard the meow-bark again.

At that moment I started losing confidence in my ability to speak the Queen's English, yet I addressed him again in the same manner. Before he had even finished his courteous meow-bark reply, the floor supervisor Mr. Russell broke in, "Val is from the old country – he can't understand a word you saying!" Everybody around burst out laughing.

Another time I was asking for a loaf of bread at an Italian bakery in Astoria, Long Island, where I was living at the time. The woman behind the counter didn't answer me at all. "I would like to buy that loaf of bread," I repeated again and pointed at the brown and crusty piece. At last she said: "Novanta centezimi," and handed it to me in exchange for 90 cents. God almighty! I was not the only one who had problems with the local language! That woman didn't speak it at all.

In the following years I encountered many expatriates who had clung to their particular communities – Brighton Beach (Russians), Chinatown, Spanish Harlem, a French-speaking village near Montreal – and never ventured outside of them. It has always seemed strange to me.

One day a friend of mine, Michael Bransburg, an aspiring drummer, called: "Valery, Art Blakey and the Jazz Messengers are at the Five Spot this coming week."

I dialed the number for the jazz line to hear who was playing in the City that week and at which club. The recording played its usual maze of Bleeker Street – meow-bark-Boomer's etc. The idea that my friend had played a trick on me started to formulate in my mind when all of a sudden I distinctively heard, "Art Blakey and the Jazz Messengers... Five Spot."

Art Blakey at the Five Spot?! The Five Spot was the legendary club where Sonny Rollins, Booker Little, the Monk quartet featuring John Coltrane, and many others played and recorded live. Art Blakey! I dialed the number again. No mistake about it, "Art Blakey and the Jazz Messengers...meow-bark... Tuesday through Sunday...meow-bark...Five Spot."

Needless to say, Tuesday night I was sitting in the closest possible proximity to Art Blakey and the Jazz Messengers. The band was all ready to play. Bill Hardman was on trumpet, David Schnitter on tenor, and to the left and slightly behind was the legendary Walter Davis on the piano. Right behind the front line was the bass player Chin Suzuki, from Japan, and to the right, next to him, behind the drum set, oh my God that's Art Blakey!

One, two – one, two, three – just like on the record I am still crazy about, "A Night at Birdland" featuring Clifford Brown. The same voice, the same intensity and just like on the record, the band came in after the count of three. Only this time instead of "Quick Silver," the sound of Clifford Brown's classic "Joy Spring" embraced the audience.

I was beside myself. That's one of my most favorite tunes. I had transcribed Clifford's solos from both versions. I had managed to get a hold of recordings of them in Moscow, in F and in $E^b$ a long time ago by then.

I learned the language of jazz from transcribing the solos of my favorite musicians, at first mostly those by Clifford Brown. As a result melodic, harmonic and rhythmic patterns derived from those transcriptions were firmly rooted in my musical speech.

Everybody sounded great. The band was talking to me in the language I learned so far away from its origin and the country where it is practiced the most. Waves of such familiar tunes, lines and accents, harmonies and rhythms were splashing all over me. I closed my eyes for a second – it felt like I was back in my room in Moscow, listening to jazz out of my tape recorder. I literally pinched myself to make sure it was not a dream. But it wasn't: Art Blakey in person sat behind the drums playing that incredible accompaniment.

I was not on the stage, but still I felt like I was right in the middle of those warm waters. It seemed like the Jazz Messengers were luring me into a conversation.

Before I knew it the set was over. All the messengers and Art Blakey with them got off the bandstand for the break. "So that's what he looks like!" I thought: short, stocky, broad shoulders, muscular, happy, confident.

As he descended down the steps to the ground level, a couple of fans, or maybe they were friends of my hero, went up to him. Right away Mr. Blakey started telling them some kind of a funny story. All I heard was: "That old witch." Later I realized Art was saying, "That old bitch," referring to somebody at the end of the bar. I got out from behind my table and moved closer.

There he was, just about my height, maybe an inch taller. He had a common look about him, looking very much like, believe it or not, some of my friends in Moscow from Mazutni drive, a not fancy, down-to-earth neighborhood. Guys like that would be sitting in the backyard cracking a bottle: coal miners, conveyor belt operators, car mechanics, ex convicts, labor camp alumni. Guys like Goga, Sasha Terekhoff or Rossin – known for his debaucheries and labor camp manners.

Very often, they even appeared as dark as Blakey, not having had a chance to wash the dirt off their faces while on break from hard work. If Rossin ever were to find out that he looked like Art Blakey, he would drink himself to death that very day, being so flattered.

But the leader of the Jazz Messengers was not an ordinary man. This was the man who possessed the spirit of jazz music. He was the rhythm and the time of jazz music period – past, present and future. There is a certain quality to jazz which remains unchanged through time. Take that ingredient out and it's no longer jazz music, like a key ingredient missing from what would otherwise be a precious metal.

With only nine grades of formal education, he was able to steer the band through myriad visible and concealed obstacles for over 40 years, and to record innumerable LPs and CDs, which register as a colossal body of the most inspiring music.

I don't think Art had any kind of formal music education, yet he was solely responsible for taking Clifford Brown, Lee Morgan, Freddie Hubbard, Wayne Shorter, Cedar Walton, Reggie Workman, Curtis Fuller, Benny Golson, Johnny Griffin etc-etc-etc to the highest level of musical performance. Although most of the Messengers acquired the status of big name musicians or superstars of jazz after being with the band, and all of them created beautiful music on their own or with other groups, none of them ever got to quite the same heights again.

Back in Moscow my friends and I considered Art Blakey, along with Louis Armstrong, Duke Ellington, Count Basie, Charlie Parker, Clifford Brown, Sonny Rollins and John Coltrane, as the Gods of jazz. Now the Rossin look-alike God was standing right in front of me. A musician, one of the guys I recently jammed with, also came up to join the small crowd, which gathered around my hero.

Right off the bat he said, pointing at me, "Look Bu, this guy is honest to God Russian, he plays like Clifford Brown." Art Blakey scrutinized me.

"Valery Ponomarev, trumpet player from Moscow," I confirmed right away.

"Where is your horn?" the God asked me in a very down to earth hoarse voice.

"It's at home," I said grasping something behind his question. "I'll bring it tomorrow," I added in a hurry.

"We'll see you then," Mr. Blakey said and turned to his friends, seeming to lose interest in me. That was my first lesson from the master – don't go anywhere without your horn.

The break dragged on and on. Finally Art Blakey walked on stage and tipped the bell of his K Ziljian. The rest of the Messengers appeared on the bandstand momentarily, coming from different sides of the club.

"One, two, one-two-three"... The second set began.

I have never seen a drummer who played with so much energy.

Blakey played like it was his last chance to sit behind drums, like it was his last day on Earth. By the end of the concert he was wet with sweat, having spent probably more calories than a boxer after fifteen rounds.

The next day I showed up with my trumpet solidly soldered to my hand. Just like the night before, I got out from behind my table as soon as the first set was over and went up to Art Blakey. "Good evening Mr. Blakey. Can I sit in with you?" I phrased the question that was such a recent addition to my vocabulary, but which was already so firmly rooted in my consciousness that I couldn't say my mother's name better.

"Yeah, at the end of the last set," said Mr. Blakey, noticing the case in my hand, and moving off to the bar to say hello to somebody.

But he did not forget about me. Actually, in his own way, he paid a lot of attention to me. Once during that break, when I was sitting at a table talking to my aspiring drummer friend, a black hand stretched right from behind my shoulder and grabbed matches off the table. I turned around. A sound of surprise escaped my mouth; it was Art Blakey.

A few minutes later the same thing happened, only this time the hand grabbed my unfinished bottle of beer. "Mr. Blakey!" I exclaimed struck by vision of the deity again.

I was not surprised, that he not only remembered me, but also he didn't confuse me with some crazy tourist on vacation. I had seen enough of them getting high from the city and trying to do something outrageous. Most musicians can identify another musician in a crowd and almost right away can tell you what sort of a musician he or she is and on what level.

The perception of one of the greatest personalities in jazz had to be much higher than average. Art identified me right away. I saw that knowing look in his eyes, a look of recognizing his own. He knew I was the messenger from Russia.

A few years later, when I was already in the band, Art would say,

"Valery was a messenger long before he joined the messengers." Another thing he said was: "The night when Valery sat in with us for the first time, Monk was in the audience. Thelonious told me, 'Get this guy, he is for real.'"

Trumpet player Woody Show was a messenger of previous editions of the band who occupied the number one spot in the critic's choice poll for trumpet in the most prestigious jazz magazine, "Down Beat." That night, he and Turmasa Hino, a great trumpet player from Japan, came by the club. By the beginning of the third and final set, both of them had their horns out and were ready to play. And play they did.

It didn't become a jam session or anything, the band was still playing its program, but the presence of two more trumpeters on the bandstand made it more informal. It turned into a trumpet player night out. The heat was rising. It was becoming harder and harder for me to sit still at the table next to the stage right in front of Art Blakey and the rest of the band playing their hearts out.

Blakey had told me himself that I could sit in at the end of the third set. This was already the end of the third set. That's my place there too, right in between Bill and Woody, I can take my horn out and speak the same language, that's where I belong!

Nobody could tell me otherwise, I just knew it. That's why I had risked my life escaping from Soviet Union.

"Mr. Blakey," I pleaded silently," take notice of me, please. I am sitting right here in front of you with my horn ready. You told me yourself I could sit in!"

The last tune ended, and all horn players left the stage. Art Blakey put down his drumsticks, got out from behind his drum set and moved towards the microphone, apparently to announce the end of the night's performance. The stage started to feel more and more out of reach, as far away as Mazutnii Drive from New York. My heart was sinking rapidly.

My whole musical life was flashing in front of my eyes, scene after scene after scene. I didn't remember the guys from Mazutnii not keeping their word. This was the End.

Right before my ticker hit the bottom, Art Blakey winked at me and made a commanding gesture with his hand, which had only one meaning: Get on the bandstand now and play. This is your moment.

He didn't need to say it twice; I ripped the case from under the chair I was sitting on and got my trumpet out in record time; it must've taken one hundredth of a second flat. As I would witness many times later, Art had a custom of bringing a young guy from the audience to sit in on drums for the closing tune. That evening I just had a moment to realize that there would be somebody else playing drums after Art called another guy with drumsticks in his hand onto the stage and said to both of us, "Play the Theme Song."

The other guy was just as quick to get behind Art's set and begin to rearrange it. With no time to even get disappointed, I just took a spot in front of the rhythm section facing the audience, right where Bill Hardman had just stood, and, closing my eyes as I always do when playing, thought, "Theme song it is, off we go. One-two, one-two-three coming in on the four."

Everything I had learned was no longer just the rhythms or time or hard swinging phrases over intricate changes by Fats Navarro, Clifford Brown, Lee Morgan, Freddie Hubbard, Charlie Parker or by any of so many musicians I had learned from, mainly through transcribing and analyzing their solos. By now, all of these had become particles of speech, sentences, nouns and verbs, commas and periods, exclamation and question marks, grammar rules, vocabulary.

These things, once committed to the subconscious, are the tools for composing, for expressing oneself, for communicating with other human beings.

This is my story, hear me out.

One had to be a genius to invent the changes to this tune – it's such a great vehicle for improvisation. Actually nobody in particular invented this set of changes. It evolved into a form after generations of musicians had been playing at a myriad of jam sessions. That's what you call "collective genius," or "public domain."

The drummer sounded good. I am pretty sure it was Jimmy Lovelace, one of the best swinging drummers in town, but at the time I didn't have a chance to take a good look at who was going to play instead of Art Blakey. I just knew that Art himself was sitting out. Suddenly, there was a strange stumble in the high-hat. When drummers sit in and have to play somebody else's instrument, they very often feel uncomfortable.

"Not like us horn players," I thought, and threw out a call. In response I heard a thunderous roll and the crash of a ride cymbal as only one drummer in the world could play it. Time omnipotent now as it was meant to be since it first started ticking.

Drum stick against the rim of the snare drum on two. A big, fat, yet such an elegant sound now came from the drum set behind. Rhythm Glorious.

I threw out another call.

A kick on the snare drum and the ride cymbal filled the remaining space of the phrase in response. I repeated my question – am I initiated, admitted, do you identify me as one of the guys, do you understand me? You know I am not a blabbermouth. My speech is well developed, coherent. There was the same affirmative response.

I multiplied the phrase.

A kick on the snare drum and then on the big cymbal simultaneous with the foot pedal hitting the bass drum. Repeat and repeat and repeat. "I hear you, I hear you. You are with us."

There was no need for me to see who it was, but I turned my head and opened my eyes anyway to make sure, that I was not in heaven, but on stage with Art Blakey behind the drum set. The other guy was still tightening the screw on the high-hat cymbals, positioning them where they had been previously set, at a much wider gap. It is an unspoken obligation of a drummer who has just been replaced to help the next keeper of the flame to have the instrument set to his liking.

This was one of those moments when you don't know where you are, your subconscious self is coming forward, shutting off everything else. This is the Moment of Creation.

Crash on the ride cymbal marked the end of my sitting in, or so I thought.

"Play a ballad, Valery."

I heard a familiar hoarse voice pronouncing my name very close to its original sound. I turned around to make sure that I understood the God correctly.

"Play a ballad man, any one you want."

Rubato C$^\#$ resolved into D in time, befitting a walking ballad tempo which followed. There was no need to ask Walter Davis if he knew, "What's New." A couple of bars down the road I was already sure that my chops were in the finest of order, off in another dimension – that's all I can remember...

I loved that song from the very first time I heard Clifford Brown play it. What a magnificent sound he had, what a precision in time, pitch and phrase. Every note, if there is room for it to vibrate, vibrates precisely in time – triplets, sixteenths and so on. One can literally hear every word of the lyrics.

Actually whatever ballad Clifford played was always the same – nothing short of a masterpiece. Every time I listen to Clifford Brown, it reminds me that emotion and the ability to think puts us, human beings, one whole level above the rest of the Animal Kingdom...

. . . Here comes the end of the melody: "… I haven't changed, I still love you so." Retardando, fermata. Chin Suzuki hits the root, Walter lays out a beautiful widespread chord of a dominant quality for me to play a cadenza, rest…

…"Blow your instrument." I heard the voice from so many records, encouraging Clifford Brown, Lee Morgan, Freddie Hubbard or whoever the soloist might have been at the time.

Quotes from Clifford Brown's cadenza on "Once in a While" recorded on "A night at Birdland" and my own interpretation came next. As I held the last note soaring above the applause, the audience whistled and screamed and Art continued to drum right over it all. For the second time "Theme song," signifying the very end of the show, broke out …

"Blow, blow, blow your ass off."

Oh my! My cup runneth over.

"Blow, blow, run it down your legs."

I came to my senses after the last sounds died out only after I was already off the stage. I don't even remember how I packed my horn. Art Blakey was right there. Before I could say anything, he hugged me so hard I couldn't even break away from him, God's sweat all over my new shirt.

"You will be playing with my band, you will be playing with my band," his hoarse voice kept repeating above my ear.

A little crowd gathered around us. "Mister Blakey, I play with Val. I am a tenor-player." (Mitchell Frohman. Later became a star of Latin Jazz. Composer, arranger. Have been part of the sax sections in the orchestras of Tito Puente, Mongo Santamaria, Charlie Palmieri, Machito, Topica 73, Artoro "Chico" O'Farrill, Willie Colone, Blood Sweat & Tears, Louie Ramirez. On 3 Grammy Award winning CD's. Sax soloist on the theme song for HBO's hit "Sex and the City. Currently the saxophonist in the Grammy Award winning "Spanish Harlem Orchestra." Runs his own

Latin Jazz Band "The Bronx Horns.") A guy that I jammed with a day or so before, tried to introduce himself.

"You won't play with him for too long, he will play with me," answered Art, forgetting to even ask the guy's name.

At that moment I thought Mr. Blakey was just being polite and that this was his way of welcoming a musician-refugee to America, but as it turned out, he meant exactly what he said. Two years later when Bill Hardman left the band I got the call.

From the very end of 1976 through the end of 1980 I traveled continuously all over the world, playing at the world's greatest concert halls, festivals, clubs, and on radio and television shows, recording eleven albums with "Art Blakey and The Jazz Messengers."

# Chapter 4

# At the Jazz Headquarters of the World

I was a new man – I had played with Art Blakey! Rumor spread around New York like wildfire. "The Russian trumpet player sat in with Art Blakey at the "Five Spot" and brought the house down". From that point on everybody was treating me differently. My friends, musicians, fans, neighbors, even my wife. Not that I was mistreated before or something, no, but everybody was looking at me in a different way now. Yes, I knew I had touched the Divine.

A lot of people told me later that they knew it was just a matter of time before I would become a regular member of the band. Art Blakey himself later said: "Valery just needed to hang in the city a little longer, before he was ready to go on the road with us."

Nevertheless, the idea of being in the band did not surface from the background layers of my consciousness for the next couple of years. No, to me it was still too far out.

To be one of them. Me? A foreigner. – No! – Fortune like that? – No! That is too much. That is for other people. Somebody else is always that lucky. Me? – No!

Just like before the results of final exams are out. You know you did well, you know you deserve to graduate, but you are still on your previous chops – you are still in the old, the longest. Years of preparation are coming to an end, when the unknown future is just ahead, around the corner, just a jump away. You are at the border. New York, New York, here I am.

A week or so after sitting in with Art Blakey I was in my apartment, when the telephone rang.

"This is Horace Silver, may I speak with Valery Ponomarev?"

I thought somebody was kidding me. Besides it seemed to me that there was some kind of an accent in the caller's voice. My first reaction to it was to think that it was Michael Bransburg, trying to play a joke on me.

"Are you kidding Mike?" I said in Russian. "You think it's that easy to fool me. Why would Horace Silver call me.

"I am sorry. Do you speak English?"

"What? This is me. I am sorry, I thought it was a friend of mine, trying to play a joke on me."

"No, no, it is Horace Silver. Bill Hardman recommended you. I would like to hear you play. We are having a session the day after tomorrow at ... (the noise coming from the window stopped and I heard clearly that it was not Michael.)...Broadway around 80th street." He gave me the address of the studio and the time.

"Mister Silver, I will be playing at the West End Cafe tonight. Would you like to come?"

"No, for me is much more convenient to meet you at the session. Do you want to come?"

"Oh yes, absolutely, I will be there."

"I am looking forward to meeting you".

At the appointed time I was at the session. The room was already full of some guys with instruments whom I had not met before. A rather tall guy was unpacking his tenor sax.

"You Valery? I've heard about you. Bob Berg. Nice to meet you."

"Nice to meet you too." We shook hands. Then Horace called a tune,

I think it was one of his recently written ones, and Bob called out changes for me right away. By the way I was looking at him he realized that I did not quite understand him, so he repeated a couple of times: "A flat – flat five – sharp nine".

In Russian, the same code letters for chords I knew very well, but hearing them in English I could not right away associate the symbol with its sound representation. So Bob just played the chord for me from the root up.

"Oh God! Please! Flat five, sharp nine. Thank you Bob."

At the drums was Jeff Brillinger, Chip Jackson was on the bass. All were great players and, as I learned later, the newest arrivals on the jazz scene. They had come to the city from different parts of the US. Horace Silver on the piano! The guys in Moscow would never believe it.

To this day, no matter where he plays – the Blue Note or Grant's Tomb in riverside park on 122nd street – if I have a chance to say hello to him before a concert, Horace, after introducing the band, announces: "Dear ladies and gentlemen, in the audience we have my co-messenger Valery Ponomarev."

\*\*\*\*\*\*\*\*\*\*\*\*\*\*\*\*\*\*\*\*\*\*\*\*\*\*

In the meantime, I was getting more and more accustomed to life in New York. A couple of commercial studio recordings, twenty dollar jazz gigs and then regular scale club dates – social functions like weddings and bar mitzvahs – followed, first, with a band of Russian refugees of the so-called Second Wave.

Second Wave meant post WWII arrivals of Russians, who, for different reasons, got stuck on the western side of Europe after the War and the devastation it had brought with it stopped and split the continent in two. Most of them narrowly escaped forced deportation back to the Soviet Union.

After years of unspeakable suffering at the hands of Nazis, back in their motherland, with a government of criminals, they could expect only execution or slow death in Stalin's forced labor camps.

Boy! I heard some stories from these guys: hundreds of thousands of Soviet troops being taken prisoner because of the incompetence of the Red Army's high command at the outbreak of hostilities, life in concentration camps, starvation, escapes, conversion to the enemy's side, heroism.

Mostly Nick Romanenko, the band's leader and saxophone player, shared his stories of survival with me on the way to and from the gigs. The ex-freshman of Moscow Conservatory, with a standard army rifle of 1898 design, was taken prisoner in July 1941. His doom took him through fascist death camps, German military school, most European countries and then to New York City where he ended working as a musical instrument repairman and playing club dates on the side for Russian, Lithuanian, Polish, French, Ukrainian, Georgian and German parties. While on his travels he learned to speak fluently English and all those languages plus Yiddish.

"How did you manage to learn all these languages?" I asked him once.

"I was born on the Georgian side of the Caucasus Mountains into a Russian-Ukrainian family, so my first three languages came naturally, and the rest I learned in concentration camps," was the answer.

"But what about Yiddish? You would've ended in a gas chamber, had the camp guards taken you for a Jew"

"No, no, Yiddish I learned from my first employer in New York. In a concentration camp you don't, if you can help it, speak Russian or

Yiddish, unless you decided that you've had it," Nick instructed me, as if I were going next week to check myself into "Treblinka" or "Osvencim".

Nick, in his New York days, was big: over two hundred pounds and all muscle. Even the WWF had tried, unsuccessfully, to recruit him for its show. In the concentration camp his weight, because of endless starvation, dropped to 40–50 pounds.

"The human body has a tendency of rebuilding itself better after such a cleansing," he would say very often. On one of the rides to a gig he dug deeper into his memory bank and granted me an exclusive extension to his collection of horror stories:

"Once in the concentration camp two short, bowlegged tartars offered me fresh meat in exchange for cigarettes. I followed them into the dusk of a tent, where in the far corner, behind a partition, hidden from everybody's eyes, was a stretched pile under a dirty bed sheet. By then I thought I had seen everything. No, surprises were still coming."

I think nobody can measure how low or how elevated humans could be. I think there is no limit in either direction.

Nick paused and then resumed. "One of the tartars lifted the sheet slightly from one end, revealing a man's head; the pupils of his eyes were very slowly moving. That's how they knew that the body was still alive and its meat edible. Those tartars kept a nameless victim heavily sedated and continued cutting pieces off him for as many days as the pupils of his eyes were moving, prolonging their own lives."

I think Nick was trying to clear his mind of those visions, which 30 years later were still haunting him.

That evening we played for a mixed wedding. The groom was an American Jew and the bride was a very pretty German girl. Her parents were stunned by hearing the bandleader speaking flawless German.

After the party I drank a little too much and Nick drove me home instead of saying goodbye at a subway station. On the last portion of the trip we were driving next to a bus full of black people. In one of the windows I saw a young lady in a wedding gown and the rest of the passengers being very animated. I think the festivities were still on.

I was coming from a wedding myself, where I was confined to a role of a passive onlooker. This time I had to join in. I stuck my head out of the window and screamed my best wishes for the newlyweds.

"Valery, stop this immediately, you will cause an accident. Valery, you have nothing to do with their wedding. Don't disturb people you don't even know," Nick kept on driving and screaming at me, trying to put some sense into my head, to no avail.

I kept on yelling and waiving my hands until the bride noticed me and alerted the rest of the wedding train. Some passengers also opened windows of the bus and heartily thanked me for my best wishes. One guy even tried to pass me a bottle, but was pulled back by a more sober partygoer. At that point Nick made a sharp left, right into my street and the bus disappeared.

"Valery, this is America, you are not supposed to crash on other people's weddings," said Nick, looking at me sympathetically when I thanked him for the ride and got out of the car.

On and off I played Russian, Ukrainian and Polish polkas, Mendelson's march plus some pop songs with Nick's band for two-and-a-half years, right until it was time to join The Jazz Messengers.

About half a year after arriving in New York I had enough work to support myself, and my now long-time ex-wife. She felt terrible at first being unemployed. I could not understand her. Why would she not just enjoy being at home?

There was enough money. My salary at B. Altman's covered the rent, food and drinks. Even before I started working as a musician, we still had a little money left to spend on clothes and movies.

Then came the first club dates. Our living standard really jumped all the way up – continuous cooking and drinking could testify to that. We had an eight-year-old Chevrolet Impala and a sewing machine, which I had bought from a vendor for $50.

New York, America, Prosperity. It took me a long time to get used to the sights of vegetable and fruit stands overloaded with everything that grows under the sun. Some of the fruit I had not even heard of. Mango for one. What's mango? Grapes without seeds! What a miracle of agriculture.

At first, seeing those stands would always bring a memory of me as a kid standing in line and holding my mother's hand in a cold, dark and dirty enclosure full of people, with one door leading to the storage room of a supermarket, portraits of Stalin and his cronies overlooking the scene from the dirty walls. The line was, I think, organized spontaneously in response to a rumor, which would surface in one section of town and die out, only to reappear in another part of town and vanish again.

"Oranges! Oranges! Oranges will be delivered to the local supermarket, in limited quantities of course, available for the general public to purchase."

I still remember my mother, a beautiful woman then, rolling up the sleeve of her coat and then shirt, to show a number, written in ink pencil on her hand, I think it was number 34, which meant that we were 34th from the window, which, in case the rumor proved to be true, would open.

And then the magic of exchanging Soviet rubles for real oranges would begin. A crude woman in a dirty robe over a padded jacket would open the window in the door and release the ration into the hands of a lucky shopper.

"We are in America now. Something will work out," I used to tell my now ex. She was a very good dental technician and could not stay idle, I guess. While I was at B. Altman's, she would go around Astoria, L.I. in search of any kind of work.

A very pretty young little lady then – she still can not speak any English, with the exception of a few shopping necessities – she had a hard time memorizing the simplest of words. I taught her how to say: "I am looking for work. Do you have any openings for me?"

She looked so cute and pitiful at the same time, trying to pronounce words absolutely foreign to her language. She would bring home stories of her would-be employers making dirty jokes in response to her version of "Do you have any opening for me?" I felt like killing those assholes. Finally I had to ask her not to go around anymore.

One day I noticed a sign on a building, not far from where we lived: "Master Touch Dental Laboratory". I went to check out the place the next morning. When I got there, I saw a gray-haired chubby and short man in pince-nez, wiping the asphalt in front of the entrance door. I asked him where I could meet the manager of the laboratory. "I am its owner. How can I help you?" answered the man in a very heavy accent.

Dr. Nagi, the owner of the laboratory, was an emigrant from Hungary of 20-some years himself. He suggested that my wife should come some time and just sit around for a working day or two. She ended up working there for 20 years; right up until the time when she was ready to open her own business.

She was absolutely not into American culture and would never have come to America were it not for me. Funny thing was, we divorced anyway, when, after leaving the "Messengers," unsteady schedule of my profession had done its damage.

Not that I did not make money. No, sometimes I made very good money, but work came very sporadically and I had to be away from home a lot and that is exactly what she could not learn to deal with. That is a musician's lot. Every musician I know learns to place in the back of his mind worries, which are stirred by the blank spots on his business calendar.

Not their wives. No matter how much they used to love their husbands, no matter how much at the outset they vowed that nothing mattered except being together forever and ever, for better or for worse, with this particular musician and his instrument. The image of a beloved fellow playing on the stage would stir less and less passion and the rigors of life with a musician would take its toll instead. Love for a musician is a very special love, not every woman can deal with it.

She now runs her own dental laboratory, something she would never have accomplished in the Soviet Union, and feels pretty comfortable in her adopted country.

It turned out that Art Blakey played in town rather regularly. Every two or three months, between tours of foreign countries or the States, he would be playing in New York. The places mostly were the Village Gate on Bleeker Street in the Village or Michel's. Needless to say, the audiences in those clubs would never lack my presence. At both of them, the bouncers and owners got used to me pretty quickly and let me in like a member of staff.

The Village Gate was a huge place with three levels full of people everywhere. On the ground floor there was a cafe, separated from the street by huge ground-to-ceiling glass windows. Carefree people behind them were lounging around between shows. A wide staircase at the West entrance led to the room below. There was a lot of space. Between thick pillars supporting the ceiling, there were tables and ever-pretty waitresses were fussing around with large trays of beer mugs and drinks.

A big and high stage dominated the room. Dressing rooms for musicians were situated to the left and to the back of the stage. A short flight of stairs at the east entrance led to the upper level where rows of chairs in front of the stage gave the room the look of a church interior.

And, of course, there was a big bar on the right. That's where I met Art DeLugoff, the club owner. "My parents were from Russia," he introduced himself. In New York almost every second person is from Russia originally. The rest is from the other parts of our big wide world, so it seems.

The other club, Michel's, was a much smaller venue, located at 96th Street and Amsterdam Avenue and patronized mostly by black people. Just like the Village Gate, Michel's was always full of guests and had a festive atmosphere.

Every time Art spotted me in the audience, he would invite me to sit in. While I unpacked my horn, he would announce me as a "new star on a modern jazz horizon from Russia". At the time I thought that Mr. Blakey was just being polite with me, but after I joined the Messengers, I realized that he had been already then treating me as a member of the band.

One night, after such an announcement, somebody in the audience expressed his skepticism, "Yeah – yeah, Blakey, you would tell us stories. From Russia and playing jazz. Enough bullshitting, I want to hear some music." Somebody tried to calm him down, but it was already too late.

"Oh Yeah?" said Art, almost angrily, "Valery, do your trick, play a ballad, any one you like". I played "Willow weep for me". As I held the last note, the audience broke out in a storm of applause.

"OK motherfucker?" victorious Art addressed the offender, who was standing in the crowd with his mouth open, eyes bulging out. "They do it in Europe, they do it in Japan, in South America, in Russia, everywhere," Art rubbed it in some more and started drumming an intro to the next tune.

Once at the Village Gate I was sitting near the stage and listening. Art signaled me to the stage, which triggered an instantaneous reaction in me – with perfect muscle coordination I snatched my trumpet out of its case in a split second.

"Ronnie is a dynamite Lady" by Walter Davis was the next tune.

"Mr. Blakey, this is an absolutely new tune, I have never heard it," I tried to find my way out.

"You have ears, don't you? Come, come, play," he said ordinarily, like everywhere else in the world musicians played with the world's greatest bands tunes they had never heard before.

What do you say to that? My trumpet was already out of its case. Everybody was looking at me. At this point it would have been more embarrassing to pack it back in and run than get on the stage and make a fool of myself.

When it was my turn to play, I was sure only of the C pedal, signifying the end of the form. That was where I finished my solo after blowing, in absolute delirium, enough notes into the air.

"Art, this is a brand new tune, he played it like he wrote it," Walter Davis jumped off his seat in excitement.

Walter definitely favored me. I had to have made enough mistakes, having tried to grab the roots and chords with my ears for several choruses. Walter Davis, what a great guy he was! He had the same quality in him as Art, maybe not to the same degree, which was to bring out the best in people. Many a time he would help me in the future.

After listening to the Messengers live and sitting in with them I was even more inspired to play whatever jazz gigs happened to pop up. Club dates were an entirely different proposition though. These were not where you played music. On a club date everything is moving like on a factory conveyer belt: a bossanova set starts exactly at the time specified in the contract. The band plays, soft, pleasant tunes for the guests to come in and find their seat assignments.

The bandleader makes, very cheerfully, an announcement: "For your listening and dining pleasure". Fifteen minutes later, at the command of the caterer, the band starts the first dance set, the volume is jacked up considerably, 15 minutes after that at the command of the "supreme ruler" the guests go back to the tables.

They have their main coarse, 10-15 minutes later, at the command issued by the same agency, the second dance set starts, the volume is jacked up further. Then the throwing of the garter, the bouquet, then: "And now for the first time as husband and wife," by the bride's wish and everybody's command, which is almost always: "My eyes adore you."

We play the number one pop song of the day, then the bride is dancing with her father – "daddy's girl". Dessert time – song of the flame, last set – the sound system is blasting, total musical chaos reaches its apogee, bum-bum and here comes the last song "The party is over."

For the bride and groom it would be an everlasting exciting experience, even if they went through it with a different cast of characters, at center stage, a couple of more times in their lives. But for a jazz musician to play weddings every weekend, in June five or six times a week, even with an ethnic variation – hora set at a Jewish wedding, Tarantella, Italian, Green Sleeves or Danny Boy, Irish etc – is too much. Everything is too loud, pitch is of no importance, on the way home vicious melodies of the wedding still ring in your ears.

A couple of years of that later my iron endurance started to show signs of erosion. Somewhere close to the middle of the wedding – when it's hardest – I started praying to God. I pleaded in full seriousness: "Dear God, please make a miracle, please make Art Blakey walk in and say that he wants me to join the Messengers from tonight's concert on."

I was absolutely ready for the appearance of the messenger of God and would know exactly what to do: even before he would begin saying something like "What the hell are you doing here? You are supposed to play with my band. We gotta go to the concert right now, go take your place in the car, it's waiting outside." In my mind's eye I was packing my horn and running off the bandstand to the cheers of the band members and the stunned wedding party.

One day, Vladimir Chizhik, a friend of mine from Moscow, called. He had legally emigrated to Israel where he had real relatives, and showed up in New York a few months later. He was a very good lead trumpet player, playing the most prestigious gigs in Russia – radio, television orchestras etc.

In New York he had a hard time finding good work as a musician at first and had to submit to working as a car dealer and playing Hasidic weddings, where he excelled very quickly. I think Chizhik had real American spirit in him – start with whatever is available and go from there, unlike some other immigrants, who wait for some mythical executive positions to be offered and end up doing nothing for years. Chizhik is a millionaire now, not playing trumpet though.

"Valery, please sub for me tonight, I've got two weddings at the same time. The music is very easy, you will read it right on the spot with no problem. It pays $150," Chizhik shot in one breath.

"$150 on Monday?"

"Yeah, yeah, $150."

In 1974 it was the equivalent of $300.

"Wait a minute, one of those ethnic weddings you are doing?"

"Yeah. You would need to wear tuxedo and a kipola."

"What's a kipola?"

"Yarmulke. It's a little head dress, just like the one the Roman Pope wears."

"Oh, man, I can't wear that, I am a Russian orthodox. I wear a cross, you have seen it."

"I like your silver cross, it says "save me and preserve" on the inside of it, but it doesn't matter, you still put the Yarmulke on your head and go to work. Look at it like it's your uniform."

"Can I not wear it?"

"No, no, you will offend the party."

"I don't want to hide that I am a Christian?"

"You don't need to. I already told the bandleader about you; they don't care what religion you are. As long as you play the music, you've got the gig. You are in America my friend – do your job well, you will be all right anywhere. They need trumpet players. You can end up working there as much as you want to. It is a lot of work and very well paid too. And in between, you can play your $20 jazz gigs. Valery, you can't be like that doctor, who treats only common colds. You ought to be able to do the work which is available to you as a musician, you gotta earn a living by playing your instrument, not driving a taxi."

$150 on a Monday! Are you kidding? Nobody needed to talk me into it for too long. I was on my way to my first Hasidic wedding. Work is work, Chizhik was absolutely right. Even my Mother, when I first started playing professionally, didn't mind my playing at a party on an Easter Eve, because I was working, not hanging out.

"Here is your Yarmulke and keep it on your head when you are at a wedding, if you want to stay in this business," Moisha Shwartzberg, the band's leader, told me. Just like Chizhik said, reading the music was no problem. It was a multitude of short melodies repeated over and over again.

Moisha would yell a number and another novice on trombone and myself would frantically leaf through the book of songs with the titles in Hebrew hieroglyphics, while the band leader would go through the first section of the song, which he called the "high part."

Sometimes he would just reach out to the book while we were still playing and open it on an appropriate page. The front line was completed by an alto sax. The alto player was a tall guy with a black moustache and young just like me, and the trombone. He looked like someone from the Caucasus Mountains. This guy knew every song by heart and had a very good sound on both alto and flute.

In a way, the wedding was similar to the ones I played with Nick, but in many ways it was different: men and women were separated by a partition and danced each on their respective side, very often holding hands. That reminded me of Russian singing and dancing in a ring. Sometimes women would peep through the fence and some of the men, in order to keep the propriety protocol, would chase them away.

The music was loud, like any wedding, and almost bizarre, too different from jazz. During one of the breaks I went with the trumpet in my hand to the staircase outside of the reception hall to give my ears a chance to rejuvenate. Then, before I knew it, I was blowing jazz lines into the space around the staircase.

All of a sudden somebody's high-pitched voice startled me. "It's you! From Russia, on a Hasidic wedding, playing lines like that? God almighty! I will be right back." That was the alto player. His handsome face was distorted in amazement, eyes bulging out. He ran through the doors back into the stale air, which hung like a cloud over the reception hall only to reappear a minute later on the staircase with his alto in his hands. Right away he started blowing. Those were the same lines I just had played.

"What?" It was my turn to be surprised. He was a real virtuoso. I threw another leak at him. He repeated it after me. I played it a fourth higher. He followed. I proceeded further on the four/five cycle. The alto player stayed with me. So we went through all 12 keys. Then he played a phrase, I followed him through the whole succession of tonalities.

We hugged like two lost souls which had just found each other.

"Marty Laskin, sorry I didn't have a chance to introduce myself before the gig. I just knew that you are from Russia. There are a few Russians in the business now, they are all very good musicians, but not jazz musicians. Man I am shocked."

"I am Valery Ponomarev, I've arrived five months ago."

"Are you Jewish?"

"No, I am not, I am subbing for Vladimir."

"How did you get out of Russia?"

That was the question I had to answer every time I had met somebody for the past few months. Little did I know that I would be answering that question for many years to come. In response I gave him an abbreviated synopsis of my story, which I had learned to deliver on automatic pilot.

"You speak good English. How did you manage to learn to play like that?"

That was the next most asked question. I delivered the next synopsis just as smoothly.

"Man, I hope you will stay in the business, it'll be great to have you around, to play some jazz over the dance tunes. I am playing jazz gigs every once in a while, but they don't pay anything, so I can't afford to turn down a wedding, otherwise I will be out of business. Are you busy tomorrow? Come to my house, we will practice, listen to music. I will introduce you to my wife at the end of the wedding, she always comes to pick me up to drive home together."

Beautiful Beth, Marty and I became very good friends. At the next wedding, during a break, Marty broke his leg. At first I thought he was kidding, because I hadn't seen him colliding with anything. Very calmly he informed me that he had just broken his ankle, no pain grimacing, nothing, he just couldn't move, so I carried him on my back to the stage.

The next couple of weddings I had to miss, because of a jazz gig at Sea Fort L.I and at Churchill's ($20 each), popped up out of nowhere. But then I was back at work in appropriate attire next to Marty in the front line. Marty's leg was in a cast, crutches neatly stacked over his alto case.

On those weddings I started seeing visions of Art Blakey walking in almost at the very beginning of the first set, then another set and then another. Sooner or later, the whole thing would come to an end and I would be free, after getting paid, very often in cash, to jump in my car and drive to the Village. Some clubs were open till 3 or 4 AM and I had a chance to catch the last set and even sit in.

Very often I would go to "Boomer's" on Bleeker Street, where a big black guy, by the name of Bob, would always, somewhat patronizingly, rush me through the doors. In spirit "Boomer's" was very much like

"Michel's," only a Village version of it. Later I learned that Bob Cooper was the owner of the place.

Back in the Soviet Union a director of any establishment, no matter how miserable it might have been, would be sitting in his office like a little god, with the personnel running around him, trying to catch any whim of the guy. Here, club owners were doubling as doormen, doctors wiping floors in front of their laboratories. What a miracle peculiarity of capitalism!

*With Woody Shaw after concert at Lincoln Center.*
*photo by Lev Zabeginski*

Woody Show, Junior Cook, Slide Hampton, Harold Mayburn and many other jazz stars and superstars hung out at "Boomer's" on a regular basis. I could easily imagine Lee Morgan hanging with these guys. But what a crazy story – he was shot and killed by his estranged wife a year before I came to the states, while playing on the stage of "Slug's," a club not very different from "Boomer's" or "Michel's."

Regardless of whose gig it might have been originally, it would always turn into a free for all towards the end of the night, with everybody blowing their hearts out. I met Freddie Hubbard there for the first time too. He was sitting like a regular customer by the bar and drinking something. Bob, the owner, or one of the musicians, introduced me to him.

Freddie was very curious to hear me play, but my chops, after withstanding several hora sets at the wedding I had just came from, were absolutely not in condition to play in front of the greatest. One day, years later, after my "Live at Sweet Basil" CD came out, I was listening to the messages on my answering machine when I heard: "Hi Valery, this is Freddie Hubbard, I just heard you play "Theme for Ernie," you sound beautiful, you sound great. Thank you."

Oh my God! I was listening to the message again and again. What a compliment from the greatest himself! What exactly happened was this: Freddie Hubbard was at Vartan Tonoian's (the manager then of a beautiful club in Denver CO). The host asked Freddie if he wanted to hear a Valery Ponomarev recording. Freddie said, "Yes, Live at Sweet Basil."

Vartan was surprised that the Greatest knew my recordings. Naturally, I took the tape out of the machine and put it in my desk, only to take it out of its resting place in my drawer, at first several times a day, and put it back in the machine to play it over the phone for all of my friends – musicians and jazz fans. They certainly can't get this recording of the world's number one trumpet-player today at any of the HMV outlets, or any other stores.

As great as Woody Show and the rest sounded on records, they sounded even better in front of the Boomer's home audience, which came to the club already charged with expectations of great music. Once the first set began, it wouldn't take long before sparkles in the form of applause, tapping feet, shaking heads, yelling and screaming and even wise cracks at the artists on the stage, started flying around the club in response to the music. From the audience back to the stage, from the stage to the audience and back again.

Usually by the time I got to the club, the alternating current was already set at its peak, reigning supreme. Musicians, music and the audience were blended in one dazzling alloy and it did not matter what component of the alloy you were, as long as you were a part of it. Nothing is like live jazz.

"Barbara's" was another place which kept its doors open till very late. On Wednesdays, it hosted a jam session for would be stars. Aspiring musicians from all over the world used to eagerly pay a $3 admission to have a legal right to blow on the blues changes as long as their energy bank allowed.

The rhythm section couldn't complain. On a jam session night there would be a herd of guys with instruments, waiting for their names to be called. Some girls used to patronize the place too, mostly pretty little "would be Billie Holidays". No matter what part of the world she had come from, her answer to the question "what would you like to sing?" would be: "My Funny Valentine".

That proved again and again that whoever came up with the anecdote: "How many girl singers does it take to sing My Funny Valentine? – Apparently all of them," was absolutely right. On the highest emotional plateau and with an air of great sophistication, rehearsed no doubt in front of a mirror for hours, she would try for several bars to come in and then in desperation squeak in the first words, in the wildest of articulations and pronunciations, off beat and pitch, completely upsetting the equilibrium of the form.

"Barbara's" – What a Treasure Island it was for Professor Higgins to study all of the World's accents!

I did not have to pay admission there, because my new friend – tenor saxophonist Jeff Hittman was in charge of the sessions and would always invite me to play with his band to kick the real thing off. So his girlfriend, beautiful Nancy at the door, would always let me in for free.

*With Kleinot.*

His band included Joe Jones Jr. on drums and Earl Clark on the piano. The bass player's name I have forgotten, but believe me, he was good. He had to be, to play with the guys like Earl and, particularly, Joe, who had learned to play from his father – one of the greatest drummers jazz world had ever seen. To any jazz fan in the world that would be more than enough credentials.

When I first met Jeff, it struck me, as it did many times since I had moved to America, how alike people in Russia and in the center of the Capitalistic World looked. This time it was my Moscow friend Vitally Kleinot, who looked strikingly similar to Jeff. Not only did these two guys share the same facial features, body structure, light blond hair and blue eyes, they also were both dedicated Sonny Rollins' fans and students, with Jeff actually taking lessons from the living legend.

There were a couple of differences though. Jeff had an enormous collection of jazz LP's in his apartment.

*With Kleinot's Double (Feff Hittman).*

First thing in the morning, after smoking enough pot with or without Nancy – Kleinot would drink vodka now with or without his future wife Marina – he would either practice his tenor saxophone or transcribe solos of his favorite musicians, mostly his teacher. Just like Kleinot had been doing back in Moscow. Only Jeff would transcribe them right off the LP being played on his record player, picking up the tone arm with the needle and putting it back on the revolving disk by hand each time he needed to figure out the note or a string of notes.

There are very many notes in each solo, even if it is short. I had seen him work. Sometimes he would get the sound right away, but normally it would take him from three to 10, or even 20 stop-and-gos. No doubt, had he looked at the surface of his LP's at least once, before his regular daily routine got on the way, he would've thought of some other way of transferring sound to paper. Or, maybe, he was too anxious to get the precious notes or perhaps he thought that he would always be able to buy new LP's, who knows. After all, Jeff grew up in the land of prosperity.

How was he supposed to imagine in the early seventies, the time when there would be only CDs available and LPs would become collector's items. His enormous collection would have been worth a lot of money now, if it were not all in worn out, sometimes to the holes, grooves.

Many times I had heard Jeff telling a story of meeting his teacher.

"When I was a little kid, I was living in the same building on Grand Street, which is not far from Brooklyn Bridge, as today. One day, my Dad and I were standing in line to pick up freshly made bagels – the bakery on our street is the best in town you know – when I saw him. I violently pulled the sleeve of my Dad's coat, screaming: 'That's him, that's the guy, I want to learn to play like him. I have seen him on television. Dad, do something.'

"My dad went up to Sonny Rollins and arranged for the lessons right on the spot. Years later Sonny always picks up the phone when I call and sends me Christmas postcards. I send him one too. I already have about twenty of them. Once, I even drove by his house upstate, on the way to a gig in Montreal."

"You want to go with me next time, Valery?" He would always add.

I can't even imagine what Kleinot would have done, had he had an opportunity to study with his idol. He would probably screw his own head off his shoulders, being so happy. Once he snuck into a Moscow-Prague train, which was taking a group of Moscow musicians and Komsomol youths, approved by the appropriate agency, to the Prague Jazz Festival.

Maybe he thought somehow everything would work out, but it didn't, of course, and he was taken off the train at the very first stop. He was lucky he didn't end up in jail.

Once I arrived at Michel's too late, when Art Blakey and other Messengers were already walking out of the entrance door.

*With Art.*

"Hey Val, what are you doing these days?" He spotted me, when I was getting out of my 10-year-old monstrosity.

"I do some work here and there, practice. Thank you for asking. How was the gig tonight?"

"Oh, we had a ball, where were you? You look like a waiter," Art knew, of course that I had come directly from some kind of a social function gig and was simply teasing me. I just laughed it off.

One winter evening that year I was walking down Bleeker street in the Village, when I bumped into John Marshal, a very good trumpet player and a friend of mine.

"Hey Val, what's going on? I hear that Bill Hardman had left the Messengers and a couple of guys had already tried for the band. That's your gig, you should be there."

Hearing John say "It's your gig" made that idea of being in the band jump to the foreground of my consciousness. Yes, why not? I could play. I knew that. After being in the city for two years, I didn't need anybody to tell me that. What do I do? The same evening I ran into Bob Mintzer, the great New York tenor player.

"Bob, What do I do? John Marshall just told me that Art Blakey is trying trumpet players."

"Just come up to him and say that you want to work with him, he is in town. Almost every night he is hanging at Boomer's."

The rest of the day I spent composing a statement, which was supposed to project the idea that there was nothing else in the whole world with any meaning to me except playing with The Jazz Messengers.

Just like Bob said, Art Blakey was at Boomers that night. He was already there when I arrived, sitting at a table with a couple of friends, engaged in some kind of a discussion. From the way he winked at me I understood that the three of them didn't welcome any interruption. So, I took a seat far enough from Art's table, but close enough to have that whole space covered by my peripheral vision.

Some time later the discussion at the table ceased to be as acute as at the beginning of the evening and then Mr. Blakey got up and moved towards the exit. I got up from my table too and walked towards God's Messenger.

"Mr. Blakey, I want to play with your band so much, nothing else is important to me," I heard myself saying the words, which were not part of the prepared script at all.

"Oh Val, your name had already popped up several times. Give your telephone number to our road manager Jim Green, there he is," Art pointed at a rather tall man, who was standing by the exit.

"Thank you Mr. Blakey".

"Mr. Green, Mr. Green, I am Valery Pono..."

"I know, I know, we had talked about you many times. Give me your number. We start rehearsing soon. I will give you the time and the address of the place later," he said with an artificial air of importance, which only unimportant people could have.

He looked to me like he was daydreaming. Maybe because the pupils of his eyes had sort of a gray-yellowish lining. I just hoped that he was not coming down with, God forbid, eye cataracts.

"Thank you Jim, here is my number."

He gave me his and Mr. Blakey's. We shook hands. His was considerably puffed up, like after a nasty mosquito bite. That's when I first met Jim Green, the road manager of the Messengers, which meant that he was responsible for setting up the drum set on the band stand, driving and some other petty jobs.

That was December 1976. Later I learned that Jim did have a really important function in the band, which he could perform better than anybody else. Art Blakey always held it in high esteem. But that was later.

I walked out of Boomer's knowing that the longest was over, the future has begun. Oh my God! He did say: "We start rehearsing soon. We had talked about you." What a Christmas and a New Year present! Oh my! I don't even remember how I got home, or even where I had gone. I think I was just walking streets aimlessly, reliving again and again the jump over the border between the Past and the Future.

That was the era right before my first answering machine. Every time I came home, my first question would be: "Did I get any calls." Every time the telephone rang I would drop whatever I was doing, including practicing, and grab the phone. Oh, no, not again, some advertising or equally unnecessary call would take place of The Call, delivering the time and the place of the rehearsal. I didn't worry though, knowing deep down in my heart that I was in.

That continued for a couple of weeks and I started to think that there must have been a reason why, in America they say: "Don't call us, we will call you." I had learned from other immigrants that it was considered bad manners to bug people about your business. If they don't call you that means they don't need you.

But Jim did give me his and Mr. Blakey's number, should I call? What if they say: "Don't annoy us. Don't bother us" or something like that. What if they didn't mean anything they said, but played the role of "polite people," who promise a lot, and meant nothing.

That was already January. All of the holidays were over: Christmas, New Year, Russian Christmas, the Russian old calendar New Year. Only my birthday was still a few days ahead. If they didn't call me by then, I decided that was it. They did not need me and the rest of it was just Western politeness.

I have heard too many times musicians telling each other: "You play your ass off. You should work," or "You sound real good," just to cheer the other fellow musician up. Everybody knows how difficult it could get sometimes in any of the arts professions, particularly in jazz. Yes, I think it is right to support each other, at least with a well wishing word, if not with a gig, but I thought that Art Blakey was above those games.

My birthday was fast approaching, but The Call still didn't come in. If it was some girl, not wishing me happy birthday or something, I would never call her, but that was The Jazz Messengers. I was supposed to have had rehearsed with them already. He did say: "You will be playing with my band."

Manners or not, to hell with it, I decided to call anyway. What do I have to lose? If they said that I was supposed to wait until Mr. Blakey says it's time, or something like: "Why do you disturb us? Did we call you?" – Than so be it. At least I would know what's going on.

I felt like a little kid back in my school, having to go to the principal's office with a summons, handed to me by our class councilor. Oh boy! What is it going to be?

"Hello, who is this?" I heard a slow unsteady voice in the receiver.

"Is it Jim Green's apartment? This is Valery Ponomarev."

"Who? This is Jim Green. Who is this?"

Here it comes. What a fool I had been, to build up all these fantasies!

"This is Valery Ponomarev, a trumpet-player from Russia. You gave me your number. You had said that you would call me with the directions and time of the rehearsal. At Boomer's, remember."

"Oh, Valery, where have you been?" Jim sounded very much like Goga or any of other Muscovites I had known, while off the wagon for weeks. "You are supposed to be at the rehearsal tomorrow, Art Junior's address, Hotel Camelot."

"What?"

"I am in the middle of something. See you there." Said Jim Green in the same shaky voice, and the line was cut off.

Tomorrow! Tomorrow! Camelot Hotel!

# CHAPTER 5

## JOINING THE FAMILY

Ten minutes to 4pm I was at 202 West 35th Street, between 7th and 8th Avenues – the address given to me.

"What Camelot hotel? I have never heard of any Camelot hotel around here. There is one on 45th Street," a passer by told me. I asked the next pedestrian the same question.

"Never heard of it," was the answer.

Oh man! I was at the wrong place and it was already the down beat time. God almighty! I dashed to the nearest phone. What else is new? When you need a phone, there are only broken ones around, just like in Moscow.

I ran across the street, then across the avenue, then across another street, further and further. Then I saw, across yet another street, behind a glass window of a delicatessen store, a girl at a phone booth talking. That one must work. I decided to play it safe and wait for the girl to finish her call rather than keep on running from one phone to another wasting coins.

Upon my approach the girl turned her behind to the rest of the world and kept on talking, totally merged with the apparatus. Obviously this public phone worked very well, because she kept on talking and talking and her well built bum, highlighted by a tight mini skirt, didn't show any signs of planning on getting out of the booth.

Oh man! How long can she talk? Oh God! Women can really talk.

What is it with women anyway? Why do they need to talk that much? Two women, at a lunch table back in Italy, came to my mind. For an hour and a half they were talking about polka dots on one of the women's new purse. An hour and a half!

The Italian language is so rich and beautiful, why couldn't they put it to a better use than nonny-nonny - tirra-tirra all the way through all of the courses until espresso was served and beyond about the same stupid design. I had thought those two were the champions. No, it started to look more and more like the American team could beat them. Every once in a while the girl would sneak a look at me, to make sure that I was still there, put a new coin in the apparatus and turn back to her interlocutress.

"... He doesn't know how to treat you . . . I am a woman of the seventies . . . he is not listening to me . . . she dances like a cow . . . he bought me dinner . . . she would've never hooked up with Mike for so long, had I not given her my yellow, with red bows, dress for . . . I am not a sex object . . . she gave him everything he has . . . he can't hold onto a job . . . she can't cook . . ."

My ear was picking up fragments of the conversation, which was definitely heading, in content and length, towards the new Guinness-Olympic-World record. "Stars are not in the right position today, that's obvious," I just thought, when a miracle happened – the bum in front of me moved in a new pattern and I heard the girl saying: "Call you next break". She did actually hang up and, not before thoroughly inspecting the insides of her handbag, vacated the premises (moved her ass out), giving me a look of absolute superiority.

I got the scrap of paper, which Jim Green had given me originally, out of my pocket and dialed Art Blakey's number.

"Alt Blakey lezidence," I heard a woman's voice, with a Japanese accent, on the other end.

"This is Valery Ponomarev, can I speak with Mr. Blakey?"

"No Mistil Bleki hom. Alt Bleki Vi bettar Elvin jons vaif."

"Do you know what's the address of the rehearsal?"

"Ah? Lilhelsal? Alt Bleki juniol?"

After a considerable discussion I figured out, that the address for the rehearsal was correct, but the name was wrong. Hotel Camelot was located at 45th street and 8th Ave – that's where Art Blakey lived. The rehearsal was exactly at the address given to me, but it was not "Camelot," but Art junior's apartment, which served as a rehearsal studio sometimes.

I rushed there, totally upset, that I was already very late. Oh God! What will they think of me?

Run, run. Here it is, one flight of stairs, ring the bell. No answer. Ring again. I heard some sounds inside, but nobody opened the door. I rang again. This time I heard light footsteps.

"Who is there?" a pleasant woman's voice asked me.

I announced myself.

"Give me a second, just a minute." Clanging metal sounds and sounds of keys turning in the locks followed, then the door opened. A very nice lady welcomed me in. "The guys should be here any time now. You are Valery, the new trumpet-player, welcome, welcome," she said.

I thanked her and walked in. On my right side I saw a big cage with a fair sized monkey in it. The monkey grabbed the fence and stretched itself full length along the cage and then jumped back and then again did the same thing, making the sounds I had heard from outside.

"Do you like our monkey? I am Art junior's wife, my name is Audrey."

"Nice to meet you."

"Please come this way." And we walked to the next room of a small apartment. There was an upright piano there and a drum set.

"Make yourself comfortable," Audrey said in unison with the doorbell which rang to announce somebody's arrival. I was not even late. A big weight fell off my shoulders, once I didn't have to explain my lack of punctuality.

That was David Schnitter. He looked even smaller than at the Five

Spot. Dressed in a vest, he didn't appear very happy. Right away he asked me something about time off. How would I know?

By that time Schnitter had been in the band already for three years. He wound up being in the band for six years. That's about the longest for any messenger. A star at the rehearsal – that's what he was. Only I couldn't see him that way. Nobody was a star enough for me except Art Blakey.

*On the stage of Avery Fisher Hall Lincoln Center. (Left to right - Walter Davis, David Schnitter, A.B., V.P., B.W., D.I.) photo by Lev Zabeginski*

*On tour*
*( Left to right - James Williams, D.S., Bobbie Watson, V.P.)*

David said something else and the doorbell rang again in response, announcing somebody else's arrival. A tall wiry young man walked in with an alto case in his hand. He had sort of a lost puppy expression on his face, waiting for instructions to be given. That was Bobby Watson.

Next, another young guy, this time with blond and curly hair, carrying a bass, showed up. He had a funny coat on, which looked like a cross between a military coat and a bathrobe. A pair of house slippers made of very thin cloth covered his feet. Slippers like that would be too light even for a bathroom, but that was January with its sleet and rain outside. Door to door taxi, I guess, had to do it. That was Dennis Irwin.

*Clowning with Dennis in an airport, Italy.*

Right after him Walter Davis walked in, looking very comfortable at Art Junior's. He walked to the piano and gave everybody music. That was the new edition of the Messengers, which jazz critics and fans all over the World were already anxiously waiting to check out. Those were my new brothers in the Messengers. Art Blakey would repeat in the future many times: "You didn't just join a band, you joined a family."

The rehearsal quickly progressed. We were checking out a brand new tune by Walter Davis – Gypsy Folk Tales – when Art Blakey showed up. He just walked to the drum set, made himself comfortable and started playing. With the first sounds of the drum part being played, the tune was metamorphosed into a masterpiece. The whole arrangement: solos, the head out, coda, everything, fell into place, everything played its role and contributed to the overall sound effect.

"I can't wait to record it," said Walter

"Had the new guys get "Uranus" yet?" Art addressed his question to the musical director.

"Not yet, we covered a couple of new tunes: 'Gypsy Folk Tales,' 'Jodi,' and 'Ronnie is a dynamite lady.' Take out Uranus guys."

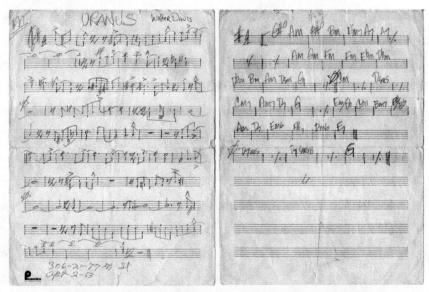

*Left: Uranus melody (Walter Davis Jr.)   Right: Uranus chord changes*
*Copyright © 1975, renewed 2003 Twenty-Eighth Street Music*
*Used by permission.*

Uranus was a great tune, complicated like hell, but great. It was a new tune recorded for the first time by the previous edition of the Messengers only a few months ago. I had heard them play it at Michel's a couple of times and still was not quite sure of its form or chords, which changed every two beats in some bars at a neck breaking tempo. Boy! What an exciting tune that was anyway.

With the music in front of me, it was entirely different matter. I loved playing it, the lines kept coming out one after the other all by themselves. Bobby and Dennis also got into it. The band sounded strong.

"Man, we should rerecord it, it sounds so good." That was the musical director's comment on our reading.

I could only wish that everything stayed as impressive as it seemed at first. I don't know about the other guys, but I had trouble with "Uranus" for sometime onwards. I was frustrated with myself. Every time, before the following concerts, Art would ask any of the new guys if we got Uranus. I would say yes, pretty sure that the band's support I would play it by memory with no problem like any other tune.

But not "Uranus." Time after time, even if I ended my solo at the right place, I would still make enough mistakes to be unable to look squarely into Art's eyes. I did get it finally. Now, years later, I think of Walter and his great tune a lot. I will rerecord it on one of my own albums one of these days.

Art Blakey also loved this tune. So many times he would say: "Walter composed a lot of tunes, he sure wrote this one."

There was no Xerox machine around, so after the rehearsal was over I collected the music and looked around for a space to lay down the manuscript paper and the parts, about ten of them altogether. There was a fair sized round table to the right and behind me. A new man was sitting there with a pencil in his hand. He must have got in while we were rehearsing. With a very friendly smile he cleared the table and got up welcoming me to make myself comfortable. I did just that, thanked him and started copying my parts, knowing full well, that it would be wrong to ask to take home the originals.

Some people left. Art and Walter were still hanging around. I knew I was holding them up and was copying as fast as I could, but was still not going fast enough. Any increase in speed would have spelled out mistakes creeping in before I knew it.

"We can trust Valery, let him take the originals home Walter," I heard Art Blakey's voice.

"Hey Val, it's alright. Come here, meet Oscar Pettifford Jr."

Oh my God! The man, who was sitting at the table before I needed space to lay the music, was Oscar Petifford's son.

"Very pleased to meet you," I said and stretched out my hand. He grabbed it with his strong hand and squeezed it so hard, I thought he would break it.

"You play beautiful, my Dad would've loved your playing," Oscar said finally relaxing the squeeze and handing me a piece of paper. That was a very good sketch of me playing my trumpet.

"That is a very good sketch," I said, noticing definite talent. "I finished an art school in Moscow myself before taking up music on a full time basis," I couldn't help but identify myself as an artist too.

"Come to my house one of these days, I will show you my work."

I thanked my new friend and everybody headed towards the door.

To rerecord "Uranus"!? Man, did I understand Walter correctly? When Art Blakey, Walter Davis and I were on the street, I asked Walter what he meant.

"No, no, it had been just recorded. No, we can't rerecord it that soon. We have a whole bunch of new tunes to deal with anyway."

I ran home as fast as I could. The next rehearsal was only a couple of days away. I had to learn to play the tunes by heart. The rest of the evening of that day and most of the next day, with the exception of practicing and some responsibilities around the house, I was busy memorizing the music: trying to bring up the sound of it in my mind, think of it, look at it, repeat. Look at it, close my yes, open them, close them. I was applying every technique I had learned from different books on memory.

For the next rehearsal I was at the right place at the right time. I think the monkey recognized me. At least it seemed to me that my very distant relative wanted to share his banana with me, when Art Junior's wife let me in.

Pretty soon Bobby showed up. While waiting for others to arrive, we were unpacking our instruments and talking. Turned out that Bobby was from Kansas City, Kansas and had just graduated from Miami University as a composer and the alto saxophone was his second passion.

*Playing My One and Only Love.*

"My composition teacher had told me: 'It is not enough just to compose good music. If you want other musicians to play it, you have to learn to play your instrument very well so you would have a chance to promote your tunes in the bands you'd be playing with.' Now I am into playing as much as into composing," said my new brother in the

Messengers and took out a chart to show me. "Time will tell" was very professionally written in a good handwriting.

Of all the Messengers I hung out with the most, at first, it was Bobby. Oh boy! Some brothers coexist very well, some fight like cats and dogs. Bobby and I were the funniest siblings I have ever seen or heard of – the best of buddies one day and the craziest of rivals the next. And a lot of fun in between. That could happen in any family, as far as I am concerned.

Soon the rest of the band members showed up, including Art Blakey himself. Bobby and David unfolded their music stands and placed them in front of themselves, Denis took a spot to the left of the front line, Walter at the piano to the right and Art Blakey, facing us, completed the circle.

"Get out 'Gypsy Folk tales' guys. Where is your music Valery?" There was a little impatience in Art's voice, who was ready to get on with the rehearsal.

"I got it." I answered.

"I don't see it," said Art, this time with a definite sign of annoyance in his voice, and pointed at the empty spot in front of me.

"I got it," I repeated.

"I want..." Art started saying something in a very new tone of voice.

"He memorized it," interrupted him Walter Davis, pleased with himself for solving the puzzle before everybody else.

Art's eyes assessed the situation and the one, two, one-two-three-fore count followed.

The first few concerts were the most difficult ones. Every time after finishing my part, I would turn around to look at Art – he was still playing and that fascinating sound was coming from his drum set. That was incredible!

I couldn't help but step away from the audience's view and close my eyes – it would be just like being in my room back in Moscow, one on one with my Mag8. I would pinch myself and open my eyes – Art was still there. It was not a dream. I got used to it eventually. After one of those concerts Art asked me: "What kind of a passport do you have, Valery?"

"I don't have a passport, but I do have a "green card," which is given to legal residents before they become citizens of this country," I explained as well as I could.

"Can you travel outside of the US on it?"

I didn't know what to answer. I just knew that it was a complicated matter. From other immigrants I had heard different theories. Some said yes, others said no. I didn't really pay any attention, because since coming to the United States I didn't have any need or urge to go anywhere.

"Let me see it."

I handed it to him. Art looked at it this way and that way and then asked me to lend it to him for a couple of days.

Then Art announced to everybody, "We are recording next week for Roulette Records. 'Sound Ideas' studio on 46th Street." What? A couple of rehearsals, a couple of concerts and already a record? I was stunned.

"We need to play this repertoire on a good tour, really work on the material. It would sure sound different after playing it every night for a month or so. Then record it," said David when Walter, he and I were in my new "Monza 2+2" driving back to the City. "Why is it always the other way around?"

"Sure, sure, you want to run the tunes back and forth until they become your second nature," broke in Walter. "Not in Art's band." That was only the end of February.

\*\*\*\*\*\*\*\*\*\*\*\*\*\*\*\*\*\*\*\*\*\*\*\*\*

A few days later, while I was warming up for the recording session,

Bobby showed me yet another new tune of his: "Hawkman," which was just as well written as "Time will tell."

"I dedicate it to Coleman Hawkins. It's his nickname. Did you know that?" Bobby asked me.

"Yeah, I have heard of it," I said. "You sure, we are going to record it? We didn't even have a chance to rehearse it."

"He said we need more tunes. So, I brought one. Here, here," Bobby pointed at a passage. "Play from here."

"Sorry Bobby, I can't right now, I gotta warm up first, charge the batteries, you know. You reed players got it easy – put the reed in the mouthpiece and off you go. Not us brass players," I had to say.

"What are you saying Valery? You know how many reeds I have to go through, before I find a good one? Two-three boxes, even that is not enough sometimes. We got it easy!"

Bobby turned away and walked over to Schnitter. Two guys, the studio employees, were fussing around with the wires and microphones, setting up partitions between the bass and the horn-players. For the drums they had a separate booth, with the drum set in it. Even the cymbals were already in place. Jim must have visited the studio before everybody else. Those two guys looked and acted very much like stage hands at the Moscow Drama Theatre, where I held my first professional job.

A sound engineer, separated from us by a huge glass window, was supervising them from his control room – just like a play director. Headphones, personal volume control boards, everything was ready. The stage was set, only Art still didn't show up, so we went through "Hawkman" for a sound check.

Finally, the protagonist entered the studio. Dressed in a bright red shirt, he walked directly to the booth, saying: "Very bright, ha?" to everybody for "hello," made himself comfortable at the drums, and checked his headphones. He looked happy and ready to have fun, like he was about to kick off his own birthday party.

"Get Gypsy Folk Tales guys," he said, which sounded like "get your glasses ready, Champagne is about to shoot up the ceiling."

"Tape is running," I heard in my headphones. Trumpet in my hands, I looked up at Art. He was surveying the studio, making sure that everybody and everything was ready for the festivities and the "one, two, one-two-three-four" count, followed by the Jazz Messengers, breaking out.

Sounds of cymbals, snare and bass drums, saxophones, trumpet, bass and piano united in one incredible blend. I heard firecrackers, screams of excited partygoers, corks popping, women's shrieks, confetti shooting in the air. The party was on. Everybody played their hearts out.

After the last sounds of the crash cymbal at the end of "Gypsy Folk Tales" died out, everybody took off their earphones and headed towards control booth, only Art waved his hand at Jim and pointed at the drum pedal. "We should make another take," somebody said after the head in, all of the solos, the head out and coda was anxiously listened to. Nobody had any objections to that. I certainly thought I could play a better solo, so did Bobby and David.

Through the glass wall of the control room I saw Art and Jim in the booth finish setting up a new drum pedal. "Can I hear the head out again?" asked Walter. "Sure, give me a second," the sound director complied with the request.

He rewound the tape and clicked the play button. Art walked in when "Gypsy Folk Tales" to coda was being played by the Jazz Messengers again.

"We can do better on the solos," somebody said.

"Not guilty" was Art Blakey's verdict. "Let's get on with the next tune. If the arrangement came out good, there is no need to do another take.

You think you will play a better solo on the second or the third take. You think you made mistakes and want to correct them, you probably will, but then you will find something else in the new solo you are unhappy about. Do you know what Miles [Davis] said at a recording session, when a sound engineer asked him to replay a tune, because the tapes were not running? 'We've already played it.' That's what he said. And that was it. They didn't come back to that tune even at the end of the session. First take is always the best one."

Bobby started saying something apologetically and heard "Just play your ass off Bobby" for an encouragement in response.

From the very beginning Art treated us sidemen like members of his own family, like we were his children. So many times he would stick up for us, go far out of his way to help us or protect our interests, sacrifice his own time or rest. I knew there was more to it than just joining a band and being able to play the music. Many of the world's greatest musicians at different times had worked in the band; that alone had a profound significance.

"You joined a family," kept ringing in my ears. That was it. Now, for the first time on foreign soil I realized I was not alone. I had a family. And what a family at that: Horace Silver, Clifford Brown, Lee Morgan, Freddie Hubbard, etc were all my uncles and brothers, and, of course, with Art the father of us all.

He gave musical life to so many artists, young and unknown at first! Who else but a father can do that?

He meant what he said, and it manifested itself time after time. I had a first proof of it on my first trip to Europe with Art Blakey and the Jazz Messengers...

Being a refugee from another country in the US is a very unsafe status. A lot of things could spell out a lot of trouble. The major one, of course, is the documents. It could even spell out a loss of family in some cases.

I had to deal with documents right after joining the band. "Get your papers together. Go to your embassy or something. We are going to Brazil next week, to Europe right after that," that's what Art told me – after the first rehearsals and even the first concerts were safely in the past – and gave me back my green card.

"Next week?!" Miss Barankovitch exclaimed in amazement. "It takes three months at least to process an application for a reentry permit, which in a refugee's case is a substitution for a passport to present at border patrols in foreign countries. In case of a death of a close relative one can get it fast, but that is an emergency situation. You can't go anywhere, if you plan on becoming a citizen of this country. Forget about going abroad with that band. What do you call it? Wait for two or three more years, get American citizenship, then travel anywhere you like."

I hated little miss Barankovitch. "How could you say that? I just got out of a country with a totalitarian regime ruled by a dictatorial government, where one can't move freely even from one apartment to another, let alone from country to country. I am in the free world now. I should be able to travel," I could hardly control my emotions. Helpless rage, like a dark cloud, was covering all my senses. I had no doubt, that the I.R.C. official knew the rules.

Art will hire somebody else. God knows there are so many trumpet-players who would give their right arm for a chance to play with the Messengers. Oh my God! I am out. Blind with panic I ran to Jim Green's. Bobby opened the door and stepped back, eyes bulging out. "What happened?"

I just walked through the corridor to Jim's room, which was in its usual disarray, and sat on the sofa.

"What is it Valery?" I heard Jim's booming voice above me.

The American phrase "a man's gotta do what a man's gotta do" kept flashing in my mind till my speech organs started moving and I described in detail my latest visit to the headquarters of the International Rescue Committee.

"Don't worry, Art will let you rejoin the band after you get your citizenship, it's your gig now," Jim tried to give me something to look forward to. Bobby couldn't even talk – he just curled the fingers of his right hand into a semi circle and bit on them with his teeth. I was not sure whether he was horrified at the turn of events or happy that he would never have to see me again.

Jim started saying something, but I couldn't listen, so he went to another room. I just knew that if Lady Luck comes to you, you had better be at her service, and if you are not, she never comes back.

"Be Cool, Valery. Listen, Valery," Jim shook me on the shoulder. "I just spoke with Art. Go to Jack's office, get a recommendation letter to whom it may concern. Go to your embassy with it."

Goodness Gracious, Jim couldn't imagine, of course, that the last place on earth I would turn to for help was the Soviet Embassy.

"Who is Jack?"

"Jack Wittemor is our booking agent; he will write you a good letter. We don't work for him – he works for us," stated proudly the road manager for the Messengers.

"We are expecting you," Jack's secretary told me, with a broad smile and polite concern on her face. Her name escapes me, but otherwise I remember her very well: kind of a plump woman in her early forties, impeccable manners, always a friend.

"Please wait here, Jack will be with you in a moment. I will walk my dog in the mean time," she said and pointed at a tiny little Chihuahua dog which, at the words "walk my dog," came running from another room.

At that moment, the dog was balancing on three legs in front of the door and picked up its left front paw in the air. The big, out of proportion, misty eyes of the miniature dog were begging for immediate attention. Then the little creature started barking in a tiny squeaky voice: "It's too much. Please have a mercy on me. I had always loved you with all my heart. My bladder is filled up well over capacity. Its contents can burst out on the shining parquet at any moment."

Finally the dog's prayers were answered and Jack's secretary opened the door. Man's best friend sprinted out of the room at the speed of lightning, filling up the dark stairwell with the sound of its hysterical barking: "Free, free". His mistress followed the lead and I was left in the room by myself.

Large picture portraits of Art Blakey, Elvin Jones, Horace Silver, Count Basie and Duke Ellington on the sparkling clean walls overlooked a very neat office, fitted out with expensive furniture. On the window sill there was a crystal vase with fresh oranges in it.

A few minutes later a short man, even shorter than I, came from another room. He had an envelope in his hand.

"Jack Wittemor," he introduced himself. "Valery, right?"

"Yes," I said.

"Very nice meeting you finally. I have heard a lot of good things about you from Art. Here is the letter. Present it, when you apply for your 'reenter permit.' Obviously you need to return to this country after the tour is over. You don't want to go to the Soviet Union. Would they arrest you?"

I thanked Jack for his well wishing and a very well written letter, but, in all sincerity, I didn't believe it could make any dent in the United States immigration law.

Next, from the corner of 39th Street and Park Avenue, I ran, in absolute despair, to the Federal Plaza 26, Visas and Immigration Office, what else. The sight of crowds of people speaking all of the world's languages all at once, exasperated officials losing their patience (officials at the windows are changed every 20 minutes), trying to explain again and again that rules are rules and every one has to follow them, made me almost scream in helpless rage.

All of the studying and practicing, getting records on Moscow's black market, escaping from my own country meant nothing on Federal Plaza 26. What do I do now?

Something must have led me or looked after me, because just three hours later I walked out of the building with a "re-entry permit" in my hand.

If you are from the Soviet Union, dealing with lines is your second nature. I could classify them instantly: long wait, short wait, medium wait, extremely long wait, wearisome, with some entertainment, boring like hell, useless wait etc. This one was in the category of lines, which close, after a long and agonizing wait, right in front of you.

There was no doubt, that even if I did get to the window at the end of the day, there would be no time to deal with the issue. I remember myself looking for the last time at the morose dragging lines in front of every window and walking off the floor through wide doors, leading to the staircase.

To the left, I saw a door with a plate on it, saying: "Floor Supervisor." I knocked on the door and a short, brown-like-chocolate lady opened it. Behind her I saw a table with two telephones on it and further behind, glass doors separating a man at a desk from the rest of the office.

"What is it?" She asked me in a tone of voice indicating that she did not tolerate any waste of time.

"This is an extreme emergency. Please help," I said and produced the letter from Jack Wittemor.

She took a quick glance at it and a faint smile on her face replaced the nonchalant mask of a seasoned official. "Wait here," she said and disappeared with my letter behind the door. A couple of minutes later she reappeared and invited me inside the office.

"I know Art Blakey, I used to go to "Birdland" to hear him play some years ago," said the man behind the desk, when I was passing through the glass doors of his office. "So you are his trumpet-player. From Russia, playing like that! Good for you. Where is your green card?" I gave it to him.

"Listen, come back in a couple of hours, we will see what we can do. Evelyn, please go upstairs, get a blank for a reentry permit," he addressed the woman and turned back to me. "Its not really our work, it's all done on the next floor," he said and stopped.

I thought that the usual "How did you get out of Russia?" And "How did you learn to play jazz like that in Moscow?" would follow, but they didn't. The all quiet meant that if I wanted to contribute to my issue being dealt with on the best possible basis, I should vacate the premises and let the man get back to his regular work. So I thanked him and did just that.

Two hours later I knocked on the same door again and the same lady opened it. In her hand she had a white long-shaped booklet reminiscent of a passport. "My name is Ms. Morgan," the lady said. "Please sign here. By the way, what should we write in the space for nationality?"

Well, all my life I was Russian. Soviet Citizenship I renounced over three years before then, when leaving the Soviet Union. U.S. citizenship was still two or three years away. "Russian," I said. "What else can I be?"

She quickly typed everything in, my name and all, and pushed the booklet into my hand. I stood there in daze, afraid to believe I got it.

"Go, go," Ms. Morgan said. "Everybody is already gone, the office is closed." I realized that she had stayed there longer than she had to because of me. What a nice lady she was! Isn't it something? I had just joined Art Blakey and the Jazz Messengers, the world of Lee Morgan, Clifford Brown and Freddie Hubbard. Of course Clifford Brown been my greatest inspiration and trumpet hero, and such a nice lady by the name of Morgan helped me so much. What if she is Lee's relative?

I was like in a cloud, suspended over the staircase. I grabbed her hand and squeezed it in eternal appreciation. "Thank you Ms. Brown, thank you Ms. Brown," I repeated several times and ran away. Something was out there, had to be.

"Why did you call her Ms. Brown? You stupid fool you" flew like a lightning through my mind a half an hour later, when I was already almost home. "Oh, please! Ms. Morgan did so much for you! How stupid you must look to her now! Oh, man!" My other self was never more disgusted with me in my entire life.

"What should I do now? Go there tomorrow with apologies? Explain to Ms. Morgan that Clifford Brown is my greatest musical love of all, that he, just like Lee Morgan, was a star of the band I had

just joined. That my first reaction was to call her by the name dearest to my heart?"

"She would think you are crazy," my other self was merciless. "No, you could only hope that Ms. Morgan would figure it out by herself somehow." This time my eternal supervisor-tutor-guardian angel-police-critic-judge-executioner showed a sign of having humiliated me enough.

Jack Wittemor, Art's agent, called the European office right away to find out if my document was acceptable. They said yes, no problem. It was the first time there was a Russian in the Messengers.

The next day I met with the Brazilian promoter, Steve, a rather tall and flabby gentleman, very reserved.

"The Brazilian Consulate in New York won't accept your paper for visa processing. There is very little time left to figure this out, so we have to give them your substitute trumpet-player's passport, but you will go on tour instead. I can arrange it," Steve assured me before I even had time to get flustered again.

The next day Steve and I went to Brazilian Consulate, where he went directly to the door for employees. I don't know how it all worked, I only remember that Steve asked me not to tell anybody, once we were in Brazil, that I was not Frank Gordon. I think he worked out some kind of a collective visa for the band plus our road manager and Runny, Walter Davis' girlfriend.

One way or the other, I didn't need to use my reentry permit on this trip. I did need it for Europe, where we were to fly to the same day we would return to New York from Brazil.

"Do you mind flying one day earlier, before the rest of the band?" Asked me Steve.

To go to Rio de Janeiro one day earlier? Was he kidding? Any time. "Of course," I said.

Time stood still or rather moved so quickly that before I knew it, Steve and I were already in the airport, walking towards our gate. There was plenty of time before boarding. In front of us, dressed in a red blouse and a black skirt, a petite young lady was walking.

I have never seen a walk like that before. All parts of her well-proportioned body were moving as if in a dance, so effortless, elegant and charming.

"She is Brazilian," said Steve, having caught my eye. I came closer. Her carefree face was pretty too. Not that I didn't trust Steve, I could recognize a Russian girl in a crowd myself, but I still wanted to hear it from her.

"I just put a friend on a plane to Rio. Myself, I return to Rio tomorrow. Where are you going?" She asked me right away. So I told her. The conversation sprung up like a wild flower. Steve went to a bar in the meantime.

"Oh, how interesting. I would love to come to your concert," she spoke good English, with a very cute accent. In the end she couldn't give me her phone number for some reason and I didn't have a clue as to what hotel I would be staying at.

It didn't feel right to go to Steve and ask him about it. To appear to a promoter of a Jazz Messengers' tour like I was picking up girls in the airport? No, no, no. So we parted with a vague prospect of meeting again at one of the concerts.

That was alright; I was happy anyway. I had my reentry permit safely in my pocket. I had brought it to the Village Vanguard the night before, where the new edition of the Messengers was meeting the audience of the legendary club for the first time that whole week.

In the back room everybody was looking at it, happy for me: Bobby, David, Dennis, Walter, and, of course, Art. He was so proud for one of his own. He kept telling everybody: "He said: 'give me that paper, I just got out of the Soviet Union. I should be able to travel. I am in a free country now,' and they gave it him."

Steve turned to be a very nice and friendly guy. After going through "How did you get out of Russia?" and "How did you learn to play jazz like that in Moscow?" he went on talking about Brazil, of its many contrasts and beauty. His English was not perfect, but good enough. I learned that he was not a full time promoter.

When I asked him what was he doing for living, he was not sure how to put it and the answer came out blurry. So I decided that he didn't know how to translate it into English. Also I learned, that the famous Brazilian Carnival had just ended, but a lot of people were still partying out of inertia. No, there was no chance to go to "Marakana."

"You will see a lot of soccer anyway," assured me Steve. "It's all over and everywhere in Brazil. Probably like chess in Russia." Steve brought up a parallel, for me not to worry about missing any of the Brazilian Genius.

Almost the whole tour we were to stay in Rio, because most of the concerts were in the city or driving distance from it with the exception of Sao Paulo for a concert, two concerts on the road and two concerts in Bahia. All together, three weeks in Brazil with Art Blakey and the Jazz the Messengers.

# CHAPTER 6

# THE WORLD – VALERY PONOMAREV, VALERY PONOMAREV – THE WORLD. (INTRODUCING VALERY PONOMAREV)

Rio de Janeiro, crystal dream of Ostap Bender, antihero of one of the most loved books in Russia. Actually it is not one book, but two, or one book in two volumes, whichever way you want to look at it.

One is called "The twelve chairs" and the other is "Golden fleece." Ostap and his friends make you laugh continuously. Ever an optimist, he is treasure hunting in new Russia, or rather the Soviet Union, inspired by the fact that, quoting the hero, "If there are monetary banknotes floating around, there must be people who have a lot of them and, at least one of them should be more than willing to bring a million or two to me on a silver platter with a ribbon tie."

After delivery of the silver platter he is planning on going far away from the communist haven – to Rio de Janeiro, where he had never been and was not ever destined to go. According to Ostap, the whole male population of Rio de Janeiro wears white slacks and sings a little rhyme about a cute girly, who is in possession of a tricky little commodity. When his friends displayed their curiosity about the mysterious city, he would cut them with "don't touch the crystal dream of my childhood with your dirty paws."

131

I am not Ostap Bender, but I am in Rio de Janeiro, looking out of the window of a double room on the 22ⁿᵈ floor of one of the uncountable hotels, which stretch like a forest in both directions to the horizon along Copacabana beach.

Copacabana turns, at the horizon to the right, into Ipanema beach, where Antonio Carlos Jobim met, some time last century, his legendary and eternally beautiful girl.

A two-way street in front of the hotel runs along the forest of high-rises, and behind the street the beach itself comes out of the ocean. One can not confuse it with any other beach in the world, because it has its unique Brazilian stamp on it.

A goal is in the sand, then a hundred and ten meters to the right and to the left is another goal, then another and another marking soccer fields all the way to the horizon on the right and the left.

There is no single blemish in the southern skies, which are as blue as they could be in the northern hemisphere too. Sun is blasting at full force, chasing life in any form off the sand.

Copacabana is deserted. There is no single soccer player on it until around 4pm, when the celestial body decides to take mercy on the life beneath it and turns down its thermostat. Then they come. They come from everywhere.

By 4:30 the beach is packed. Every soccer field features a game at the highest level of performance and virtuosity, as it could be played only in Brazil. They play – that is exactly what they do, they play.

At most soccer matches I had seen prior to coming to Brazil, players looked like they carried out some hard work or solved, with somber faces, complex war game puzzles or proved something to somebody. American players look to me like they don't think of soccer, but of baseball, which is a totally different game.

In Brazil they play, they play like happy children, make merry, rejoice, laughing, celebrating, cheering each other whether in the same team or the opposing one. No wonder players like Pele and Garrincha crystallize out of the collective genius of Brazilian soccer for every World Cup.

How can one do his best in any sport, particularly in soccer, if he is constantly under pressure? The mind is fogged. Muscles are bound.

My trumpet teacher used to demonstrate this point very well. He would tighten up his neck muscles and force himself to speak. His normally clear voice would turn harsh and he would say: "When you are tense, you can't even talk. How could you play?"

I believe that the Russian national team will soon win the World Cup too. With the heavy responsibility of representing a totalitarian state and its rulers as God's gift to humanity on the international stage off their shoulders, Russians will be able to display to the fullest their own ethnic genius and inclination for sports. Provided, of course that no other obstacles get in the way.

Boy that will be a day – Russia, in a beautiful and close game, beats Brazil in the final! Hurrah ... Hurrah ... Hurrah ...

The next day the rest of the band arrived. When I went to the ground floor, Art and almost everybody else was already off to their quarters. Only Dennis and David were still fussing with their luggage.

"Hey Val, how is your room? You and I double up." That was Dennis.

"Oh man, my room is great. Windows face the ocean, a lot of space. I am going to practice a little, get some fruit for the room and then I'll go to the beach. Good plan?"

"Yeah, sounds like a good plan to me. It'll be good to hang with you Val. We didn't really have a chance to talk yet. Did you notice that water drains from right to left? Isn't it weird?"

Then Dennis went through the classic "How did yous," and learned from me how to get LPs on the Moscow black market, how to get a forged visa – the whole package.

"Man! You know it was almost the same for me."

"What? I thought you were an American."

"Yes, I am an American, American Adrued, but I am from Atlanta, Georgia. There is nothing there, no clubs or jazz radio stations. I went to Atlanta University as a clarinetist for a couple of years and then switched to bass."

"What's American Adrued?"

"Oh, well, you know, its a little American sub-nation . . ."

"Yeah, yeah" I thought to myself, "almost the same for me."

After practicing and getting fruit to the room I packed my swimming trunks and a towel in a little shoulder bag and went on with executing the next part of my plan. Upon entering the elevator car, I came almost face to face with Art Blakey, who was standing there among other people, just like a regular hotel guest.

Nobody was trying to get his autograph, or find out about the tour. Everybody, including the superstar himself, was standing there with a gloomy face. Maybe they were unhappy that I had interrupted their smooth descent towards the ground floor.

"Hi Mr. Blakey, it's me, Valery."

"Hi Valery".

"How was your flight?"

"Good, thank you. Are you off to the beach?"

The sea was not really calm. Every once in a while a good-sized wave would smash itself on the sand and then retreat back to the sea dragging with it whatever it could find on the shore. Looking at the vastness of water in front of me I couldn't help but think of how far I was from Russia.

Until very recently I could only dream, like Ostap Bender, about

Italy, Austria, America. I was in South America now. In three weeks I would be touring Western Europe with Paris, Madrid, Lisbon, Berlin and London on the itinerary.

"Oh man! You forgot yesterday to look up the Southern Cross in the night skies. You are in the southern hemisphere! Damn!" My other self was a little disappointed and astonished.

"That's alright", I gave my assurances. "There is plenty of time. Maybe tonight".

I dropped my little bag and ran to the water past the crest of the wave. Wow! The shore past the water line turned out to be pretty steep. It wasn't like that in Italy or Long Island NY, where I swam in the ocean the previous summer.

Back In Russia I was caught in a current once and it carried me further and further away from a wild shore of the Black Sea. If it hadn't been for the coast guard, who happened to notice me, I would probably have had to stay in that water for a long time.

This time I was right at the shore, but each time I got close to the water line and stretched my leg to find rescue in the steady ground, the wave, having smashed itself on the sand, would pull me back into the ocean. Finally, I saw a big wave coming and decided that I should get on the crest of it and let it throw me on the sand past the water line, rather than keep on trying to swim to safety by myself and exhausting my muscles completely instead.

Boy! It did smash me on the sand pretty hard. It felt like not one, but three waves were twisting me and ringing me like I was a piece of cloth, trying to break me in two at the lower back. At least I was on the safe side of the water line. Realizing that my body was still intact, I moved out of the tide's way, picked up my belongings and went back to the hotel. So much for swimming for today.

"You are already back from the beach? Art asked me, when I entered the lobby, where he was lounging around with agents, friends and newspaper writers, Brazilian radio and television people.

"The shore is steep. It makes it hard to get out of the water. Besides I can't take too much sun in one day," I answered. "It could result in sunburn. I have heard that if one takes too much sun before the tan settles in, then the sunrays do a lot of damage. They cause not only peeled skin, but swelling of the embouchure and blisters on the chops as well. I take sun gradually".

"I have heard of this too that's true," broke in Ronnie. "Be careful Valery."

I knew how to sunbathe. Being predisposed to sun anyway, a few days later I was already almost as tanned as Art or Bobbie.

"Boy, you tan fast. Back in America they will expel you from your neighborhood," Schnitter joked, when he and I were walking towards the Rio de Janeiro Opera House, where our first concert in Brazil was to be held.

"Man, I feel like on a vacation, living in this hotel, practicing, hanging out on the beach, going to restaurants, exploring town. Is it always like this?"

"Oh no, far from it. When we hit one-nighters in Europe, you will see how different a tour could be. This is heaven on earth." Schnitter circled around with his hand and we made a turn. The Opera House looked very much like Bolshoi Theater, the big square in front of it stretched ahead of us. There were so many people everywhere that the theater looked like a fortress under siege.

"All these people came to hear you Valery, how do you like this?" David asked me.

"Oh, please David, they came to hear Art Blakey, not me."

"Of course they came to hear Art Blakey, but you will be playing too." Schnitter wouldn't calm down.

After being in the band for three years, he got used to the idea of contributing to the show, I guess, but myself, having just joined the Messengers, I couldn't see it that way.

"No, no. They came to hear Art Blakey," I insisted, as we kept on making our way through the crowd.

As we got closer to the house there was already a solid wall of people looking for tickets, so we walked around the building and got in through the service entrance. Before going to the dressing room I went to the toilet.

As soon as I closed the door of a little enclosure behind me and was one-on-one with the toilet bowl, I heard an urgent knock on the window from outside. Then I heard something being said in Portuguese. The voice sounded like it was pleading and ordering at the same time. I saw some shapes in the darkness outside and cursed them out in English.

"Open windov. Let mi in." The same ordering-pleading voice switched to broken English.

Now I could make out the forms a little better. I realized it was a guy, trying to get in the theater through the toilet window. I could open it, but how did he expect me to remove an iron fence in front of it? I shook the fence with all my might to assure the guy that the theater administration must have expected this kind of a turnout and had taken necessary precautions.

Without wasting any time, the guy moved away, no doubt in search of an alternate way of getting inside the building. I understood him very well. I would have tried anything myself if, let's say, Art Blakey and the Jazz Messengers were playing at the Bolshoi and I didn't have tickets.

After completing my warm-ups before the concert I was sitting in the dressing room, engrossed in thinking of the changes for Walter's "Uranus," when two of the most beautiful girls – as only in Brazil girls could be – walked in. Art got up from his seat to welcome them in and brought them over to where I was sitting.

"That's my son VaLery." With a flicker in his eyes, he introduced me, like a proud father would introduce his grown-up son to a new business acquaintance.

I jumped off the big and comfortable chair screaming "Yeah...." with my fists up in the air.

Instead of hugging the girls Art and I embraced as only father and son could, as if we had just won a World Cup or something. What a day that was!

At that concert and at all of the remaining ones Art, in full seriousness, was announcing me: "Frank Gordon on trumpet". For a feature I played "Blue Moon", a beautiful singing standard and got tons of applause for it. One of the girls turned to be the wife of a musician in a famous Brazilian pop orchestra called "Novos Baianos". Since there were no public concerts of the band at the time, she invited us to come to their house to hear the guys play. The other girl from that evening on and for the rest of the tour was calling me "Mister Melody".

*The Jazz Messengers on the stage*
*(L.to R. James Williams, D.S., V.P., Dennis Irwin, B.W., A.B.)*
*Photo by Christian Ducasse.*

After the concert Art announced: "We are invited to Steve's tomorrow. Bring your instruments." The announcement sounded more like a required band activity than anything else. So my schedule for tomorrow was cut out for me. Cool, hanging with the Messengers.

The next day Walter, Ronnie, Bobby and I were sitting at a table of an outdoor cafe near our hotel, waiting for the ride to the tour promoter's.

"Bob," I said.

"Don't call me Bob, my name is Bobby, not Bob," my brother in the messengers answered, sounding offended.

"I am sorry Bobby, I didn't mean to be impolite . . ." I started apologizing, when two little children, maybe six or seven years old, came by the table and broke into our conversation with their tiny subdued voices. I didn't understand a word they said.

"Do you know what they are saying Valery," Ronnie asked me.

"No," I said, "I don't have a clue."

"What do you think that girl is doing?" Ronnie pointed at a pretty girl slowly walking back and forth in front of the hotel.

"Well, I don't know, she appears to be no older than fifteen."

"That's a lot older than these kids."

"What?"

"Yeah, yeah, they offer sex for money."

"No!" I was stunned. "I have never seen anything like this, not even in the Soviet Union."

"Valery, there is a lot of poverty in this country. Their parents can't support them most likely, or they are simply homeless."

We all dug into our pockets and gave the children a lot of coins. They softly said "Obrigato" and moved to the next table.

"Wow!"

Two big cars drove up the driveway. "Must be our ride," Walter said. So we paid for the drinks and left the cafe. The rest of the band came out of the hotel's lobby and crowded around the cars. Now I had a chance to take a closer look at the girl. She was really attractive with her tiny waist and slim body. At close scrutiny she looked even younger than fifteen.

As if she knew I was looking at her, the girl glanced back, catching my curious look, and smiled at me. What a bewitching smile she had on her pretty face! White Fang's mother (from Jack London's novel) must have had the same smile, luring his prospective fathers to their deaths.

"Valery, Valery get in the car." I heard Ronnie calling, so I got in the back seat next to her and Walter, Art was in the passenger seat in front.

"We live in the mountains, away from the City, but the ride is not long at all." Steve said as the car engine started and we took off.

Soon we were driving on a winding road, up and down hills. Vegetation and foliage around us was so thick that it practically grew into a tunnel around the road, making it darker and much cooler there. Then we drove along a dusty road for a minute.

"These are our factories." Steve pointed at two big and dirty buildings standing near the road to the left. The car drove past the factories and went into a wooded area again.

When we arrived, there was an American woman to meet us. It seemed like most of the band members and Ronnie knew her from the States. It was such a joyful scene, with all of them hugging and kissing, being so happy to see each other that far from New York.

"Did you have a chance to see Sugar Loaf yet?" The lady asked me, after I was introduced.

"Oh, yes, of course, with a statue of Christ on it. With the arms stretched out. From a distance, the statue looks like a cross on a peak of a mountain. It must be enormous in actual size, ha?"

"Oh, yes, it is 120 feet high. Do you know there is one exactly like that in Portugal, also on a mountain, overlooking Lisbon?"

"I have heard of it. We will be in Lisbon on our European tour, maybe I will see it then."

"I understand that you will be rehearsing later. There, to the left of the main house." The lady pointed at a three-storied building. "There, on the second floor you will find Steve's office, leave your instruments there. Feel free to look around. In a minute drinks and hors d'oeuvres will be served here."

Servants dressed all in white, tuxedos made of light fabric, shirts and bowties were already building a stand out of two tables, having put them next to each other and covered them with a white table spread.

I took my trumpet to Steve's office and went for a walk on his property. First I crossed a soccer field, then a stream with a company of ducks in it. Then I came upon a little open zoo with very cute baby animals in it.

Behind the zoo I saw a beautiful lake, but decided not to go that far and turned back towards the main house. Everything was clean and harmonious everywhere. Freshly-cut grass, neat footpaths, no single cigarette butt or a beer can in sight.

"What would you like to drink, sir?" Asked a uniformed servant, when I came up to the table bearing a multitude of drinks, goblets, wine glasses, drinking glasses and delicious looking appetizers.

I wanted to drink champagne, but asked for mineral water, because of the rehearsal I had to go to a little later. I had learned a long time ago not to drink alcohol and play the trumpet, because my chops swell considerably after even a small dose of the green monster.

"I'll grab some at the dinner," I told my own police-tutor-guardian angel-etc. to allay his worries. My other self's ears would always prick up at the word "alcohol."

Steve turned out to be a very generous and hospitable host. We used his music room with a Steinway in it for the rehearsal and when the time came, went to the dining room, where an elaborate dinner had been served by the same team of servants, this time dressed in black tuxedoes.

I, for sure, and I think Bobby too, drank a little more champagne than we should have, but who cares. After all, we were at a dinner with our family and friends.

The next day we were off again, perfect for a band activity. All together we went to Novos Baianos' house and were met at the door by the hostess, who had a baby in her hands. That was a surprise. We all marveled at a heavenly beautiful baby girl. Her name I remember, it was Consuela. The mother was so young, it was hard to imagine her being a mother even with a baby in her arms.

I figured in Brazil, as in many other countries with a hot climate, the stork sends children to very young parents on a regular basis. We learned that Novos Baianos had recently bought and moved into this house, which had just been built, and used it as the headquarters for the band.

Being on tour most of the time and dealing with a brand new baby, they didn't have a chance to fit out the house. For the most part, it had bare walls and floors. If not for the mattresses and couches in some rooms and a couple of chairs, the house would have been standing there just like the construction workers left it.

After checking out the ground floor we all went upstairs and crowded into one room, where three guys were sitting on a couch like young yogis. Each held an instrument, two guitars and a mandolin. When we came in they were already playing and smiled at us apologetically as if they were saying: "Your are welcome, make yourselves comfortable, feel at home, but sorry we can't get up and shake your hands: that mean breaking the music and that is something we cannot do."

It looked like they had been playing since the inception of the

Carnival or even before it, and were extending the annual event as long as inertia allowed them to. There was no music in front of them, they did not look at each other, they just played and sang without any breaks, changing songs and keys, tempos, switching from bossa-nova to samba without as much as winking an eye at each other.

"Here," somebody stretched his hand, generously offering me a little butt of a self-made cigarette.

"That's alright," I said. "I've tried it before and turned to be very much disinclined to it." This time my alter ego did not need to worry about me at all.

It was already very late, but nobody showed any signs of trying to change the scene.

"When are we going back to the hotel?" I asked Walter, being concerned that we might have outstayed our welcome.

"We are not going anywhere, we are staying here. If you are tired, just go to any room and sleep. Don't worry, you won't offend anybody."

That's exactly what I did. There was a couch in the corner of the next room, so I made myself comfortable on it and fell asleep. I woke up maybe a couple of hours later and went back to the room where everybody was hanging out.

The three musicians were still sitting and playing in the same poses as when I first saw them. It was rather dark in the room and I couldn't tell with certainty whether the guests were sleeping in their seats, charmed by the music or listening. Eventually we did go back to the hotel, but I don't remember now what time it was or who drove us.

The next day somebody brought a newspaper with a review of the first concert in it. There was a picture of the band too. The review was very favorable, and in particular it praised Frank Gordon for playing "Blue Moon" beautifully.

A funny thing happened on the road. We were staying in a small hotel somewhere in the middle of the country. Before the concert Bobby and I practiced a couple of heads together in my room. When it was time to get ready for the main event, Bobby went to his room to take a shower and dress up and I went to the bathroom to take a shower myself.

I thought that there was nobody in the hotel except for the messengers, so I didn't bother closing the door of my room. After taking a shower I had just a moment to put boxers on, before Bobby, also in boxers, came running in.

"I took my saxophone with me, didn't I?"

"I didn't really watch, when you left." I looked around the room, but didn't see the alto case.

"Maybe you put it under my bed."

We both fell on our knees to search under the mattress, where I kept my trumpet, but there was nothing there, no alto, no trumpet.

"What???!!!"

Scared out of our minds, we ran to Art's room. Art and Jim were there, sitting around a night table with a lamp on it.

"Art, our instruments were stolen, trumpet and alto are gone." We screamed in perfect unison and froze in horror at our own words.

Art looked at us for a moment and burst out laughing: "Jim, give them back their instruments."

"Oh my God! Nobody had played this kind of a joke on me since I was a kid. Oh, please!" All I could think of, as my mind and body quickly unthawed and I started laughing myself, was being overjoyed to hold my large bore 72 bell Bach Stradivarius in my hands. "God!"

"You gotta learn to close the doors of your hotel rooms guys, you are on the road, you don't know who might be staying next door to you. I wanted to teach you a lesson." Jim muttered in his usual manner. "If your instruments were really stolen, it would've been a big trouble for the whole band, not only for you". The safety course professor rubbed it in some more, with somewhat apologetic overtones in his voice.

"I couldn't hold off my laughter when I saw Valery and Bobby in their boxers petrified in the middle of my room." Art would tell and retell this story many times in the future.

I sure learned my lesson well and in the future, I would be always extra careful to lock my door if Jim was anywhere near it.

Back in Rio everybody got paid for the whole tour, so I called my now long time ex to inform her that we were millionaires.

"Really?" I heard in the receiver.

"Cruzeiro millionaires, it equals 2,100 dollars. I am coming back on the day after tomorrow, the same evening we are flying to Europe. Prepare my alternate luggage." I issued an order to my, then, future ex and went to buy post cards.

At the bottom of the stairs, leading to the hotel, I saw the same girl. This time she was talking to a short gray-haired gentleman. Just like the first time, the girl glanced back and caught my inquisitive look. She recognized me. I felt like she had established some kind of a bond between us. Her eyes were saying, "I'd love to talk to you, but I am busy right now". I wondered what the "Mister Melody" girl would say about this.

She and "Novos Baianos" came to every concert of ours, if it was within driving distance of Rio. The next day after the end of the tour they went with us to the airport to see us off.

Consuela's mother brought beautiful garlands made of flowers for each one of us. There we were, sitting on a bench in a small terminal, waiting for our plane to take us back to North America.

Soon it would no longer be somewhere there, to the North: On the contrary, South America, the Southern Skies, Brazil, Rio de Janeiro, the Sugar Loaf, Christ soaring above the whole city, our hotel and the girl in front of it, Copacabana and Ipanema beaches, soccer fields, the Opera House would be somewhere there, to the South.

Walter was sitting next to me and staring into the space in front of him. Ronnie put her slender arms over his powerful shoulders. Tears were rolling down his cheeks. What a great guy Walter was! I always knew he was sensitive, to play and write music like he did, one had to be sensitive.

After the last goodbyes, hugs and kisses, the Messengers plus Ronnie and Jim as one group, went through the luggage check and passport control. Our Brazilian friends on the other side of the glass partition were still waving their hands and calling out our names: "Goodbye Art, goodbye Walter,...Bobbie,...Jim...Ronnie...goodbye Mister Melody ..."I am sure everybody else, just like me, was wondering: "When would we come to Brazil again?"

As soon as the doors of the plane locked, the Brazilian tour fell into the past, although our friends were still only a hundred or maybe 200 meters away and probably figuring out who would drive who back to the city. They were locked out in another hemisphere.

The routine flight progressed very smoothly. An hour or so into the flight I was standing up and talking to somebody a couple of rows of seats over when the plane plunged. A dead silence was cast over the plane, I was the only one who was still standing and talking. Then the plane plunged again, this time much deeper as the collective cry of the passengers shook the plane.

My whole body tensed in a standing position, hands grabbing onto the seat in front of me and legs to the floor in a desperate attempt to keep my balance. Then I fell into my seat.

"This is the flight commander speaking. There is nothing to be alarmed about. Please fasten your belts, we are experiencing a little difficulty," was announced through the speakerphone in the passenger compartment and everything quieted down. The rest of the flight the passengers spent talking about air pockets, black holes in space, and my standing and talking, they thought, nonchalantly, like nothing happened.

"New York, New York!!! We are in America," was ringing in my mind. Six hours later, with my alternate luggage and reentry permit in my pocket, I was back in JFK, looking for the flight to Amsterdam.

I still couldn't believe it was real. Art Blakey and the Jazz Messengers was the world's most loved, famous and greatest band. I, VaLery Ponomarev, a nobody, just a refugee from the Soviet Union, am a member of it, holding the trumpet chair in it!

Jim Green woke me up: "We are in Amsterdam now. You've been smiling for the past hour in your sleep. Too bad nobody had a camera to take a picture of you."

It was hard to get used to the new reality. Everything was so shining and different. Even after a Dutch officer stamped my paper and handed it to me, I still didn't feel like I was fully awake. For some reason, Jim Green's words: "In Holland everything is cool," kept ringing in my ears.

Well it was a long day, everybody was tired. Art's many friends came to the airport. He introduced us all to them, Bobby, Dennis and me were new. Everybody was anxious to meet me – a Russian in the Messengers. Can you imagine?!

Soon we said goodbye to everybody. (Art, contrary to his habit, didn't hang out long in Holland.) We had to get to the hotel, it was pretty far, in Germany, and everybody was already tired enough. So we got in two cars, the first one with our luggage and a Dutch roadie, the second one with all of us musicians.

It was so warm and cozy in the back seat of the rather small car, sitting next to the great Walter Davis. The car kept rolling, and the nagging feeling of trouble moved to the back of my mind. Suddenly we came to a complete stop. The driver opened the window, and an authoritative voice said with a heavy German accent, "Your passports please."

The sight of a German patrol officer in a military uniform didn't make feel very good. Something was the matter. I felt like a partisan in one of those Soviet movies, which I've seen many of, caught by Nazis.

Everybody handed their passports to the officer. I handed him my new re-entry permit. He disappeared into the station house for a few minutes. It was hot and uncomfortable in the car. The air was stuffy, and I could only see the darkness of the back of the front seat before me. I raised my head as I heard him coming back. In one hand he had a stack of dark passports, in another he had the elongated white booklet, called a re-entry permit.

I started to get out of the car before he even tried to pronounce my name: "Va-lery Po-no-ma-rev"! Out!" The movie was definitely still on.

I was escorted by two German soldiers to the border patrol station house. I didn't have any maps of German positions on me, no weapons, nothing incriminating. "This way," one of them said. They kind of pushed me into a small enclosure behind a bar. The room was full of soldiers and officers in hostile uniforms.

A senior one, short with a blank face, asked me, "Are you VaLery Ponomarev?"

"Yes," I said.

"A Russian passport looks different," he snarled. "You are passing for an American, mixing among these guys. You must be a spy."

His right hand rose up with a gun facing me in it. I knew only too well what was going on. The dream was over. No Art Blakey, no family, no America, no jazz, nothing. I was back to reality. Next they'll throw me in the concentration camp, torture me, make me work, put me to hard labor.

So many times, back in Moscow, I would wake up in the middle of the night from the dream of New York, jazz music, the West, only to realize that I was still in my room with the play button of my tape recorder within reach, so I could push it down first thing in the morning.

Boy! What an awakening this time – German solders all over the place, I was captured and a muzzle o a gun pushed into my face. I stood there in a stupor, knowing only one thing from long experience: once I woke up, I woke up – and nothing could bring back the dream.

"Put that foolish thing down," I heard all of a sudden, a harsh voice, so familiar from many records, even more familiar lately. "Put that foolish thing down! That's my trumpet-player, VaLery Ponomarev!"

To this day I don't understand how Art managed to sneak into the enclosure, where I was pushed behind a bar, and stand shoulder to shoulder next to me, facing the same gun. But there he was, the world's greatest drummer and band leader, a superstar of modern jazz, Art Blakey.

"Call this number. They will confirm his identity, he is no Russian spy."

It was hard to reach anybody in the American embassy. At 2am Sunday morning, everything was closed, and everybody was gone. Finally, many calls later, they woke somebody up, and made somebody go to the computer and identify me.

I got a visa for two days and was recommended to go to the German Consulate in Copenhagen, where we were to play Tuesday and Wednesday, to straighten everything out, so I'd be able to come back to Germany afterwards.

On Tuesday, in the waiting room of Consul General Herbert Fon Der Bank's office, there was a long line of applicants. A very pretty secretary came out and called my name first. "Mr. Ponomarev, would you kindly, please, come to the office? Mr. Fon Der Bank is upset that you are waiting." It sounded like she was talking to somebody else, except she was looking at me and smiling.

Mr. Von Der Bank rose when I entered and stretched out his hand. "Art Blakey! I love his music," he said, "I have been collecting his records for years. I am so happy to meet his new trumpet player. It's such an honor. Also please accept my apologies for the incident at the border. Soviet tanks are right at our eastern border and it makes everybody extra sensitive."

"Of course I understand," I assured him.

"I knew you would," Mr. Von Der Bank said and handed me my booklet with a visa to enter and exit as many times as needed for half a year. "If it's not enough, I will extend it longer. You have to change your traveling document anyway. In the space 'nationality', in the paper like this, must be written 'Stateless' since you are no longer a Soviet citizen, and only an American resident."

I had many troubles being stateless for another three years: I was expelled from Norway (another story), I had to fly to East Berlin with a personal bodyguard, I was detained in Switzerland and France, and more than once missed planes. Many times in the future I would just hold back my reentry permit, even if all the visas were in order.

Every time I saw that the border patrol officer was careless, not looking inside the car to count all the passengers, I would just sit back like nothing happened, not bothering to hand in my document. A couple of times I didn't have a chance to get a visa to some countries (I forget which ones) and it worked.

Boy! I lived dangerously. All of that was going on until October 9, 1979, when I became an American citizen. Bobby took pictures of me with an American passport crossing the border for the first time.

Art Blakey would always stay by me, and would never let anybody mistreat his trumpet player.

# CHAPTER 7

# AT HIS MAJESTY'S SERVICE

I used to love postcards. I still send a lot of them, but not like when I first started to travel. Then I used to put hundreds of them in the mail for my friends and relatives. To my mother and my godmother – her best friend – alone I had sent from the first tour probably 50 just from Paris.

My godmother was born and raised in Paris. As a young and naive ballerina she moved to Moscow to continue her study of ballet at the Bolshoi Theater Dance School. There she met the love of her life – Innokentii Vasilievitch, who I used to call "Uncle Kesha," a tall, studious gentleman with a goatee and mustache – and stayed in Russia past the point of no return.

I had never heard her, or anybody in her presence, talking about Paris. There had to be some reasons for that. One of them, of course, was that it was not a good idea to publicize one's capitalistic origins in the Soviet Union.

I knew she had to be thinking about her hometown, called by Hemingway, "A Moveable Feast." Only in my godmother's case, the legendary city of her youth was not with her, but existed out of reach somewhere far away in her distant memory.

My mother, on the contrary, used to fantasize aloud about London, Madrid, Paris of course, Athens, Berlin, Delhi, Rio de Janeiro – you name it. She knew them all very well from books, but had never had a chance to visit any of them.

My mom and her best friend, beautiful women in their youth, used to sing at parties with friends a dream-like song about "Bananoysh-Lemonysh Singapore…drowning in magnolia blossom."

My godmother's full name is Galina Anatol'evna, but my mother always called her Galia for short. In my mind's eye I could clearly see my mother calling her best friend: "Galia, Galia, I received a whole avalanche of post cards, this time from Paris, they are all signed in Valery's handwriting."

"Me too, me too. They are all signed, 'Your Godson' or 'Valery.'"

In Paris we played for three days at a club in Montmartre, the bohemian section of town called the Latin Quarter, which was popular with the tourists. Routinely there was a mob scene at the entrance every night.

The jazz lovers were pretty rude: when I walked confidently towards the door – some angry yelling and even hand pushing ensued for a moment, until, "That's Art Blakey's new trumpet-player" rang in the air.

Then, first with a dose of suspicion, with reverence and a little bit of jealousy the astonished crowd gave way, letting me through. "Take me with you," I heard somebody yelling out to the right and behind me, in a timbre of tone very similar to one of the angry voices that had tried to chase me away a moment before.

The performance was to take place in the cellar, which had been converted into a jazz club. The scarcely lit alcoves, pillars and stone floors of the club gave the impression more of an ancient basement in royal quarters, where evil schemers would gather to plot a palace coup, than a place for modern tourists to listen to jazz.

"You know why the floors are wet?" Walter asked me.

"I guess they have been washed recently."

"No, the club owner just wants water on the floor, so the audience won't sit there. Standing they take much less space."

"Oh, that's what it is, so the owner can sell more tickets that way." I guessed the trick of a capitalist promoter.

"You got it."

I barely had time to warm up, when people started pouring in. Sure enough, in about half an hour the club was completely packed. A solid wall of people occupied benches, chairs, the area by the bar, the open space in front of the stage. A perfect illustration of the saying, "packed in like sardines," the equivalent of the Russian "like herrings in a barrel."

We were just about to start. Everybody held their breath and quiet descended over the club in anticipation of the first sounds of the Messengers, when Art all of a sudden got out from behind his drums and came to the microphone.

"Somebody call the club owner," he demanded in an angry voice. That was something he would never do – show his anger in front of an audience.

"What is that?" he barked and pointed at the wires and microphones attached to the ceiling near the stage. I saw them too, but took these, much smaller ones, for an innocent addition to the microphones on the stage. Somebody was already making his way towards us, pushing people aside.

"This is only to record for the needs of the club. This is absolutely non-commercial." The man, obviously responsible for the extra sound equipment, took his chance in convincing Art of his most honest intentions.

"You setting up a recording and not breathing a word about it to us?"

"I am sorry mister Blakey, I am sorry mister Blakey. We thought you wouldn't mind. It's only for the use at the club, for advertisement and promotion. We didn't mean to make an LP out of it, or anything like that. Please trust me." The man was still trying to catch his breath.

"Tear all this down right this minute, if you want the concert to go on. To do something like that behind our backs!" Art rubbed it in some more and went to his drums in the back of the stage, while the club owner was already on a ladder, dismantling the very carefully set attachments.

"I was just about to be recorded on a bootleg record with Art Blakey: Jazz Messengers! Live in Paris!" flew through my mind, when the first sounds of the drum intro to Jodi cascaded from behind, turning well developed boos into a storm of applause.

Here we go. "Blow your horn, blow your horn."

For an intro to my feature that beautiful spring evening I played fragments from "April in Paris" and then came on with a tune of my own choice, "Autumn in New York." The parallel was immediately noticed and commented on by our musical director.

Every round of applause easily qualified for standing ovation status, since the audience was just as excited as anywhere else and most of them had spent the entire evening on their feet.

Oh man! If I could only play with Art Blakey again!

After the second concert we went to a local jazz club to hear a band, led by an American expatriate, the legendary Kenny Clarke. Art was absolutely natural in the position of an ex student who had become a successful band leader himself. He used to talk with a lot of respect about drummers he loved and learned from – Chick Webb, Sid Cattlet, "Philly Joe" Jones, Kenny Clarke.

On the third night we had a real jazz dignitary in the audience. Chen Parker, Charlie Parker's widow, came with her daughter to hear us play. After the concert, instead of going to the hotel room to pack and go to bed early, we were sitting at the restaurant above the club and listening to

Chen talking about her life in France and her daughter learning to sing. In general she loved the life in Europe, but missed the States.

*************************

Going to bed early almost never happened. For the most part the road schedule of the Messengers could be safely carved in stone: first take a plane to what could be anywhere in the world, arrive, check into a hotel, shower, meet half an hour later in the lobby to go to the concert location for the soundcheck.

While the microphones, wires, speakers, monitors where being prepared you warmed up. After telling the sound engineer enough times "once you establish the volume, don't change anything," the sound check is considered to be over and everybody is headed to a restaurant to grab something to eat before the gig. In some variations of the schedule there were sandwiches served after the sound check.

It had happened more than once that we would get stuck somewhere on our travels and arrive at the location right before the audience started filling up the place, or even when the audience was already waiting. In that case you would get on the bandstand and play, skipping all of the preliminary steps except warming up.

After the concert, there was a dinner organized by the promoter with all of his friends, sponsors and friends of sponsors invited. If there was any jazz club within driving distance, we headed there to hang out, returning to the hotel in time to pack, maybe sleep for a couple of hours and then drive to the next gig or head to the airport early in the morning to catch the first plane out.

It could be to a place we had just come from the day before, like when we made it from Sicily to Paris and then right back to the South of Italy the very next day, to repeat the same travel-arrival-hotel-sound-check-concert-dinner-hang-hotel sequence again.

That schedule would repeat and repeat until the string of one-nighters was broken and we would find ourselves in London for a two week run at "Ronnie Scott's." Or at "Domicile" on Leopold Strase in Munich for a Thursday through Sunday engagement. Or any of the world's capitals for two days to a week.

Or we simply got stuck in the middle of nowhere in a hotel for a day off. Japan, Europe, or the States – it didn't matter. The Sisyphean labors would go on unchallenged 52 weeks out of a year.

All four years of my being with the Messengers now seem like one big tour. Even being in New York didn't feel like being at home, but rather in a city on the itinerary – only the hotel room was bigger and had more personalized services.

If we happened to play in any of the bandmembers' hometowns, Art Blakey would make a point of announcing: "Atlanta's own," or "Kansas City's own." and the audience would go wild with the pride of having a messenger coming from their ranks. Once we were real close to Russia. Just thinking of it brings out in perfect detail that now distant moment...

The band had just flown from New York to Helsinki, Finland. First stop – the Pori Jazz Festival, a rather long ride from the airport. No time for the hotel or anything of the sort, we went directly to the concert location instead... I am standing under the tent, which separates me from pouring rain, and chewing, between warm-ups, on a quite stale sandwich.

Russia was so near, yet it was so far behind the Iron Curtain. That's when Art's husky voice startled me with: "Did you wanna be a musician, Valery?"

He thought I was going in my mind over the drawbacks of the music profession. No, he was wrong this time, I was thinking of St. Petersburg, which was only a bus ride from where we were, but it was not very likely

I could take that ride any time soon. It turned out to be 17 years before I could return to Russia for the first time.

*Pori Jazz Festival (L.to R. - Walter Davis, D.S, V.P., D.I., B.W., A.B.)*

But those or any drawbacks of the music profession never distracted me. Music, that's all that mattered. To get to the stage, to play with Art Blakey, that's what mattered first and foremost. And that was the same for my brother Bobby or any of the messengers.

**\*\*\*\*\*\*\*\*\*\*\*\*\*\*\*\*\*\*\*\*\*\*\*\***

Early the next day, after completing the Paris engagement, we packed into three taxis and proceeded with our schedule. Drive to the airport, the flight, the arrival – in Oslo, Norway this time – customs.

Oh no! Not again! The customs official, with scorn on his face, pushed back my reentry permit.

"You are declined entry. Your paper is no good."

Minutes later, word got to the organizers of the Norwegian part of the tour, mostly students of the local university, who were waiting for us on the other side. One of them was allowed to come over to where I was.

"We will show them! This party is no good. The People of Norway need another one." He kept calling the names of the rivaling political parties, which I don't remember now. "Election is coming up. We will make scandal. We will make fools out of the old party. Not to let a musician in our country! This is an outrage! They are violating human rights!"

My friend sounded very much like big John from the West End Café; only John's Norwegian counterpart was much shorter and spoke with an accent. "They will get theirs," he kept assuring me as a security official escorted me out of the small terminal and walked me across an open place to a two-story prison-like building, which turned out to be a hotel for transit passengers.

"You will have to stay here until tomorrow, since there are no more flights out today." The official checked me into the hotel and left, but the student remained to hang with me a little longer.

"Mister Blakey said that you will have to fly to Amsterdam tomorrow and wait for the band there. This is the number you should call and ask for Fuzzy."

I knew who Fuzzy was. She was Art's good friend, a petite and very charming young lady, who came to the airport in Amsterdam to meet us, when we first landed in Europe.

"I will come in the morning to make sure there are no more problems. Your flight is not until 1pm anyway," my student friend informed me before saying goodbye.

He, of course, had introduced himself initially, but I couldn't concentrate on anything and didn't get his name, because I kept thinking that this visa business could not go on like this forever and that Art would say sooner or later, "That's enough."

The next morning the student came with a whole bunch of newspapers under his arm.

"Valery look, look! These are the major newspapers of our country," he exclaimed, all excited, and opened the front pages. There I was in a picture, sitting dumbfounded. Another newspaper featured a picture of me writing a declaration that I would leave the next day.

"I told you! Valery you will see, we will have a new party after this election. I guarantee you."

I was already walking up the stairs to get into the plane, but my student friend was still assuring me that the brighter and better political future of his country was firmly on the way.

*Norway customs with reentry permit.*

\*\*\*\*\*\*\*\*\*\*\*\*\*\*\*\*\*\*\*\*\*\*\*\*\*\*

I never actually checked if the ruling party had to step down or not, but when a few months later I went to the Norwegian consulate in New York to get a visa before our second European tour, I was treated like a god – "Oh, Mister Ponomarev!" "Oh, please Mr. Ponomarev, your reentry permit," "Oh sorry Mr. Ponomarev," "Please wait just a minute Mr. Ponomarev."

The two secretaries fussed around me as if I were the most important customer they had ever had and then disappeared into the depths of their office to reappear literally a minute later with my document in their hands. They were both carrying it as if it were a crystal vase or a burning hot plate of gold or something.

"Mr. Ponomarev here is your visa. We hope you will enjoy your visit to our country. You are most welcome. Please come again."

I thanked both ladies wholeheartedly and left, totally convinced that whatever party was ruling Norway at the time I would vote for it without any reservation.

**************************

I got to Amsterdam with no problem and spent the rest of the day walking the streets of the hospitable city. It was already late evening when I decided to sit down in a bar before going back to the hotel, and descended stairs leading into the first one on the way. There were a lot of young people, some were dancing, some were hugging. I made myself comfortable on a low windowsill, but didn't stay for too long and called it a night.

"Valery, what were you doing at a teenage club yesterday?" Fuzzy asked me the next day, when I called to find out if she had any news from the Messengers. She laughed as she tried to sound flabbergasted.

"What teenagers' club?" I couldn't understand what she was talking about.

"You were spotted at a club on such and such street late at night yesterday. That is a kids' hang out."

"Oh, I know what you mean now. I didn't realize it was teenage hang out. How do you know where I was yesterday?"

"Oh, please Valery, I have my sources." She laughed again.

"You know the bartender at the club? Was he at any of our previous concerts or something?" I guessed.

"No, my 15-year-old daughter was there."

"You have a daughter?"

"And a son too. They love your playing. They are Art's adopted children you know."

"Oh my! I would never imagine you having children that big."

"Oh yes. Anyway, Art called. They played a concert yesterday and may play another one tonight, but they are definitely coming to Amsterdam tomorrow. Art said that there is no Jazz Messengers without trumpet and canceled the rest of the concerts in Norway, so you guys will have unplanned vacation in Amsterdam."

"He canceled three concerts?!"

"Don't worry Valery, it's not only that. I think he wants to hang in Amsterdam with me and the kids too."

"Oh God!" I could only say and made an appointment to meet Art the next day.

It was a beautiful sunny day. Art was smiling, coming right at me. I couldn't understand how he could be smiling with me anywhere in sight, having just lost so much money because of me.

"I am sorry Art," I said. That was all I could come up with for the day's greeting, having been prepared for the worst.

"Don't worry Valery, you've made hundreds of thousands of dollars worth of publicity. Enjoy Amsterdam. We will hang here for three days, and then go to Copenhagen again. Did you like it the first time?"

"I didn't really have any free time then."

"You will this time. We are playing at "Montmartre" for three days. Hotel is right above the club."

"The name is just like in the Parisian Latin Quarter."

"Yeah, just like it."

I liked it very much. There was no need to look for the club, you just kept on walking down the stairs to the next level, then another one, and another one, opened the door and you were in the club. Turn right and there was an office.

"Hi Valery," I heard somebody say. There was a man sitting behind a desk.

"My name is Chris, I am the owner. Feel yourself at home." He spoke to me like he had known me for many years.

"Nice to meet you."

Except for the club itself, which was different in interior from the club in Paris, everything else at Copenhagen's Montmartre repeated itself as if in a movie which you liked the first time and came to the theater to watch again. There was a packed house, Art's many friends, excited people and tons of applause. During the first break I was making my way through the crowd when I saw Mister Herbert Von Der Banck at the end of the bar.

"Oh, mister Von Der Banck, so good to see you. I am sorry I didn't send you an invitation. I didn't realize you would have time to come to the club," I tried to conceal my embarrassment as well as I could.

"Don't worry yourself with an invitation, I have an annual membership here. How is your tour progressing?"

I told him what happened in Norway, hoping that the worst was over, since the remaining three weeks we were to play in Germany, Holland, and one day in Paris and Denmark where visas had already been taken care of. Back in America I didn't expect any problem changing my reentry permit and status to "stateless."

In the second set for my feature I played "Blue Moon," at Art's request, and got a storm of applause for it. After the set Art was relaxing at the table with his friends when I passed by, feeling proud of myself.

"You need to learn the lyrics to the ballad you're playing," I heard Art saying from the table.

"When you work on a ballad, you need to learn not only the melody and changes, but the lyrics too, because when people listen to your performance of their favorite song, they recognize right away when you know what you are playing about. At least familiarize yourself with the words, so you know the general mood of the tune."

I heard Art telling that to David and Bobbie, when they tried a new ballad for their feature number, but he never said anything to me about this. I knew he liked my treatment of "I Remember Clifford", "My One and Only Love" "Autumn in New York" and other ballads, because he had been featuring me every night and even twice sometimes. Also I didn't know the lyrics to any of the songs I was playing.

I went closer.

"Sit down," Art invited me. "You see Valery, you have a beautiful tone, and you feel the tune so well, but you still need to learn the lyrics."

And he went on with the whole lecture, which I listened at full attention, knowing that Art had heard something wrong in my rendition of the famous standard. He taught us many things, verbally and in action and he always knew what he was talking about.

I had something on my mind when I asked him, "Is it only the horn player who needs to know the lyrics, or the rhythm section players too?"

"Of course, everyone should know them," was the answer.

Art had never become just one of the guys for me. As long as I knew him, he remained a living legend and my hero.

*Calendar 1980.*

"Art," I began, "we are in Denmark. Where will I find the lyrics now? Please write them out for me."

The atmosphere around us tensed right away. Everybody was looking at me with a serious judgment in their eyes, as if they were asking: "Are you sure you did the right thing, putting the great superstar on the spot?"

It seemed to me that even Art looked at me with sparkles of annoyance in his eyes. Without saying anything, he just took a pen and a piece of paper. The pen didn't look very comfortable between his fingers, which were used to drumsticks, but he was moving it in a slow and steady rhythm without any deviation.

I thought I saw that funny look in his eyes again when he handed me the paper.

"It will help you to play the song like you know it," he growled.

"Art," I said, "please sign it for me: for Valery to play better, or something." He broke into a big smile of a flattered man. "Come on Valery, you are kidding. You are a Messenger. You don't need my autograph."

*Close up playing trumpet.*

He kept on smiling as he was signing: "Written for Valorie by Art Blakey."

*Left: Autograph; Right: Autograph front page.*

His daughter Evelyn to this day calls me Valory instead of Valery.

One more little incident occurred on that tour, when my traveling document came under the inspection of a border patrol officer at Orly international airport in Paris. He was just about to stamp it, when I heard Jim Green's unsteady voice booming from above and slightly behind me.

"Be cool Valery."

In his mind Jim was contributing to my successful passing through the border, but he achieved exactly the opposite result. The officer took a long scrutinizing look at him, then at me and put the stamp away.

"You have to wait," he said and moved my substitute for a passport aside.

"I can't wait for too long, I will miss the plane. Besides my paper had been checked already. Everything is in order."

"Don't worry, my superior will be here soon. Wait over there." He pointed at a bench in the corner.

Jim in the meantime hurried away to catch up with the rest of the band. I was staring at a clock on the wall, watching minutes go by.

Boarding time! Minutes kept on marching on – still no superior. He did show up finally, when our plane was supposed to be already in the air, gave the OK for my crossing the border and walked with me to the gate.

When I entered the tunnel leading to the plane, I saw Art at the end of it sitting on a chair in front of the wide open door of the plane, disregarding the flight attendants fussing around him. From the expression on his face they should have realized already that this plane was not going anywhere until "The Jazz Messengers" was complete.

When he saw me, he got up, not saying anything, waited for me to pass through and matter of factly followed me onto the plane, thus allowing the plane attendants to lock the door and proceed with the flight.

\*\*\*\*\*\*\*\*\*\*\*\*\*\*\*\*\*\*\*\*\*\*\*\*\*\*

The rest of the tour breezed by without any problem. It always amazed me how whatever events in life moved from the future to the present and then into the past. Where did the time go? Like nothing had happened at all five weeks later, it would be eight and even ten week tours, we were in the Amsterdam airport ready to go back to New York.

Bobbie and I were standing by the luggage check in counter and talking about the past tour, about an oncoming engagement at Washington's "Blues Alley," when we heard: "Give me my money," pronounced in a very firm, all too familiar hoarse voice. We both froze, eyes staring at each other.

"Give me my money," the voice repeated, this time a little louder,

making us slowly turn in the direction it came from. There they were –
Art, raising his head to meet the stare of much younger and taller Wim
Wigt, the tour promoter from Holland.

"Art, please not so loud, there are people around us. I had told you,
that the last check didn't clear. I will bring the money to New York next
week. I…"

"Give me my money," Art repeated louder still with the same firm
resolution in his voice.

"Art, please speak quiet. People looking. I don't have any money. You
have to trust me; I will bring it next week, when the last check goes
through." Wim's rosy cheecks were shaking and his eyes blinking at every
two or three words.

The pressure in the atmosphere around them was quickly rising,
sparks were flying in all directions, ready to ignite an all-out battle.

"Give me my money"– " Please speak quiet. You have to trust me,"
the call and response kept on going like that for a little while longer until
Art's voice reached its loudest decibel, Wim's cheeks turned red and his
eyes were blinking steadily.

That is when the miracle happened. At Art's last "give me my money,"
Wim's plump hand reached into the breast pocket of his jacket and
produced a neatly folded rather thick envelope. He handed it to Art
without any commentaries.

The pressure started to drop right away and by the time Art had put
the envelope into his pocket, in a second at the most, he and Wim looked
perfectly natural, like two business friends, discussing a very promising
business preposition. Bobbie and I turned back to our initial positions
and stared at each other once again.

"Learning?" we inquired in perfect unison. A trumpet-player and an
alto-player cannot be a part of the horn section in "The Jazz Messengers"
for nothing.

\*\*\*\*\*\*\*\*\*\*\*\*\*\*\*\*\*\*\*\*\*\*\*\*\*

"Your mother called. I told her that you are on tour," Tatiana informed me after the first hugs and kisses on American soil. "She didn't really believe me you know. I hope she didn't hear that stupid KGB rumor."

"She wouldn't take it seriously. She knows better than that," I calmed her down.

The telephone rang almost as soon as I put my bags down.

"Valery is that you?"

"Ma!"

Dead silence and then uncontrollable sobbing followed.

"I had never believed that stupid rumor. Synok, synok."

"Ma!"

"Synok, synok." She kept repeating and slowly took control of herself. "What do all these postcards mean? Rio de Janeiro, Paris, Berlin, Amsterdam, how could you be in so many places at once?"

"I have joined Art Blakey and the Jazz Messengers. We were in Brazil for three weeks then flew to New York, changed bags and later the same day flew to Europe for a five-week tour. Just came back. We are going to Washington next week."

"Who is Art Blakey?"

"Remember the pictures on the wall?"

"Yes"

"On one of them was a picture of Art Blakey."

"Ah, that's what it is. Now I understand everything," my mother said very slowly. "Which one is Art Blakey? That handsome one with trumpet?"

"No Ma, that is Miles Davis. Another one with a trumpet is Clifford Brown. Art Blakey was with drumsticks."

"God bless him. Write from Washington."

\*\*\*\*\*\*\*\*\*\*\*\*\*\*\*\*\*\*\*\*\*\*\*\*\*

Washington, Washington, the worst of what could happen to a trumpet-player, the ugliest nightmare of all, had happened to me in Washington: a – fever blister.

And when! At the worst possible time: it was still my first months with Art Blakey and the Jazz Messengers. O yes! Everybody wanted to hear and see The Messengers. The band set a new precedent: a Russian holding the trumpet chair. The news sent shock waves all over the music world.

Many a critic, promoter, an agent and what not told the leader of the most sought after Jazz group: "What are you doing Art, who needs a Russian in the Messengers? Couldn't you find somebody else?"

"Don't tell me who should play trumpet in my band, I decide who can play my music and I don't care where the guy was born. Valery Ponomarev was a Jazz Messenger long before he joined the Messengers." That was the answer.

Nothing could change Art Blakey's decision. "When you know you are right, don't be afraid to say it," was another phrase we all heard him say very often. I still hear Art Blakey's hoarse voice in my ears.

We were all set for our premier appearance in the capital of the United States at "Blues Alley" the most prestigious jazz venue of the time in Washington DC.

What a nightmare: my lower lip was swollen, sound was not coming out, almost no sound to be exact. "It's like playing saxophone on a broken reed," I was trying to explain to Bobby (Watson my newly-found brother in the Messengers, a great young talent.)

Also since he played alto saxophone not trumpet, I knew he would understand what a mess I found myself in.

Even at close scrutiny one can't tell the difference in appearance. To the audience a musician on the bandstand would look just the same, broken reed or blister; a fan would never notice the difference. But one for sure can hear when a musician cannot command his instrument. Also, no saxophone player would ever in his wildest dreams think of playing on a cracked reed.

I had heard of things like that before and even seen trumpet players living through this infamous brass-player's horror, but it had never happened to me. I thought I was exempted from this ugly experience. I was always careful anyway.

Brazil came to my mind. What a trip that was: blue ocean, blazing sun in February, miles of beaches, soccer fields allover the place, people, Brazilian music, the "mister melody" girl…

Now, only two months later, I was in Washington, alone in my hotel room, in total panic, knowing for sure Art would say: "Yes, with a lip like that you can't play, we'll call somebody else."

God knows most trumpet-players in the world would give their right arm for a gig like this. No question, my days with the Messengers must be over.

Upset and dispirited I went to Walter Davis, he had seen all editions of the Jazz Messengers and not only played with almost all of them, but as a musical director had written a lot of the most inspired music for different editions of the band.

What a guy he was – always a friend, always wishing you to succeed, always ready to help. But as friendly and kind our musical director always had been, I knew he would not be able to help me. A blister is a blister, no one can argue with it.

The whole morning I kept rehearsing in my mind how I would go to Art and beg him: "Art, please don't feature me this evening, I can hardly blow." That phrase became a fixture in my head and kept repeating and ringing in my ears.

I just had to talk to somebody before I went to Blakey to hear his verdict, and our piano-player-musical director was the best.

"Whatever you do, don't tell Art about it," instructed Walter Davis, who had seen Art Blakey – one of the greatest bandleaders of all time – dealing with the band members for many years.

"What?"

"Don't tell him about it" Walter repeated. I stared at him. "How could you not tell Art about it?"

"Trust me," my confidant assured me. "I'll tell you what happened when Lee Morgan, and many other trumpet-players, came to him with the same very problem.

It would never occur to me that any of my predecessors in the Messengers, all of them my heroes, could have been in the same predicament. In total amazement, with my eyes and ears open, I listened to Walter.

"Once Lee Morgan fell sick," he began "High fever, his body temperature must have been up to 105. He was all upset, in bed the whole day, lips swollen, taking pills and what not. He asked me to call Art. Half an hour later we all went to Lee's room. He looked awful: face swollen, towel on the forehead, chops in blisters.

"With a weak, trembling voice, the trumpeter, legendary for his powerful sound among other amazing attributes, whispered: 'Art, look at me, I am so sick, I feel so terrible, I can't play tonight, I'll die if I only try to get out of bed.'

"Bu [Art Blakey's nickname that is short for Buhaina, his adopted Muslim name] was looking at the fallen giant with compassion, and obviously feeling bad for Lee. Art was always so proud of the trumpeters who came through the band and this young genius was no exception, already legend at the age of 20. It must have hurt him to see Lee Morgan like that. 'No, you don't look good at all,' Art admitted. 'The concert starts at eight.'

"Having said that Art Blakey turned around and left the room. He saw the sick man next on the bandstand several hours later. A packed house, as always, the crowd was roaring in anticipation. Bu counted the fastest, most intricate tune in the book. The following number you know: 'We were always blessed with the world's greatest trumpet-players'... etc."

Walter's imitation of Art's presentation of the featured artist is almost perfect. I know that presentation by heart since I hear it almost every concert now. Years later, it was the very same introduction, only the list of preceding trumpeters was longer.

"Anyway," continued Walter, "right after that mercurial opener, Buhaina brings Lee to the front for a feature. Lee Morgan couldn't do anything about it: he couldn't leave the stage and go back to the states; we were in Paris at the time. The only thing he could do was to play any way he was able to. And play he did. I mean to say," Walter continued "... there was no bristling attack or fast runs of scales or powerful notes in high register, not Lee's usual total brilliant command of the instrument anyway, but overall it was beautiful. The audience burst out in appreciation and it was long before thunderous applause died out. 'Music is not only high notes and loud sound, Valery'. Our musical director's imitation of Art Blakey was near perfect again.

"Needless to say, the rest of the concert and the rest of the whole tour worked out with no problem at all. One-Two-Three, just like that" finished Walter.

Yeah, that was a long time ago, so it seemed to me, and that was Lee Morgan, one of my heroes and Trumpet Kings. What do I, Valery Ponomarev, do now, today?

Of course I went to a doctor, knowing full well that he wouldn't be able to help me. The doc gave me medicine, a bright white spread. Yeah, sure, maybe it would reduce the swelling by the end of the week, maybe even in two or three days, provided of course that I did not play a single sound, but what do I do this evening, the opening night?

I already knew from the experience of just completed European and Brazilian tours, there would be a lot of people: Art's numerous friends, critics, media and fans, fans, fans. Everybody wanted to hear and see the new Messengers and me, Valery Ponomarev, from Moscow, Russia on trumpet.

What a mess, I couldn't even play a scale straight! Also, I was wearing the medicine, on my lower lip, but it didn't make any difference. Well, I would have to live through it. What else could I do?

I had to get away from my thoughts, get away, walk around and leave the room. That's exactly what I did: just left, locked the door and walked towards the exit. As I walked, a car approached, also leaving the premises. Of all people it was Art Blakey driving his shining new Cadillac with a new occupant in the passenger seat – the beautiful Joy.

I went up to the driver's window to say hello, remembering Walter's advice. "Hi Art," I said, trying to sound as relaxed as I could. "Hey Val," was the cheerful answer. "What's on your lip?" Blood rushed away from my face. "Art, please don't feature me tonight, I can hardly blow," I heard myself saying the phrase with a very weak voice. Here it comes.

"You should watch what you eat, it all comes from your stomach. You need to wash it well now and take some vitamins. You will be all right."

He knew I would rather die than play that night, or be driven over by that gorgeous Cadillac of his with Joy in it.

"See you at the club." That's all he said and drove off, probably to Georgetown for dinner.

\*\*\*\*\*\*\*\*\*\*\*\*\*\*\*\*\*\*\*\*\*\*\*\*\*\*

Here it is "Blues Alley" on premier night. The club is packed to the doors; there is not even standing room anywhere. I am on the bandstand in line with other members of the horn section still hoping for a miracle. The hum of the crowd subsides; lights in the house are off; only the stage is brightly lit. Art is playing an intro to the opening tune.

He would never tell us in advance, what we were going to play. There was never a preprogrammed repertoire or any discussion of what the opener, at least, would be. He would just play for 8 or 16 bars and from his drumming we would know what was coming. O my God that's "Uranus".

We hit.

A few bars later I couldn't even deal with the melody; all hopes were out the window. I could hide a little behind the saxophones during the head, but when my turn came to play solo I was totally exposed with no sound, range, staccato or inspiration. I just closed my eyes, as I always do anyway when playing, but this time also so as not to see all these people staring at us.

I knew there were writers from Washington newspapers, officials from the Russian department of Voice of America and fans, fans, fans… I would rather drop through the stage and disappear, but I had to finish the tune and stay there until the bitter end.

If I could only tell them: "it's not the way I play, don't judge me by this performance, I am sick, my lip is swollen, it's like playing a violin without strings, I am drowning."

Everybody else played great, with so much fire, inspiration, inventiveness, and command of his instrument.

The audience loved it. Thunderous applause broke out with the last crash of the cymbal marking the end of "Uranus". It was only me who was messing up.

Why did it have to happen to me, to spoil a performance of the band of my dreams? Art Blakey and the Jazz Messengers.

"We were always blessed with the world's greatest trumpet-players: Clifford Brown, Kenny Dorham, Donald Byrd, Lee Morgan, Freddie Hubbard," Art Blakey's voice startled me.

"…And now we would like to present to you…"

Who was he going to present to this audience? What was he talking about? I knew by heart this whole introduction. It was almost part of the show; it led to my feature, no doubt. He was announcing me like that since I joined the band, but who was going to play tonight?

Art always looked like he was having a great time when he was on the bandstand. That sacred space called the "Stage" belonged to him. He knew how to conduct himself, how to interact with the audience, how to handle it. And it all looked so natural.

"…a man with such a beautiful sound, so spiritual…from the far away city of Moscow, Russia – Valery Ponomarev."

There was nowhere to run; I was already there in the spotlight. The surface beneath my feet didn't break out and swallow me, no atomic bomb detonated. None of that happened. I was standing there with my horn facing the audience. From Russia, from Russia I heard intense whispers from different directions and then complete silence.

The first couple of notes into "Autumn in New York" and there was already a struggle. I was in a daze almost like watching myself from the side trying to hold on to the sound of the beautiful melody as long as I could: notes slipping from under my fingers, the tone getting thinner and thinner and then nothing, darkness. I was not quite consciously there any more.

I must have been through the melody and solo and then half a chorus of bass solo and then the melody out, because this was already a cadenza. I played the last note. Loud noise broke out. What a shame, what a disgrace! I ran off the stage through the rows of people up the stairs into the dressing room and fell into the chair with my head buried in my hands. I have never cried that bitterly, not even when I was a little kid.

Somebody knocked on the door and asked: "Can I come in?" That was the voice of the girl I had met at a Jazz-Mobil outdoor concert a couple of days before. I tried to control my voice as much as I could and said, "Please wait for me outside, I'll be there in a minute." Then I heard her light steps going down the stairs.

"Come on Val," my brother Bobby, with his saxophone hanging round his neck, was saying as he walked in to the room. "You played beautiful; they are still clapping their asses off."

Bobby and I were fighting a lot over a lot of stupid things, just like siblings very often do, as long as I was in the "Messengers." But when it was for real we would always support each other.

"Music is not only high notes and loud sound." His imitation of our leader was not bad either.

There was still loud, insistent applause. How did Art do it? Nobody could fool me, I knew I didn't play a note straight. It had to do with Art. He was the magician presenting the Jazz Messengers.

Needless to say the rest of the program was one-two-three. After going through "Uranus", then a feature, and at the very beginning of the concert, nothing was as difficult as I expected it to be.

Yes, that was it. Art would lead you through the impossible and then your mind was ready to deal with anything.

His mission was not to hire a promising musician and then two months later fire him because the novice thought he was in trouble. No, he would make a Jazz Messenger out of every one of us. That was my turn.

*Geneological Messengers tree.*

# Chapter 8

# Heir to the Trumpet Throne.

In Europe it was mostly one-nighters with some exceptions here and there. In Japan it was half and half, in the States it was a week to two weeks runs in different cities with the exception of an occasional festival or college. Since the United Kingdom is not on the European continent I would put playing in London in the same category as American tours. Besides, the language is almost the same.

Two weeks in London! At Ronnie Scott's! What could be better? – Here you have a different set of Sisyphus labors, namely: get up, go to any joint nearby for breakfast, come back to the hotel, practice, occasionally fight off the offensive of the front desk clerk, who had received a message that I was making noise, hang in the city, come back to the hotel, take a shower, dress up (the whole band was wearing overalls for a uniform), walk to the club, warm up.

Get set. Ready? Go. Play. Every night!

Monday was different. A day off is always a boring day on the tour, but not if you are in London.

I had heard many times that it always rains in London. Even locals confirm this rumor. But it's not true in my experience. With very few exceptions, to this day, every time I go to London the weather is beautiful.

My first Monday in the Capital of the United Kingdom, Carlene

Eros, bar tender from the club – "Ronnie Scott's own" – and I hung out well into Tuesday morning. It was already breakfast time when I got locked in the shower room on the first floor at her place.

She didn't have a chance to tell me to take keys to the self-locking door with me. One way or another she had to open the window of the shower room from outside the building and rescue me.

Boy! It was quite an expedition to make it back to her room with only a towel in my hands – climb out of the window into the back yard and run around the building back to the safety of her little living space. Nobody saw us, I don't think.

I put my clothes on and went outside in search of something to eat when it was her turn to take a shower. Still shaken from the experience she was squeezing the damn keys in her lovely little hand.

Sounds of clinking plates and people talking across the street attracted my attention. It was one of those hostels providing tourists with bed and continental breakfast. A big space on the ground floor was filled with people of all ages sitting around tables, busy with coffee, served in beautiful silver pots on just as beautiful silver trays, loaded with porcelain cups, bread rolls, butter and jam cubicles.

Many had cameras, some were checking the maps of the city – tourists, all excited, the vacation is on, Big Ben, Waterloo Bridge, Hyde Park, the British Museum, Piccadilly Circus, British Parliament sessions, Buckingham Palace, shopping on Oxford Street, all of it and any of it was rightfully theirs.

"What would you like, tea or coffee?" all of a sudden I heard a question, put to me by a young lady, obviously a help at the hostel, who appeared out of nowhere in front of me. "Coffee," I said. She turned around and ran away only to reappear a minute later with a silver tray and a coffee pot, porcelain cups, bread rolls, butter and jam – a complete set.

She pushed it all in my hands and ran away again. So I turned around and walked out of the same door I had just walked in, crossed the street and made it all the way to Carlene's room not spilling or dropping anything off the tray. There she was, as fresh and beautiful as a girl could be at twenty, after a morning shower, drying her rich hair.

"What is this? Where did you get all this?" Carlene was stunned and smiling that charming smile of hers, like a child, ready for a Christmas present at any time. That was May. "I love this silver set. It's beautiful."

She laughed uncontrollably after I told her how I got it. "From the hostel across the street? Oh my God! I am not taking it back, no way." "Me neither," I assured her. So we decided that the set would remain in her room, since nobody was taking it back to the place of its origin.

Having resolved that problem we set off for Ronnie Scott's, where Carlene waited for me for two-and-a-half hours while I was practicing. She interrupted me only a couple of times, asking questions about my breathing.

"I am studying to be a singer, you know. To learn your breathing technique will be very beneficial for me." Then we ate somewhere and went to Hyde Park again.

The weather was just as gorgeous as the day before. She cried bitterly when I told her that I was married. "Why is it I am always so unlucky?" she repeated a couple of times through her sobbing. "The man I had met right before you is too much older than I. He is just about your height and his hair is all grey."

We kept on hanging anyway. In the evening we only had to go to our respective places for a minute.

Out of several overalls I had, Carlene loved my light blue ones the most. So before going to the club that evening, I wrapped them up and handed the package to her over the bar right before beginning the first set. Ronnie Scott, a handsome gentleman and a brilliant tenor saxophonist, was already announcing the band.

To complete the announcement, he told the audience that two suspicious looking characters, dressed in grey trench overcoats, were waiting for me outside. Just like he did every evening of the previous week. The first time I heard it, I knew he was teasing me with a straight face, trying to make it sound like two KGB undercover agents were on a mission to capture me, sedate me, tie me up and transport me back to the Soviet Union. Ronnie was always getting a kick out of it, so I went along with the joke, pretending that I took it seriously.

That week I was playing for my feature "I Remember Clifford" for the first time. I ended up being featured on it for the next three-and-a-half years every night, with the exception of playing "Autumn in New York," "My One and Only Love," and "Nature Boy" a few times each.

What a tune! I could never get tired of playing it, even if Art featured me on it for the next 100 years. The audience really outdid itself that night. I had already taken several bows to the rows of people in the darkness of the club surrounding the brightly lit stage and turned around to bow at Art. But a storm of applause, screaming and yelling was still coming in torrential waves from the darkness around me and Art was still standing behind his drums, encouraging people to clap even more.

Every break of that evening, as any evening of both weeks, the bar and the rest of the club were packed to capacity. Only at the end of the working day could I make my way to the bar, when it was time to collect Carlene. Art was standing there too, waiting for somebody or a drink to be served maybe.

"I will be ready in a minute," she said and leaned over the bar to kiss me on the cheek. "I'll change quickly and we can go," she added and went behind the door of a little space at the end of the bar. Art looked at me in a strange way. I was standing with my back to the bar and thinking that, "You need to learn the lyrics to the song you playing," might be coming, but he didn't say anything.

He just kept on looking at me, eyes maybe a half an inch higher than the level of my eyes, hair all grey. Then I felt a small hand, patting me from behind on the right cheek softly, followed by: "Val, let me through". I stepped aside and turned around.

Carlene picked up the flat board of the bar and came out of the captivity of her working enclosure into the vastness of the space of the rest of the club. There she was, standing in front of us, dressed in the light blue overalls. They were just a little tight around the thighs, but looked so good on her, highlighting her bewitching smile more than anything else.

"Val's overalls look really good on you," Art said with the same look in his eyes. I thought his eyes were sad and helpless.

"Do you need me for anything?" I asked him, not even being sure why I said that. "No, no. You guys go hang," he answered and asked another bartender to serve him a double shot of Hennessey.

The rest of the week Carlene and I were inseparable, never discussing anything, just having as good time as we could. After the last day of the engagement in London, instead of saying goodbye, I just went to my hotel to get ready for one-nighters on the European continent. We were to come back to London a couple of weeks later to play at a festival.

After serving Sisyphus' labors for two weeks I was back in London in the same hotel and in the same room. I just dropped my bags and ran along very well known streets to the two-storied house were Carlene lived. Here I was, running up the three steps leading to the open entrance, along the corridor to the door at the end of it.

Knock-knock-knock, bum-bum-bum . . . Complete silence greeted me in response.

"Carlene," I called and received the same answer. I stood there in the scarcely lit corridor, gathering determination to turn around and walk back on the street.

"Carlene," I heard my own voice breaking the dead silence.

"She doesn't live here anymore," I heard a voice behind me and turned around. It was an old lady standing in front of an open door of her living quarters on the other side of the shower room. "She moved out a week ago or so."

"Where did she go?"

"I don't know. She didn't say anything."

"She didn't leave her new address, a note maybe?"

"No, nothing. She just left."

"Left."

Carlene-Carlene, if you only knew how much I wanted to see you that moment – almost as much as to play with Art Blakey!

At the club nobody knew where she went either. I haven't heard from her since. Years later, when I was already divorced and had just broken up with my first post-marriage love, I called Carlene's hometown – Vancouver, Canada – information and got three phone numbers for the name of Eros, one of them Carlene. She could've been an out of shape lady with a whole bunch of children by then, but I wanted to talk to her anyway.

"Can I talk to Carlene Eros?"

"This is she," a voice in the receiver answered, which could have been Carlene's.

"This is Valery, Valery Ponomarev."

"Who?"

"Valery Ponomarev, trumpet player with Art Blakey and the Jazz Messengers. May '77 in London, remember?"

"I have never been to London. You must've got a wrong number."

I dialed the other numbers, achieving just as much, which brought up a phrase in my mind I've heard or read somewhere. It sounded something like: "Whatever happened in the past should remain in the past." I guess it should.

*************************

In full accordance with the American tour variation we were to make our way to the West Coast to play at the Concerts by the Sea (in the "Parisian Room") in LA for two weeks, at San Francisco's "Keystone Corner" for two weeks, after playing at Joe Segal's "Jazz Showcase" in Chicago for a week.

"Did you hear that Walter is not going with us to the West Coast?"

"What?"

"There is a strong possibility that Horace Silver will be playing with us in LA," Bobby shared the latest news with me in LaGuardia airport, where we were waiting for the rest of the band to arrive. Bobby didn't look like he quite believed his own words.

"No Walter – Horace Silver instead? Are you serious?"

"Ye, ye, its very possible. I heard it from Jim."

"Oh my God! Just like twenty-five years ago, when they were co-leaders. That's a historical reunion! That would be something!" Bobby and I kept on talking while everybody, except Art, gathered around us.

We talked some more – still no Art.

The 11am flight to Chicago was fast approaching, but Mr. Blakey was still nowhere in sight. Somebody called Jack Wittemor's office and learned that we would fly now on the 6pm flight instead. Six hours to kill.

Well, LaGuardia airport was only ten to fifteen minutes by car from Astoria, L.I. where I lived. That's where I headed. Everybody else also found something to do.

My future ex was at work, so I didn't bother leaving any note, I just returned to the airport in time to check in for the 6 o'clock flight. This time the Messengers were complete and flew to their destination with no problem.

Only in the hotel, when I turned on the news, did I learn that the plane we had missed in the morning crashed, no survivors. Wow! I called Astoria right away.

"Ah, what?"

"I am in Chicago."

"I know you are in Chicago. That's where you flew this morning."

"Yeah, yeah, you are right." There was no point in going into any explanations; obviously she didn't hear anything.

Come to think of it, I didn't need to worry at all. Firstly she still didn't speak any English and secondly to watch the latest news would've been the last thing on her mind. Why did I even bother?

\*\*\*\*\*\*\*\*\*\*\*\*\*\*\*\*\*\*\*\*\*\*\*\*\*\*

Very often, nowhere nearly as often as "How did you escape from… etc.," jazz fans around the world ask: "Where is the better audience, in Europe, in America or in Japan?"

Sometimes the question is even more detailed, going down to the specific country and a city or even a village, and always you could see that light of hope in the questioner's eyes, which indicated hope, that you might say: "Here."

Wherever you might be, in an ancient Italian town or surrounded by a cluster of skyscrapers. As much as it's tempting to make this particular fan happy and tell him exactly what he wants to hear you cannot do that.

I'd say that in Europe the audience is coming to a jazz concert as an artistic event, bringing a centuries-old tradition of going to a theater, ballet or a museum. In Japan, I'd say, a feeling of being a dear guest prevails. Playing for an American audience is somewhat like delivering a heart felt speech to a bunch of excited experts, but that's only nuances.

In general, audiences all over the world are the same – hospitable, generous, appreciative, loving. Playing in your hometown is different. That's what I realized much later as an artist's personal feeling, but in general it's still the same audience, maybe with a slight European nuance to it. As everywhere else, I loved the fans in Chicago. What's next? The West Coast.

That was my first trip across the North American continent. After a concert at one of the Mid-Western colleges, we drove further west. The plan was, after crossing the state of Utah to turn southwest, towards LA. We did have two big station wagons, but they still didn't provide enough space for all of us.

Bobby was with his newly wedded wife Pamela. Fuzzy joined the Messengers just for this trip to the West Coast, Jim was with Miri, who he met at the Montmartre in Copenhagen on the previous tour.

All of us plus, of course, bass, drums, the rest of the instruments and our luggage – it was tight. Nobody really cared, a little longer and we would reach the "Promised Land" – two weeks in LA, two weeks in Cisco: hang on the beach, play every night. On the way we were to pass Las Vegas.

"You will know you are near Las Vegas, when we get there. Gambling machines are everywhere: in gas stations, in toilets. Sit on the John and play the machine. They make sure that you gamble." Art was holding court from the driver's seat.

I heard mockery in his voice, pitying those poor people who got caught in endless attempts to become rich overnight, wasting their time and money instead. If he added something like: "They would've been much better off spending their last money on our records," I would totally agree with him.

We had been driving for a while already, which meant that a serious stop at a good restaurant was in order sooner rather than later. Yeah, that was time to eat, even Art said that he was ready for food.

We were kind of lost anyway, not being sure where to pick up the southwest route, so the decision was made to get off the main road. Very soon we saw a sign: "Green River."

Behind it was a one storied wooden structure with the word "Restaurant" above the door, inviting travelers in a strange land in.

Without any discussion both drivers turned right into the little parking space of the refuge. Art said that he would relax in the car and asked Fuzzy to bring him a plate of food from the restaurant.

"There is the river," Jim pointed towards the trees, inviting us to look. "I was born in this area. That's how I got my name." Indeed between the trees and below I saw a glistening passage of water.

"Jim, you are in your native land, your home." He was visibly excited.

Once inside, he joined some people in the far end of the restaurant and very animatedly entertained them with some stories, maybe of his childhood. Fuzzy, Bobby , Pam, Schnitter and I made ourselves comfortable at a table in one of the two rooms of the restaurant and the rest of our traveling expedition occupied a table next to us.

There were some people in the well taken care of room, furnished with good quality wooden tables and matching chairs. The other room was empty; it wasn't as clean, poorly lit and equipped with cheap furniture. The sight and smell of well-prepared food on the other tables tickled our taste buds to the highest level of anticipation. Boy, were we ready for a good meal!

I knew exactly what I wanted – steak (medium rare), mashed potato with garlic sauce and vegetables.

"I want ..." I started, when the waitress, a rather healthy-looking young woman, approached our table.

"I can't take your order until they leave this room," the waitress said somewhat apologetically, and pointed at Bobby and Pam.

"What?"

"This room is for white people only."

"Ah?"

"They have to go to the next room, if they want to eat in this restaurant," she said with the same apologetic overtones in her voice and pointed in the direction of the other room, above the door. This time I noticed a wooden board with letters in faded paint: "For colored people."

"What? Are you serious? We can't sit at the same table?"

"I am sorry, this is the restaurant's policy."

Then Fuzzy started saying something nervously and got up. The quiet buzz of the room instantly turned into a pandemonium of angry voices. I could only make out "I am sorry, this is the restaurant's policy."

I was still sitting there dumbfounded. Harriet Beecher Stow and Uncle Tom in his cabin, that was a long time ago, in the sixth grade and that was about the times a century before then. Jessie Owens had beaten Nazis already in the 1936 Olympics.

Now we were in the fourth quarter of the twentieth century in the most developed country in the world. Duke Ellington, Luis Armstrong were the dearest guests all over the world, Art Bla . . . oh my God!

"Valery, be cool," Jim boomed somewhere above me and I felt a slight poke in the ribs. "We don't want to eat here. Let's go."

That brought me out of the stupor; I got up and followed everybody to the porch outside. Aside from us there was a whole bunch of young people there.

"We support you." "We left too." "Hell with their food." "We would've never come to eat here, had we known what kind of place this is." "We are students at UCLA on a tour." "We will write a complaint to the state department." "They should close this joint." Our new friends were talking all at once. "What a shame!"

It all really happened, Fuzzy, Bobby , Schnitter, everybody and I were there, but it still, many years later, seems an unreal crazy nightmare.

We all hugged like members of one family before saying good-bye, returned to our cars and drove off.

Art was not the only one to drive – everybody had that privilege. We all liked driving very much. I think it's most natural for a musician to be in a state of motion, particularly for a musician who deals with rhythm all the time. I was at the wheel when we crossed the Utah-Arizona border and then, soon after, Arizona-Nevada.

A few miles later I alerted Art that the needle in the gas indicator was getting too close to the empty mark.

"Get off at the next gas station Valery, let's fill up."

When we got to the gas station, everybody got out of the cars to stretch their legs and buy something at the station. I was standing next to Art when he was getting ready to pay for the gas, and watching a guy to my left putting quarter after quarter in a slot on the face of a strange apparatus and pushing some buttons on it. That apparatus was in many bright colors, something was rotating in the middle. It looked very similar to a pinball machine, only vertical.

"What is he doing?" I asked Art and pointed at the strange guy.

"You've never seen a gambling machine before?" Art sounded a little surprised, but not disappointed.

"No. This is the gambling machine? How does it work?"

"Oh! It's very simple: you put a quarter in the slot, choose a picture on the panel and push this lever. Now, look here. You see these three pictures over here? They will rotate real fast and then stop. If the picture you've chosen shows in all three windows, you win."

"What do I win?"

"Money."

"How much?

"I don't know. It could be a lot or very little or nothing at all."

"Where do I go to collect the money?"

"You don't go anywhere, the machine gives it to you."

"The machine gives it to me?"

"Oh, Valery, just try it, you will figure it out right away."

Art sounded a little annoyed and amused at my not having confidence in American technology. I dug a quarter out of my pocket and put it in the machine, pushed the button next to the picture of a running deer and depressed the lever. The apparatus came into motion.

Something inside of it was turning faster and faster, building compression in its belly higher and higher and higher still until the machine couldn't take the pressure any more and with a loud noise burst open, spilling it's intestines into a compartment below. The unstoppable downpour of metal in the shape of small disks kept crashing down into the space below, some of them even fell out of the compartment.

"What happened? I broke the machine?" I got terrified. Now I would have to face the consequences

"You won, it's all yours."

I looked closely. Those were quarters.

"That many?"

"Yes, yes, they are all yours."

Well, if Art Blakey said they were mine, then they were mine. It took many handfuls to transfer all of those metal discs, four of which put together spelled out one American dollar, into my pockets. Then I took one of them and stretched my hand towards the slot. Art's strong hand grabbed me at the wrist.

"That's exactly how they become addicted," he laughed and pulled me outside, where everybody was already sitting in the cars and waiting for us. We got on the highway and drove pass the celebrated city like it was an island infested with sirens and, of course, Art was Ulysses.

"I saved Valery from utter and complete ruin. If I didn't push him away from that machine, he would've become a gambling addict. We would've lost our trumpet-payer."

Art was telling and retelling that story of my hitting the jackpot and him "saving" me from a miserable downfall at a gas station in the outskirts of Las Vegas. He would embellish and dramatize it each time at any opportunity during the following years, pretending he was completely serious. Boy! He was getting a real kick out of it.

The last leg of the trip Jim was driving the lead car and I was following. As he originally put it: "We drive caravan style." On the road the Messengers almost always stayed together, that was a rule.

This time I didn't need to worry about directions, I didn't know them anyway. My concern was only to keep a safe distance and not to loose Jim from sight.

It turned out that Jim didn't worry about directions either. We ended up driving past our exit for a whole hour before Art woke up and told me to signal Jim to stop. Then we got off the road, made a U-turn and drove for another hour in the opposite direction.

The first time in Los Angeles, we played at "Concerts by the Sea," a beautiful club right by the beach. Our hotel was also on the beach.

When we finally arrived, I quickly unpacked my bags and ran to the Pacific Ocean. I couldn't stay there for too long, because the rehearsal with the new piano player was to start in an hour. I just dived in the water, made a couple of strokes and returned to the beach.

"Hey Valery, you realize where you are?" That was my other self again.

"Yeah, really."

"Midway, Japan, Sakhalin, Kuril Islands, Kamchatka are all somewhere out there. Isn't it something?"

"Truly."

"You gotta run back to your room, warm up and go to the rehearsal."

"Yes sir."

No, Horace Silver wouldn't be playing with the Messengers that week – his schedule didn't allow. Rumor had it that he really wanted to.

Instead there was a delicate looking, soft-spoken, young man with kind features by the name of George Cables. I loved his playing. He played with us in San Francisco too.

There, after the first week at Todd Barkan's "Keystone Corner", Dennis, myself and a couple of female jazz fans were desperately looking for anything to drink. The search around Chinatown, where our hotel was located, ended in complete failure. So we decided to try our luck back at the Vallejo Street, where, together with a police station on the corner, the club peacefully coexisted.

At after 3am our chances were very close to zero, but what else could we try. Coming closer, I thought I heard music. There was a little window on the upper part of the entrance door, so I stretched upward on my toes and looked inside.

There he was on the stage, playing piano. Dennis and I tiptoed into the club, leaving the rest of our company outside. The club was completely empty. George was just playing, not practicing or figuring out some tune, no, he was literally one on one with music. He sounded so beautiful! We stood there motionless until George switched to experimenting with some chords.

Filling up two large pitchers with beer was no problem – carrying them to the hotel was kind of pain, but worth it.

\*\*\*\*\*\*\*\*\*\*\*\*\*\*\*\*\*\*\*\*\*\*\*\*\*\*

European tours, "Ronnie Scott's", "Concerts by the Sea", "The Lighthouse" or "Parisian Room" in LA, "Keystone Corner" in San Francisco, "Michel's, "The Village Vanguard" or "Village Gate" in New York, "Blues Alley" in Washington, "Bijou" in Philadelphia, the "Brass Rail" in Boston.

Tours of Japan were following each other with regular intervals, just like spring, summer, autumn, winter, spring and so on, until time ceased to exist or stood still somehow.

We were coming back to the same place again, whether in Europe or in the States, half a year or a couple of months or a couple of days later and the time in between was just gone, like it was never there.

You stand on the same stage, you deal with the same club owner – familiar faces in the audience – or it would be the same town or museum or the same tennis court, and you had a feeling that you had never left.

Three days after the band came back from the eight-week European tour Art and I were in the car – it must have been that famous ride to Syracuse. I asked him: "Art, how do you see that? This past tour seemed endless at first and then we were sitting on the plane, seemingly the same plane, which took us to Europe, only we were flying back to New York and the time in between just disappeared, like it was never there. Even that moment has already disappeared; we are in America now, driving."

"You know what Valery? The whole thing will be like that." He kept on looking through the windshield, not really watching the road, but rather thinking about something.

"What do you mean? I didn't quite understand you."

"Life. The whole thing will be like that."

I knew right then that if I lived to his age, it would still be one and the same moment, like it had been being stretched or was standing motionless up until then.

\*\*\*\*\*\*\*\*\*\*\*\*\*\*\*\*\*\*\*\*\*\*\*\*\*\*

On the first night at the "Concerts by the Sea" Freddie Hubbard – he lives in LA – came to hang at the club. That was the first time that I had seen him since "Boomer's". He remembered me.

"Now I can see you studied a lot of Clifford. You play your ass off."

"I had studied you too."

"No, no, no. Clifford Brown is your man."

That was true, but I still wanted to boast to him, that I had transcribed very many of his solos too. Then he asked me about my diet, just to continue the conversation, but I didn't know very much about diets then, I ate anything in sight. What you would call now a "see food diet" – eat whatever you see.

On the second day Dizzy Gillespie came, he happened to be in the area. Art introduced me to his old friend in Washington, when we went to "Blues Alley" for the first time. The crowned king of be-bop couldn't stay then, because he had a concert of his own the same night, also in Washington. Boy, wasn't I glad that he didn't hear me then.

In LA, Dizzy got on the stage at the end of our first set, so the audience could see him, and clowned around a little bit.

"Your new trumpet player can play. Where do you get guys like that?" Mr. Gillespie asked his old friend.

"They come themselves," Art snapped back.

I saw Dizzy and spoke with him many times in the following years. Once we bumped into him at an airport. It was one of those big European international airports with mobs of passengers in a festive mood everywhere, with shops and eateries.

A crowd of people gathered around us right away. I proudly showed him my new re-entry permit, where it said "stateless." Ever ready to go on stage and entertain, he took the booklet and wiped over his behind with it as if he had toilet paper in his hand. "What is this 'stateless' shit?"

"I need this paper for identification," I told him not sure whether I should laugh or take a stand for my re-entry permit, for which I had had to fight so hard.

"He thought that the word 'stateless' was offensive to you and wanted to support you," Art told me later.

I didn't really care what it said on the paper as long as I could cross borders with no problems. Then I showed Mr. Gillespie trumpet valves, cut for me by Nick Romanenko off an otherwise badly beat-up trumpet, attached to a one and a half inch diameter ten inch long pipe, which I carried around with me on tour as a tool for practicing breathing and finger dexterity. He liked it a lot. "Very smart" he said, "You breathe in here and push the valves. Very good."

When a couple of years later his book "To Be or Not to Bop" came out, in my copy he wrote, "To Valerie my favorite, your main man, D. Gillespie."

The second time in LA we played at the "Parisian room." After the first set ended I stepped off the bandstand, which was higher than the floor by a foot only, and made a few paces through a thick crowd of the club's patrons, when my way was blocked by a radiantly beautiful lady. She was a little taller than me, slim and very stylishly dressed.

"You played beautifully. Clifford Brown must be your favorite trumpet-player."

"Oh yes, absolutely." I was flattered, that such an elegant lady characterized my playing with a pinpoint accuracy.

"I didn't quite get your name. What is it exactly?" I introduced myself and she made me repeat it several times, so she could learn to pronounce it correctly.

"May I have your name"? I tried to sound as elegant as the lady, being prepared to repeat her name several times too, if necessary, so I could pronounce it properly.

"LaRue Brown."

"Excuse me."

"You heard me right."

"You're Clifford Brown's wife?"

"Yes"

I knew their story very well. My hero's untimely death made me contemplate time and again: "Why is it that such geniuses die very often young?"

Pushkin, Lermontov, Mozart, Gagarin you name it, Clifford Brown, Charlie Parker, John Coltrane, Lee Morgan. What is it? Maybe God calls them back because they are too good for this world. What if they themselves, perfect minds, don't want to adapt to the imperfect world of ours and find a way out somehow leaving us here on our own devices? Who knows?

I told LaRue how her husband's music inspired me to become a jazz musician, how I studied and practiced, how I escaped. Then the sound of Art's cymbal made me return to the stage.

"I will come back tomorrow with his sister. She is a classical singer."

"Are you serious?"

"Oh yeah, she would be very happy to meet you too."

Both breaks between the sets of the next night at the "Parisian Room" I spent with Clifford Brown's family. Before driving home LaRue asked me to tell everybody in the band that we were invited to come the following day to her house for dinner. (That was to be repeated each time the Messengers were in LA)

The next day, while the roast was getting ready, I rode LaRue's little nephew on his bicycle around a very neat neighborhood

*With Clifford's brother holding Clifford's trumpet.*
*Photo by Cynthia E.Oats.*

until it was time to eat. Never in my life had I eaten such a delicious roast.

In San Francisco we held an audition for piano players. That's when we met our new brother in the Messengers –- James Williams. He wrote tunes for the very next Jazz Messengers recording and in some two or three years recorded not one, but two super trio records with the Elvin Jones-Ray Brown team (!!!) on one and the Ray Brown-Art Blakey team (!!!!!...) on the other. Wow!

For a year or so the Great Curtis Fuller rejoined the band. There had been very many cases in the past of different band members going in and out of the band.

Curtis came from the times when the Freddie Hubbard, Wayne Shorter, Curtis Fuller, Cedar Walton and Reggie Workman edition of Art Blakey and the Jazz Messengers ruled the jazz world supreme.

What a group that was – spirit, command of instruments, repertoire, horn section, rhythm section – still unsurpassed today. A direct link between generations of the Messengers was right there. Curtis accepted us like members of the family right away. Bobby and I actually treated him more like a dear uncle or, maybe like an older brother, but Curtis hung out with us like we were his equals.

First he started playing with our edition of the band at "Bijou" in Philadelphia or maybe slightly before then. There we were playing opposite the Bill Evans trio.

Imagine that! Back in Moscow everybody was in awe of his playing. One guy, his name was Vagif Seidoff, claimed, that he had held correspondence with Bill Evans through his mother, who translated the letters. We knew, of course, that Bill Evans was born to Russian Parents, but getting letters from the West, from America of all places. Where was the KGB looking? I don't think so.

Everybody was treating him like "yeah-yeah, sure". I was in Vagif's house many times, but had never seen any letters. "Yeah-yeah, you corresponding with Bill Evans himself, sure," I was thinking to myself.

There was no KGB in "Bijou". I could listen to the Bill Evans trio live every other set of that whole week and even talk to him. The trio had a beautiful repertoire of originals and standards, played as only the Bill Evans trio could play it.

The piece I liked the most was "Nardis," a very jazzy tune on the elegant side. I was coming up the stairs to our dressing room after our first set when I almost clashed with Bill Evans, who was leaving the room. He was much taller than I am. His manners were somewhat reserved.

"Hi Valery, nice to meet you. I liked your playing very much. Where are you from in Russia?"

"I am from Moscow."

"Have you ever met Vagif Seidoff?"

"Oh, sure. I know him very well."

"I used to correspond with him. My mother is Russian. She used to translate his letters to me. To write back I would tell her what I wanted to say and she would translate it into Russian."

"I have heard of you writing to this guy, but had never believed it. I thought it was a hoax."

"No, no. That's true. How did you learn to play like that in Russia?"

How about that?

The opening night was on January 19. I remember the date very well because the next day was my birthday. Philadelphia was so close to New York, that there was no question in my mind about driving back. I was driving then a sporty looking Japanese car called Monza 2+2. It looked kind of elegant, but was nothing more than just a small sedan.

"Valery, are you driving back tonight?" That was Schnitter. "Can I go with you?"

"Sure."

"Oh yeah? I'll go with you too." "Me too." Of course Curtis and Dennis were most welcome traveling companions. So our car pool swelled to a comfortable four passengers.

"Valery, tonight is a big snow storm." I heard somebody's warning, when I was saying goodbye to one of the waitresses back in the kitchen. I had to go through the kitchen door to where I had parked my car.

"It's already falling." Somebody else's voice added.

I walked outside. Indeed, healthy sized snowflakes were falling from the pitch-dark skies.

"Valery, are you sure you should go? They predict a big one."

That was the waitress, still in her uniformed T-shirt and apron, who stepped out of the warm kitchen into the dark backyard to look at the snow. My traveling companions followed her without delay.

I always loved snow and couldn't understand what she was talking about. OK, some good size snowflakes were slowly falling in an orderly fashion on the ground. So what? In the years preceding that winter I had not even seen any serious accumulation of snow in New York, only a little bit in January and February and then back to warm weather.

In Moscow, that's a whole different story. Snow very often already started to settle in November and stayed in big piles on the sides of Moscow streets, normally, until the end of March.

Only then would the slow process of meltdown start to end, as scheduled, by the beginning of April, sometimes later. I have never seen even heavy snowstorms altering very much traffic on the streets of Moscow, public transportation or otherwise.

As soon as cute starlets accumulated on the ground, big plough trucks rolled out on the streets and pushed them to the sides, turning the slush and fresh foliage into miniature mountain ranges. When those ranges grew too big, then they were loaded into open trucks and driven outside the city limits. Life went on as usual.

"What's the big deal?" I couldn't understand. "We are not in some distant village. We are going to drive on a modern super highway from one major city to another."

My confidence allayed any doubts, if there were any, of our successful completion of the mission and strengthened everybody's resolve to go home. East or West – Home is Best. We didn't have to pay for a hotel room either.

How was I to know that the world's financial nerve center didn't have funds for a fleet of plough trucks, because big snow storms in the New York's area were rare and paying for the fleet and its storage was simply a bad investment?

Off we went, four naive dummies, to meet our doom. By the time we drove up to the highway entrance, snow was already interfering considerably with the free movement of my car's four wheels. I still didn't have any clue.

"Those had been little back streets, the highway sure will be clean. Sure, sure," my thoughts were circling unopposed around those lines.

Nobody offered any other analysis. I rolled up to the entrance gate, grabbed the toll ticket handed to me and drove on the 95 north. There were some trucks and small cars following in their tracks, which they left in the piles of snow.

The five lane main artery between New York and Philadelphia was reduced to two lanes. It looked to me like two echelons of cars were moving at a speed much slower than the 55 mph limit.

"All right," I calculated in my mind, "we will be in the city an hour later."

The white stuff was falling hard in true Russian winter fashion. My windshield wipers worked tirelessly at full speed. We were in the middle of an authentic snowstorm, just like the one Alexander Pushkin described in his immortal novel "The Captain's Daughter".

That gave me even more confidence. If Grinioff, the romantic hero of the novel, and Savelich, his servant, could make it 200 years ago on a horse-driven sleigh in the wilderness of the Russian expanses, I sure could make it in a modern car with a 250 horsepower engine on a modern super highway.

Yeah, we did make it. It took us 12 hours to reach New York. Every time I have seen Curtis since then, he would always remind me of the trip and, if there were people around, he would necessarily entertain the audience with the story of that trip in detail. He particularly loved the part when our car skidded off the road, but stood firmly on all fours. I got out in search of help.

Through the wind and high piles of virgin snow I climbed back on the road and walked towards a tollbooth. There was practically no movement on a wide white blanket field which was getting thicker and thicker, with the exception of an occasional four-wheel drive truck slowly puffing by.

Compact to mid size hills on the blanket meant that there were cars under the snow. Only yesterday this was a beautiful five-lane highway, until Nature decided to demonstrate who was really the boss here. Now yesterday's glory looked not much different from a wolf's trail somewhere in the wilderness of Siberia.

"I made it to a toll booth and asked to call help," I told my companions in adversity, when I climbed back in the car empty-handed.

"What did they say?"

"The booth operator said: "Pay dollar fifty toll.""

"Curtis burst out laughing. He kept on laughing as he, Dennis and I got out after having made a collective decision to push our only hope out of the ditch. Only Schnitter remained inside.

"David, get out of the car," I ordered in Marshal Zhukoff's voice, as if I were commanding a parade in Red Square. Nobody expected from David's diminutive frame any physical help, but at least he could contribute to our effort by cutting the weight of the load.

Dennis, Curtis and I pushed the car back on the snow-covered highway and at an average speed of 10-15mph reached New York.

My car proved to be a strong vehicle; very many cars didn't make it. Manhattan was one gigantic pool of slush, but drivable. So I took everybody home and headed towards the 59th street bridge. Thirty-first street, the shortest route to Astoria, was blocked by snow, so I turned onto Northern Boulevard.

There, 100 yards later my heroic Monza 2+2 got stuck. It was already broad daylight. Snow was everywhere. It had stopped falling, but the stuff on the ground was so white! It was eerie white. Here and there I could see disabled cars, some abandoned, some with occupants sitting inside or standing around.

"Do I have to leave my car here too? Have I tried enough? No, that's it. I can't sit here forever," I was thinking when a knock on the window startled me. I rolled it down. There was a round face with rosy cheeks.

"Do you want me to show you how you can get the car going forward? I have already helped a few people," the round face asked me.

"Sure, please."

"What you need to do is to switch from drive to reverse a few times and it'll catch."

"I thought I had already tried that."

"Not fast enough. It's a strain on the transmission, but it'll get you out of here.

I applied the recipe a couple of times and my hero-car got going again.

"It worked, it worked," I yelled into the open window, overwhelmed with excitement.

"If the car stops, try it again."

"I will. Thank you, thank you," I kept screaming, but the nameless Good Samaritan didn't hear me. I saw him in the back mirror moving to another car and bending over its window on the driver's side.

"God bless him," my other self said, using the phrase which we had both learned from my mother.

We did stop a couple more times, but each time my companion responded to the "drive-reverse" command perfectly. My car found its final rest at the approach to the driveway of my garage. There, with the hind wheels on the street and the front ones on the pedestrian walk, it emitted its final breath for that day.

Snow, two to three yards high filled up everything all the way to the garage. That was too much even for my car. Many cars got caught in the snow right in the middle of the street, so mine wasn't even in the worst position.

"Don't worry Valery. Parking regulations are suspended indefinitely. You can leave it like this." That was my neighbor and friend Yuri Grabovitch.

"I am going back to Philadelphia for the rest of the week."

"Don't worry, I will drive your car into the garage if we shovel the snow out of the way before you come back."

"Oh thank you," I gave Yuri the keys and ran home.

All the festivities had to be cancelled, because the clock, when I walked in, was showing 3pm. To get to Bijou in time for the show we had to take the next train, which was leaving from Penn station in an hour and some minutes. Shower-change-sandwich-run.

The subway was running on a normal schedule like nothing happened, so I made it to Penn station with no problem. David was already there; then Dennis and Curtis showed up.

"What did that booth operator tell you? Pay toll, dollar fifty?" We all broke out laughing and walked to the appropriate platform.

On the stage at "Bijou" I was very concerned. With no warm-up, let alone good practice or sleep for my chops I had a reason to be concerned. Art told us many times: "They see you before they hear you," which meant that on the stage you were supposed to be dressed decently, act decently and, above all, never look gloomy. Yeah, I knew all that, but couldn't help it.

"Aren't you happy you were born?" Art's hoarse voice shook me up. "Play your ass off."

I did. Surprisingly my chops functioned pretty well, considering.

With all that glory, the 20th of January ride from Philadelphia to New York was not the greatest. The greatest one was from New York to Syracuse, NY three days after we came back from our first eight-week tour of Europe.

Art was late, so Jim and the rest of the band with all the instruments took off. Jim had to be on location early anyway to set up the drums. I was to drive with Art in his new Cadillac. The concert was to take place in the University of Syracuse, a seven-hour drive upstate New York.

I was sitting in the little lobby of the "Camelot Hotel" on 45th street and 8th avenue, where Art had an apartment, and calculating: "If we get going now, we will be there at 7pm. Cool, so the concert will start at 8."

I was waiting and waiting, but no Art. I had already heard the 12 o'clock news and its 1pm variant, then the 2 o'clock news, but still no Art.

I started to think that a call to Jack Wittemor's office was in order, when I heard something slamming against the revolving door of the hotel from outside, making it shake quite a bit. Then the door came into motion and made a 180-degree turn, ejecting a body of my height, the hair on its head all grey.

"Thi…s .eeeis our trumpet-play-er," Art told the doormen to whom he had introduced me already in the past. "He can pleeeeei his assss off." He added his customary praise, making familiar words hardly understandable.

"Valery, waaait here. I will be raiight back."

Art was a very strong person and could live without any substances for a long time, defying the laws of addiction, but every now and then the times when jazz and drugs could not exist without each other mercilessly pulled him back into its clutches.

On the day of the Syracuse concert those times had done their worst. Art was totally out of it. He did walk on his own towards the elevator door, but with intervals. He would make a few paces and stop bending knees, strong shoulders dropping and arms feebly hanging along his body. Then he would straighten out and make a couple more paces. I tried to help him.

"Valery, wait for me here, I will be right back." He said almost clearly that time and disappeared behind the elevator door. I had seen a lot of drunken people in Russia, but this was different.

To my surprise he reappeared very soon and stumbled towards the door; I followed him. We both got caught in the same quarter and were released with a little bit of energy outside.

On the street I grabbed him around the waist like I used to grab Goga when he needed my help and we walked across the street to the garage. On the way Art tried to slow down and bend his knees again, but was carried forward by inertia, with which the revolving door had charged us both.

At the garage he freed himself from me and made a couple of steps to the booth. There he dropped his head and bent his knees again. With his slouching hands he searched for something in his pockets and then produced a receipt in one hand and crumpled bunch of dollars in the other. He let the attendant pick dollars of the appropriate denomination and turned towards me.

At that moment his beautiful sparkling new Cadillac rolled out of nowhere and stopped. The door on the driver's side opened and one of the attendants climbed out of it. So I walked around the car and took the ignition keys from the hand stretched towards me. I was just about to make myself comfortable behind the wheel, when I heard Art's voice.

"I drive the car."

"Art."

"It's my car. I drive it."

I tried to reason with him. The supervisor of the garage tried to reason with him, but all efforts were useless. Art was hopelessly stuck in the other time, which surrounded him like an invisible screen. No matter what I said it bounced off the screen, which blocked any reason from getting anywhere near Art's senses. He was like a kid who didn't want to share his toy.

"It's my car. I want to drive it."

I got out, walked around again, climbed in and strapped myself in the passenger's seat. The attendants gave it up too. "You guys are in the hands of a higher authority . . . What will be will be . . . Whatever happens – happens," I read on their faces.

If it were Germany, they would have called the police. If we were children, they would have called our parents. "What could you do?" What will be will be.

We rolled out of the garage and made a left. How we made it to the 87 North I don't even know.

Art closed his eyes and opened them, slipping in and out of his senses several times, but each time I asked him: "You want me to drive? Are you alright?" He would answer: "I am having a ball."

We were zigzagging most spectacularly, crossing lanes two at a time left and right, speeding up and slowing down to 20mph on an interstate highway.

The cacophony of car horns around us must've been terrible, I did hear it, but it didn't disturb my nerves. I must myself have been surrounded by some kind of a screen. I was absolutely calm. I was just thinking, that if it was my time to go, at least I would go in the same car as Art Blakey.

"Art, are you alright?" I asked him again, not looking for an answer, but trying to keep him from switching off his consciousness again. In response the car turned sharply to the right and crossed into the next lane, then drove onto the shoulder, the cacophony around us reached its climax, and then, to my surprise, the car stopped.

"Valery, you drive," Art declared, got out of the car and took the back seat.

I didn't have a clue where Syracuse was. It could've been in Florida as far as I was concerned.

"Art, where are we going?"

"Straight, take a left on 90."

"When do I get off?"

"I will tell you."

"When does the concert start?"

"As soon as we get there, no later." Having said that Art stretched on the back seat and fell asleep like a baby in its crib.

I was driving and driving past many exits, not knowing if I needed to switch to another highway or take another route. Every once in a while, when driving aimlessly turned into an unbearable suspense I would wake up Art with: "Art, where are we going?" He would answer very clearly in his sleep: "Straight." It kept on going like that for a very long time and I had already given up waking up my boss, trusting ourselves to the hands of Providence.

Art didn't emit any sounds except healthy snoring for quite a while now. All of a sudden he sat up in his seat and with his normal voice very clearly said: "Take a left here." I did.

Shortly after, Art and I were entering the amphitheatre of the University of Syracuse. The house was packed. On the stage drumless and trumpetless the Jazz Messengers were playing something.

When we walked on stage, a storm of applause shook the foundation of the building, the music stopped. Art went behind his drums, sat down, checked the set and got up again.

I just had a moment to ask David, "How did you start without us?" "The wait was too long, we had to start. That's what Art wanted us to do; I know it from the past," was the answer.

In the meantime Art came up to the microphone and started his usual greetings of the audience.

"Good evening dear ladies and gentlemen..." That was past 10pm. "...sorry for the delay. It's not our policy to be late at all. It's all Valery's fault."

The audience broke out laughing. I was stunned – it was so funny. Art didn't mean to be serious. With his smile he showed the audience that that was a joke.

Still smiling he walked back to his drums and started playing an intro to "Evidence" (aka "Justice"), which we had recently rehearsed.

"Valery, take the first solo."

Warm up or no warm up, it didn't matter. We were on a stage. We were playing. Time stood still. I guess there is no time in heaven. Yeah, time ceased to exist. Only my future ex's biological clock was ticking louder and louder.

The subject was being brought up more and more often until it couldn't be ignored any longer, when we reached a point of no return. As much as I was not ready to start a family I thought it would be cruel of me to deny Motherhood to someone who, because of me, left her

Motherland behind, parents, friends, a beloved city, lifestyle and followed me into an absolutely foreign land.

Well, a man's gotta do what a man's gotta do.

At the appropriate time our doctor Isaac Weinberg – who I called Izum, Russian for raisin – informed us that the baby was on the way. Some time later, after one of the check-ups, he called us both into his office and matter-of-factly explained that the pregnancy would be very difficult.

We had to exercise extreme caution, not any kind of extra movement or anything else like that. That didn't surprise anybody; the pregnancy was already very difficult. She needed constant attention and help.

Still not speaking any English, and me being away all the time, if there was an emergency she would have been in trouble. I had to get off the road. If something happened to the mother or, God forbid, to the not yet even born child, while I was playing somewhere far away from home, I would've been blaming myself for the rest of my life.

Forget about playing music. There would have been nothing left in my soul to express except guilt and misery. I had to find a substitution for myself and talk to Art.

Art's phrase "they come themselves" came to my mind all the time, but nobody was coming for a long time, nothing serious anyway. I had to find somebody really good to bring into the Messengers.

We were in New York between tours, which meant that the Messengers would play, most likely, at one of the three places – the Village Vanguard, Village Gate or Michel's.

This time it was Michel's. The club was packed as always. In the break James Williams came up to me.

"Val, you want to meet a young trumpet-player from New Orleans. He comes from a very musical family. Have you ever heard of Ellis Marsallis?"

"Sure. Piano player."

"Yes, that's his son."

James and I came to the table across from the right corner of the stage. "Meet Valery Ponomarev," James addressed a very young man at the table, who got up and stretched out his hand: "Wynton Marsalis."

"Very nice to meet you."

"You want to sit down?"

I sat down and the trumpet talk emerged right away. Wynton knew a lot about trumpet and spoke about it with a lot of confidence.

"How old are you?" I asked him.

"Eighteen. I am here to go to Julliard School of Music. In the meantime I got me some work at a Broadway show. I played lead a couple of times at the …" He named one of the Broadway shows, I think it was "Sophisticated Ladies."

To play lead at a Broadway show, to know so much about trumpet and classical trumpet repertoire at the age of 18 was remarkable. I was intrigued.

"Do you play jazz?"

"A little bit. Not really. I don't want to be a jazz musician. I want to be a classical musician. I want to be treated well. I want to be dressed well, travel first class."

My curiosity grew even more. "If he talks like that, how does he play?"

"Why don't you sit in? Play something."

"No, no, you don't do it in New York."

"Oh yes, that's exactly where you do it. I will introduce you to Art Blakey. Come." I brought my intriguing young friend to the stage, where Art Blakey was talking to somebody.

"Art, meet this young man. He is a great trumpet player. Can he sit in?"

"Yeah, at the top of the set."

That was the last set for the evening. The first tune was "Along Came

Betty", one of the most beautiful tunes in the entire jazz repertoire with somewhat unconventional form and changes to it. If someone doesn't know it, it would be no fun to play it by ear.

I was sitting out and standing next to the stage watching Wynton closely. He didn't know the tune and kept missing the chords, but one thing was obvious – he could play trumpet. He had a beautiful clear tone and articulation, which gave away a very good training.

His whole posture was perfect, the embouchure muscles were set perfectly – an ideal picture of a trumpet-player. He kept on searching for the right notes and finding them, but when the chord was already past.

In a tune like that there is no way to anticipate the chord if you already don't know what's coming. I knew the changes were holding him back and that made me even more curious to hear the youth from New Orleans on a tune of his own choice. The next tune was "Blues March".

"He'd better play now," passed quickly through my mind as I moved to the center of the room. Boy! Was I ever surprised! Eighteen years old to play like that! Sound in all registers, technique, articulation, low register, high register, staccato, legato! I was in shock! To command an instrument like that at any age! But that's a kid! He is only 18! That's phenomenal!" Kept flashing in my mind.

Why did he say he didn't want to play jazz? He has so much feel for the blues. His jazz vocabulary is limited; that's obvious. But so what? He will build it up in no time. There is no better environment than Art Blakey and the Jazz Messengers to be in to learn the language of jazz.

If he stays with the band long enough, he could be as good as anybody had ever been. Jesus, what if it's the new Louis Armstrong? What if it's the new Clifford Brown on the stage? What if I had come from Russia to witness the arrival of a new Jazz Messiah?

Whether he learns harmony or not, builds up more vocabulary or not, I got me a sub. That's for sure.

# CHAPTER 9

# LIFE AFTER THE MESSENGERS

# (IN THE NAME OF JAZZ)

Life works in mysterious ways. I wish I could ask Art Blakey "How did I as a kid know that I'd be playing with him?" "How did I end up playing tribute to my greatest trumpet hero Clifford Brown in the quintet, which he once led, with the original members of the group: Harold Land, George Morrow, Sam Dockery and Max Roach, the co-leader? All the arrangements we played I had learned in the old USSR. How did I end up meeting Larue Brown? How did I end up not only playing at Birdland (every Sunday for several years now with the legendary Arturo "Chico" O'Farrill Afro-Cuban Jazz Big-Band) but actually living across the street from it? I can literally see the entrance to Birdland from my window. I had been living in my building for fifteen or so years before the club moved into my neighborhood.

## Be careful of dreams.

One thing I hear just as often as "How did you join Art Blakey and the…etc?" is: "Your dream came true." Yes, it did.

I didn't put it together with the epigraphs, simply because it's not a question that I needed to answer. It's just so, it's a fact. My dream came true.

Ever since hearing "Moanin'" by Art Blakey and The Jazz Messengers, I had somehow known that I would play with that band, that I belonged there, that it was my music.

Something was already in me which longed for that music, majestic, victorious, blessed, tragic, providential, joyful, confident, full of excitement, with pinpoint accuracy in sound, rhythm, pitch and ensemble work, beauty of the arrangements, logic of solos, delivered with neck-breaking virtuosity.

The Jazz Messengers spoke the truth like nobody else.

Around the time when I discovered Jazz music, I was very often visiting my older friends, a married couple by the name of Regina and Walter Bykoff. They were a dashing team, handsome, well educated (Regina graduated from the Moscow Institute of Foreign languages, majoring in English, and Walter from the Architectural Institute), elegantly dressed – as elegantly as it was possible under the circumstances in the USSR.

Walter sometimes wore a neckerchief, which made him look like a foreign movie star. Both loved jazz, with Walter actually playing very decent tenor saxophone and Regina, with Russian charm, singing American standards.

They were very hospitable people and I ended up spending many an hour in their house listening to jazz music on their tape recorder. After one of those listening sessions I declared: "I will be playing with Art Blakey and the Jazz Messengers."

Years later, already in New York, Regina told me: "When you left that day, we both felt very bad for you, because to us it was obvious that you had lost your mind. Imagine my astonishment, when in '77 I heard on the Voice Of America an announcement – ex-Muscovite Valery Ponomarev is holding the trumpet chair with Art Blakey and the Jazz Messengers. My mind immediately raced back in time to the early '60s, when you used to come to our house to get your first doses of jazz. Your dream came true."

After moving to the United States, Regina wrote a beautiful story featuring this incident and had it published in one of the West Coast newspapers.

I am still living out my dream: playing and recording all over the planet, recording my own albums with the world's greatest musicians, having my CDs rated at five stars out of five and at four out of four in the world's most reputable encyclopedias on jazz music, meeting new people and enjoying whatever comes along with it. I am absolutely convinced that had I not dreamed of it – none of it would have happened.

Dream, dream my dear reader, but be careful – dream only of things you really want, dream about "your" thing only, because . . . are you ready for this? . . . Dreams do come true.

Now, because of her work, Regina travels around the US a lot, but always calls when she is in New York to find out where I am playing.

Ten years ago my girlfriend of the time and I "adopted" her, since Regina was going with us to every one of my gigs of. So we were calling Regina "our daughter" despite the fact that I was younger than Regina by a few years and she had some serious years on my "would-be" better half.

We all loved that joke and felt like one happy "family". That was over 10 years ago.

Last Saturday, I played at Birdland in New York City, the place that Charlie Parker called "the jazz corner of the world," fronting an all-star band. During a break, I tried to introduce Regina to her present day "jazz mother" counterpart, on whom the would-be "daughter" had even more serious years than on the original one.

Regina was visibly upset and with a stern face and voice informed me: "I have only one mother." That embarrassed me a lot. How insensitive I had been all these years, never even asking about Regina's natural mother, whom I had never met.

An apology was in order. With a wave of a hand she dismissed it and reached for her handbag, producing a picture: "That's my 'mother,'" she said proudly.

I couldn't stop laughing. I remember the picture very well. I even remember taking it, over 10 years ago at a club called "Zanzibar", which was located then on 3$^{rd}$ Avenue and 36$^{th}$ Street. There they were – ever pretty "mother" and "daughter", hugging and laughing as only they could. That's what I call loyalty!

After the break I went back on the stage to play the last set of the engagement. The band sounded fantastic. I was on the bandstand of the legendary Birdland, playing my music with some of the world's finest musicians. (Check this out – Carl Allen on Drums, Reggie Workman on the bass, Dave Kikoski on piano, Craig Handy on tenor.)

The audience was beside itself clapping, screaming and yelling, at times getting on its feet. The dream was definitely still on.

When it was not possible to play any longer, I came up to the microphone and announced the end of the performance and once again gave the audience the names of the artists on the bandstand. Then, came the time to announce myself, so I delivered my usual little speech, which I, from the bottom of my heart, recite at the end of almost every concert of mine:

"You were a wonderful audience. It was a great pleasure playing for you. At this time I am looking forward to playing for you again as soon as possible, anywhere possible. Until then, yours truly, Valery Ponomarev. Thank you. Goodbye."

At this time the author is working on his next book, which will be called "Life after the Messengers," and feverishly collecting material for the book after that. It will be named "Two Lolitas."

*A star with trumpet*
*Photo by Daniel Lubei.*

*Art, Bobby and I on bandstand*

*Art talking to Bobby and me*

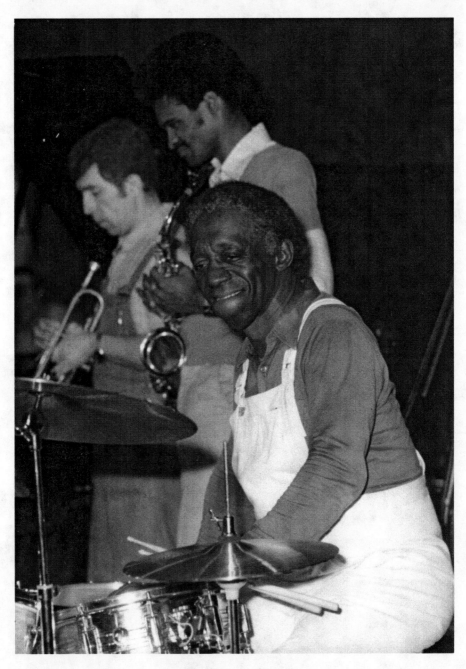

*Art, Bobby and I listening*

*Bush inauguration with Lionel Hampton*

*Newport in NY open stage*

*on tour*
*L to R: James Williams, V.P., Dennis Irwing*

*on tour*

*on tour in Japan*

*Portrait in UK*
*photo by Mark Hadley*

*Jazz Messengers Reunion. New Year's Eve 1979 at the Key Stone Corner in San Fancisco (L. to R. Eddie Henderson, Curtid Fuller, D.S., Phillip Harper, D.I., V.P., Jackie McClean, A.B., B.W., Aerto Moreira). B. McMillen Photos*

*the Jazz Messengers on the stage*
*(L.to R. - James Williams, Bill Pierce, Charles Fembrow, V.P., B.W., A.B.)*
*Photo by Anko C.Wieringa.*

*"Mother" and "Daughter".*

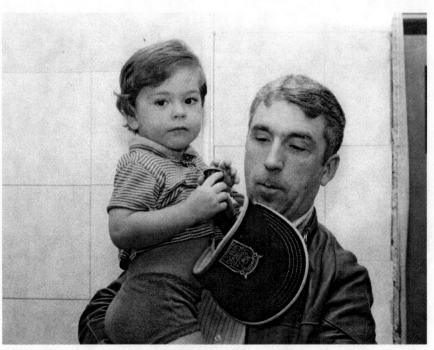

*With Pashka*

# TRIBUTE TO
# CLIFFORD BROWN

*George Morrow, Helen Merril, Max Roach on drums, VP, Harold Land.*
*© SwingJournal*

*Clifford Brown-Max Roach Quintet*
*© SwingJournal*

*With Max Roach*
*© SwingJournal*

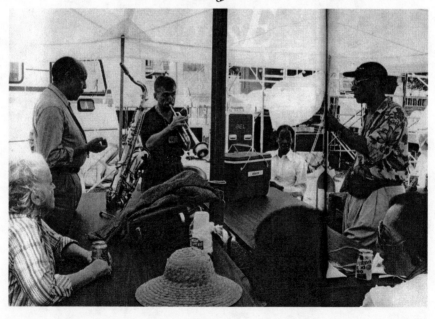

*L. to R. - Mrs. Morrow, Harold land, V.P., George Morrow, Max Roach, LaRue Brown*
*© SwingJournal*

*Larue Brown with my son Paul age 5*

# STORIES

# NIGHTMARE

Why does nobody stop them? Why is there no law prohibiting them from getting anywhere near any position of authority? Nurse Ratched, Pol Pot, Hitler, Stalin, Napoleon, etc. Remember Nurse Ratched in the "One Flew Over the Cuckoo's Nest?" Not only her, the whole nursing staff. There were reasonable people too, not just doctors, but psychiatrists. Didn't they know that a power-hungry nurse would cause a disaster sooner or later? Why did they allow her to abuse her authority and jeer at helpless patients for so long? Did they realize what had really happened after one of the patients killed himself and another one, played by Jack Nicholson, "had" to be put to sleep practically?

So many warnings came about—Hitler, Stalin, Napoleon… a lot of people knew they spelled disaster. Why is there no law demanding at least isolation of these nuts, if not rebuilding their psychological base at the very first signs of what I call human deficiency syndrome—using the excuse of position of authority to inflict harm on others; "strongman" syndrome? What a sweet feeling it must be for them to be able to force somebody else to do what he or she doesn't want and/or doesn't need to. These ghastly creatures go to incredible lengths to put themselves into a position of authority to enjoy the power. They surround themselves with their kind and then breed, attract, and spread like cancer, bringing that ugly syndrome out of others. Isn't it a menace, hazard to the society? There are "No Hazmats" signs on highways. "Careful! Mad dog" signs are everywhere. Only a couple of centuries ago ex-convicts and thieves were marked by law enforcement for everybody to be aware of. There should be some kind of "Rapist," "Child Molester," "Beware of Authority

Syndrome" signs; otherwise we are headed towards another World War or 9/11.

The syndrome manifests itself on a very low level and extends to an extremely high one. Once, as a kid, I was a witness to a scene like this: two short, old and very fat ladies, what seemed to me a spitting image of each other, dressed in identical beat up shoes and worn out overcoats, standing in front of a public toilet. A tiny black haired woman with a round face and small nose, even shorter than the ladies; a pug dog with a broom in her right hand, was in front of the open door blocking the entrance. "No, I won't let her in; I am in charge here." The tiny creature was barking at the ladies. "I am closing it." She kept snarling with the air of an unjustly assaulted keeper of the order. One of the ladies was desperately shifting from one foot to another and the other was begging in a whimper: "My daughter has a condition. Please let her in. There are no more public toilets around here."

"Give a little authority to a nobody and she will turn into a monster," commented my mother and pulled me by hand away from the scene.

What's so amazing is not just that these "strongmen" are allowed to commit their crimes, but are regarded by public opinion, sometimes for a very long time, as heroes. Take Hitler for example—if he had stopped short of unleashing World War II[1], or winning it, he would've been considered in his country the greatest statesman of all times. You think Napoleon is any better? No way, it's the same syndrome again—the guy couldn't live a day without mutilating and killing other people. But in French schools kids are learning from history books that Napoleon is their national hero and a genius.

What a hero, to cause so much destruction and misery to his own people, army, and his own country, not to mention other countries. To <u>order to blow </u>up the Kremlin Wall, of all other crimes, just because

---

1    By 1939 Hitler had already committed enough crimes to be featured, along with Stalin, in the Guinness Book of Records.

it was in his authority, when there was not any reason for it, military or otherwise! French History books don't even mention the fact that Russian Marshall Mikhail Illarionovitch Kutuzoff absolutely destroyed this "National Hero" and his military, chasing the last remnants of it all the way to Paris and saving 99.99 % of the Russian army, where the "genius," who by the whim of his authority, unprovoked, invaded Russia, wasted almost 1,000,000 troops. What a genius, what a hero! Kutuzoff let the nut leave because of the Tsar Alexander the First's orders, who wanted the "genius" to create more havoc in Europe. Otherwise this "piece of history" would've been paraded on the streets of Moscow in a cage on an open carriage with kids spitting and throwing pebbles at him, just like their predecessors did with Pougatchev[2] and their offsprings with Fascists "heroes" of Stalingrad. Napoleon was not even French to begin with. Hitler's predecessor, that's who he was; may he burn in hell, crazy piece-of-you-know-what...

I did identify the warning signs, but only in retrospect; a couple of months after the fact. Hind vision is always perfect. At the time I couldn't imagine that I would become a victim at the hands of the pug dog authority syndrome after traveling the world for so many years. Here is what happened:

On a beautiful sunny afternoon of the 6th of September, 2006, Igor picked me up in front of my apartment building in NYC and customarily drove to JFK. I looked at the ticket and checked the flight number, the time of departure and airline. The rest was on an automatic pilot—to Europe, I always flew out of Kennedy.

"You are in a wrong airport, Mr. Ponomarev." A clerk at the check-in counter, with a friendly smile, told me when I put the case with my trumpet and flugelhorn on the floor and gave him my ticket.

---

2      Pougatchev—head of the most destructive mutiny in 18th century Russia.

"Jesus!"

Now it jumped at me as clear as if it were just happening, how a few months before this trip, I asked a clerk from the travel agency to fly me out of Newark International Airport. That was the first time I decided to try a twenty minute ride by bus from the Port Authority, a block from my house, and see if it might be more convenient than a car service to JFK; car service to Newark is much longer and more expensive.

The fact that I myself arranged to fly out of Newark had been replaced in the foreground of my awareness by a multitude of gigs and various events in my NYC life, and moved to the very fringe of my otherwise very well trained memory. There is always a first time. Yeah, we do a lot of things on instinct, but it's far from 100% foolproof.

"I am sure the manager will allow you to fly out of here. You don't really have enough time to get to Newark. It's still the same airline and the flight is almost empty. There he is," said the smiling clerk and pointed to his right.

"What's the matter?" asked Igor as he walked up and put my luggage next to the trumpet-flugelhorn case.

"Oh, a little formality, please wait here for a sec." I said and made a few steps to my left.

The manager was young, taller than medium height, with kinda regular features and a little anxious expression on his face. I explained to him the nature of my predicament, anticipating hearing: "Oh, no problem. You don't really have enough time to get to Newark. It's still the same airline and the flight is almost empty. Just go right there and check in."

"Your ticket is out of Newark, so go to Newark." He tried to look indifferent, but I could see clearly how much enjoyment he was getting out of being able to send somebody on an hour and a half mad rush ride to be told at the end of it: "You are late. Check-in is already closed."

I tried to reason with him, but that was useless. I knew from the start that it would only give him more pleasure to repeat "I am in charge here. Your ticket is out of Newark, you must go to Newark." There was no time to waste either, so I just cursed him out in my mind, as only a Russian could, picked up the case and ran after Igor, who was already with the luggage at the exit.

Instead of a limo, for this trip, Igor used a Porsche-like red car to provide extra elegance. Maybe it was a Porsche; I didn't look at the insignia. Wasn't that handy! We were flying all over the highways which were, to our total surprise, mostly empty. When did you see the last time the highway leading out of JFK empty? We were flyiiiiiiiiiing....

The empty roads were telling me that we were in luck, but the time hands of my watch were spelling out a monstrously heroic, but futile effort. No way. There was already only half an hour before closing the check-in, but we were still nowhere, and besides, the traffic started to get thicker and thicker. I didn't see any point in this crazy drive any more, but Igor kept stepping it up.

"You never know, Val. The flight might be delayed. I spend more time in airports than at home and have had a lot of surprises. Anything might happen. Relax, listen to this. Tell me, who is this playing?"

Igor would always download from the internet what he thought was jazz. But very often it would be something like Chelentano, the great Italian entertainer of the prehistoric 60's, or something odious like... I have to give Igor credit though - sometimes he would come up with the real thing.

"Charlie Parker," I said, "playing 'Quasimodo,' but it won't help." The hands on my watch were showing 15 minutes before departure, which meant that the check in counters had to be closed for at least 45 minutes by then.

"What is the brand of your trumpet again?"

I had answered that question on almost every trip to or from JFK and Igor knew very well that my trumpet was the legendary Conn Connstellation, that it had been made in 1961, that most of my trumpet heroes had played, at one time or another, exactly the same horn, that it retained 99% of its original condition and was the most prized possession of my entire musical life. No, there was no way of getting my mind off the fact that the doors of the plane were not only locked, that it was not only on the runway, but must've been in the air for a little while already. Yeah, gotta look for the ticket counter, pay a penalty, wait for a few hours for the next plane, maybe even till the following day, miss the connecting flight. Jesus!

"Val, grab the luggage, I will park the car and come back to the terminal. If you are not there, I will know that you had made the flight. If don't, I will find you, we'll figure out what to do next."

A thick crowd of confused and disappointed people packed the hall. Some of them were gawking in disbelieve at the board with a flashing announcement: The flight to Paris # XXX is delayed for 6 hours. "What?! That's your flight. Wow!" My alter ego and I were ecstatic. I didn't miss anything, no need to pay penalty, change the ticket or miss connecting flight. "Hurraaaaaaah."

"You must've known something about this flight." I told Igor when he came up.

"No, not really, mostly intuition. Alright, so you are fine. I will go to the next terminal and pick up Manhattan bound passengers. Congratulations! Enjoy your trip. I will meet you on the 9th. Bye," said Igor and returned to his work.

"Ha! How do you like that? Not bad. How many times have you been to Paris?" My alter ego was a little excited and became too talkative.

"Yeah, how many times?"—Very many times. With Art Blakey alone I have been to Paris for what seemed like at least a couple of times on every European tour, from a few days to a week at a time. And those tours were two or three times a year. And of course, after I left the Messengers, trips to Paris were on the books very often. For a few years I was going to "Billboukett" two or three times a year, a week each time. "Billboukett" is something else. It's located right off San Germain du Pre Boulevard, in the very middle of crowds of tourists, and is an attraction in itself. On the ground floor it featured a very classy restaurant. But if you descend down the winding stairs to the basement you would find yourself in "Café Olympia." I don't know why the management doesn't use that space anymore, but it's still intact, just like in the late 50s/early '60s when Art Blakey played there with the original Messengers. The legendary club now looked like lodgings for a family of ghosts, barely lit and unkempt. But those sounds were still in the room, the very sounds which reached me in Russia and set the course of my life.

For a couple of years I didn't have a chance to go to France. But this year it was already my second time. Only a couple of months before then Billy Pierce, a fellow Messenger, and I together with the French rhythm section, played a tribute to Art Blakey for a week in Paris and toured the south for a week. Yeah, the French loved jazz, and The Messengers' version of it particularly.

I felt very close to the French not only because we shared love for Jazz, but also because throughout the history Russian and French cultures were very close. Traditional Russian colors are very similar to the French. Russian nobility spoke French before they spoke Russian. I don't speak any French, but my godmother did. Well, she was born and raised in Paris. Too bad this time I was not to stay in the celebrated city, but only change planes in Charles De Gaulle airport, and fly to Lyon for only one concert. The rest of the band was flying from Russia.

The gig was actually not in Lyon but an hour ride into the grape country. I had played one just like that for the same employer a couple of years before then. That was my first contact with the successful businessman of post-Soviet Russia. Ivan Vassilyevitch turned to be a very nice man of quiet manners, and almost shy. What's more, he loved my music, considered me one of the world's best and had in his collection every CD of mine except the latest recording. Naturally I gave him that one and my book, which came out in Moscow in the Russian language two years before then, as his birthday present.

That's what it was, Ivan Vassilyevitch's 50th birthday celebration. For the party, his office rented a castle in a village near Reims, an hour and a half ride from Paris, flew in his friends from all over the world, and engaged several of the most famous artists of Russia for the gala concert. The castle, incidentally, is famous for producing one of the world's most exquisite and most expensive brands of Champagne, which you will never see in your local liquor store. At a White House reception, maybe. Another attraction of Reims is the gothic cathedral, which is the largest in the country and, very possibly, in the world, Notre Dame of Paris taken into account. Coronations of all French monarchs, including the nut Napoleon, were conducted there.

I felt pretty foolish, when the fact that the fees of all Russian artists were no less than $20,000 each, revealed itself by accident. You have to agree, that being regarded as one of the world's best and quote $2,000 to the middleman for a performance where other participants, Russian style hip-hop dancers, rock artists, some vocalists charge ten times more, is not very flattering.

A storm of applause came down on me when it was my turn to get on the stage. The best Russian cats accompanied me and played their hearts out. Ivan Vassilyevitch was at the center table with his wife and daughter. He looked rather handsome and if not for his grey hair one would've never figured out his age. The beautiful lady of about thirty, who before the concert was very insistently inviting me to join her, turned out to be his mistress, and was sitting alone at the table next to the center one. A gigantic "thank you very much" went out to my intuition for saving me the embarrassment of swallowing the bait. Wow, that was close. Maybe it wasn't intuition at all, but the fact that I was too busy discussing the program with the guys, who I hadn't seen for a year.

After the concert and five-course dinner, with a loud noise in the form of songs and cheering, everybody poured into the yard and nearby streets to watch fireworks in honor of the jubilee. The villagers must have felt tremors in the middle of the night and been alerted by the noise, which was inspired, no doubt, by very considerable libations. Only the locally produced Champagne, in unlimited abundance, was served during the dinner. If there was vodka, it hadn't been visible. I didn't have any problem imagining the townies at a market making faces at each other the next morning and exclaiming, "the Russians had a party again."

The next day, everybody was invited to have a tour of the Champagne factory. Turned out that the castle was built on a solid rock and the production was done a hundred meters down inside of it. Many large rooms were full of wooden racks, holding unmarked large and small bottles of future Champagne. That precious solution had to stay there under certain temperature for certain amount of years before it became Champagne, before it was good enough for the customers and before the label with the name of the Castle could be put on every bottle. All guests, including the artists, were given a couple of bottles each for a souvenir, care of Ivan Vassilyevitch.

After lunch everybody walked to the architectural wonder of the world, which was only a mile or so away. It was more impressive than the Notre Dame of Paris. First of all, it was much larger; with many more portals, statues and figurines. But the main difference was in vegetation. I don't remember a single tree near the Paris cathedral, when the Reims' was drowning in big and small branches.

The whole place was very quiet. It seemed like the cathedral was taking a break between the main events and the royal court, crowds of distinguished citizens with their dames clothed in dresses with trains, masses of onlookers could start arriving at any time.

The next day everybody, except the "regal" family and secretary/ mistress were on a huge tourist bus en route to the airport with the stopover in Paris for a short sightseeing trip.

That was two years ago.

What was going to happen this time?

I knew it was a wedding. Obviously Ivan Vassilievitch divorced his wife and gave his secretary a status of wife, I reasoned. Ha. What can I produce for a wedding present? Think, Valery, think.

"What could be easier? Write a song for the newlyweds and perform it with the cats at the concert." Yeah, that was it. My alter ego got a big credit for it. The idea came right on cue. A simple and catchy melody was created within minutes and there was still a lot of time left before the flight.

"Why don't you write lyrics now, uh?"

"What lyrics?" I thought my other self got too inspired by the initial success and became overly ambitious.

"Yeah, yeah, lyrics, the band will play the melody, then everybody blows (slang for every band member playing an improvised solo), then we sing the lyrics and teach the audience repeat the refrain."

"Listen to you, why not?" I just agreed with my councilor-disciplinarian-executor-chief advisor-critic-interlocutor-admirer, my other self, my alter ego. Russian words, fitting the melody, started to jump up one after the other. Here is a rough translation:

Friends,

Let's raise our glasses

And wish the newlyweds

Everything in the world
Hurrah, fireworks,
Bouquets of stars will fall to us from the skies,
Kindhearted wizard cast for you
Love and happiness, Vanya & Nina.

"Check in for Flight XXX will begin in ten minutes.""What? Where did the six hours go?"

"That's your hand luggage?"

"Yeah. Can I have a window seat?"

"Sure. Is row thirty-four good for you?"

"Sure."

"Your hand luggage will be inspected before boarding.  Here is the sticker for the big bag. It's booked all the way through."

"I will pick it up in Lyon?"

"Yes, here is your boarding pass; you have a window seat. Have a good flight."

"Thank you very much."

At boarding routine check of my hand luggage followed. It's very simple. I part with my most prized possession for just a moment, when it's being rolled by a conveyor into screening. I step through the gate and pick up the horn on the other side. Sometimes security would like to inspect closer the contents of the case if something like Palm Pilot, iPod or pack of CDs hasn't appeared clearly on the screen. But most often the security personnel, I think, just want to see my treasure closely. I don't mind, but always open the case myself, so inexperienced hands won't touch the instrument.

"Oh, it's trumpet," or "You are a trumpet-player." Will follow in a sort of derisive-respectful tone and then "Have a good flight."

"Thank you."

Routine flight over the Atlantic.

After the years and years of flying, I worked out a habit of not sleeping very much the day before the flight, but making sure that I do sleep on the plane for at least three hours. That helps me very much to switch to the European schedule. 9:00 a.m. in Madrid is 9:00 a.m. in the morning for me. 8:00 a.m in Moscow is 8:00 a.m. in the morning for me, not midnight in NYC. My mind switches to the new schedule and the body follows; that's it. Musicians who know me would make sure that upon arrival to the hotel, they ask for a room as far from me as possible. Because when they check in, they go to sleep for a few hours. But for me, after breakfast of course, it's time to take my Conn Connstellation out of the confines of its case and let it launch into the air a beautiful sound as only Conn Connstellation can generate: practice time.

Anyway, routine flight, routine check-in on the next flight to Lyon followed without any deviation.

"Oh, it's a trumpet. Have a good flight."

"Thank you."

Lyon. A driver from Ivan Vassilyevitch's Lyon office met me at the airport and drove to the castle. It was a different castle, but also in the vine country. High in the mountains, from the highway it looked like an illustration from a book of fairy tales. Just wait a second and you will see horsemen in armory holding flags, drawbridge descending, King and Queen coming out of the gate to greet their subjects.

"Kings and Queens did stay in this castle many times," a young lady behind the desk in the office told me when I was checking in.

"You will be staying in the quarters which were occupied by the king so-and-so in the year of 17XX. Furniture is exact replica of what royalty of those times were used to. Of course air-conditioning and TV are modern, but the bed, bath, wash-hand-stand, parquet, carpets, chairs, stools, armchairs, table, nightstands are exactly the same.

"Wow," silently exclaimed my other self, but I calmly said "Thank you," as if I stayed in the kings quarter's every day. I do stay in very fancy places every once in a while, but far from very often.

"Are you also working for Ivan Vassilyevitch?"

"No, I am one of the team working on preserving the historical site. One of our functions is to rent the Castle out for weddings, receptions etc. Only the extremely rich or very big corporations can afford it. There are several sights like this one around the country."

"Oh, yeah, I had been at one of them two years ago in Reims."

"Yes, that is one of them, they produce Champagne. We produce some of the rarest wine in the world. Tomorrow all the guests will be invited for a tour. Today, after the ceremony, you will be invited to watch our show—knights in full armor on horses, just like centuries ago, will be staging mock fights, all sorts of competitions, etc. To you it will all look real."

"How interesting!" I said and thanked her for the little preamble.

"You will find a door with the #21 across the lawn. Here is the key; it bears the same number."

Ivan Vassilyevitch was crossing the lawn when I saw him on the way to the king's quarters.

"Hi Valery, how are you? So good to see you! How did you like your quarters?"

"It is so good to see you too! No, I haven't seen it yet, but heard everything about it. Thank you very much."

"Oh, you are most welcome. I want you to be a guest at the wedding. Today you have a free day. The concert is tomorrow, can't wait to hear you play live again. Sorry, I have to run. It's almost ceremony time. You are very welcome to attend. It's over there, as you turn around the castle, you will see the vineyards. Take the stairs to the lower ones and you will see us in a gazebo. The priest and all the guests are already there."

"Oh, thank you. I will be right there, I'll just drop my luggage."

Ivan Vasilyevitch didn't change much at all—handsome, athletic figure, gray hair, soft manners. May be even a little more humble than the last time, but that's it. He hurried away and I walked across the lawn to look for the door with the number 21 on it.

"Jesus!"

It was only one bedroom, but what a room! Just like Catherine the Great's bedroom in Hermitage. Just like it. Probably ten meters high, if not higher, ceilings, tapestries hanging down the walls, enormous bed covered with embroidered bed cover, shining parquets. That room was at least four times larger than my one bedroom apartment in the city. There were two separate rooms for toilet and bath with an adjacent closet for clothes. They were also very impressive white marble wash-hand-stands and bathtub, handmade wooden closets, thick cotton towels embroidered with king's monograms.

"You gotta get a queen in here." My other self never missed a beat.

"You are right there."

When I got to the gazebo, the service was already in full flight. Coming down the stairs all I could see were vineyards everywhere, to the horizon on the left, to the horizon on the right and to the horizon in front of me, flushed in sunlight. The tiny little structure looked like a little island in the middle of an ocean of grape vines and was packed with ladies and gentlemen of all shapes and ages dressed in tuxedos and evening gowns. It was noon and at least 95° F.

Most of the guests stayed outside of the little pavilion, so I remained on the stairs where the view was much better anyway. Ivan Vasslilyevitch was in the middle of the pack and looked lost. Next to him was a very thin girl in a wedding dress. She didn't look older than 18 and just like the groom, appeared lost. Her big eyes were staring in the crowd and begging for support. All white, in finest of embroideries, the splendid dress failed to hide how thin she was. She must've stayed on some latest French diet forever. As for me, I'd like a girl to have at least something on her. But that was not my call and there was no arguing with the fashion.

"Groom may kiss the bride" rang in the air and was repeated by a couple of lonely voices and then taken up by the rest of the guests. Now "Groom may kiss the bride" sounded like command from a higher authority and there was no arguing with it. The girl in the wedding dress blushed, for the last time turned her big eyes into the crowd and submitted to the inevitable.

"What? She had never kissed before."

"I think it's possible." My personal interlocutor-advisor-critic-secretary etc. and I were amazed.

"Everybody is invited to go to the tent next to the lawn where drinks will be served and entertainment will follow shortly." The young lady from the office made the announcement and the whole mass of guests moved in my direction, so I led the way, not allowing the masses to swallow me. Most people went to their rooms to change, and so did I. When I came to the tent, there was already almost everybody who I saw at the ceremony. A little bit later the newlyweds walked in. I wished them both happy marriage and toasted Champagne.

"Valery, I loved your book. I read it in one sitting; couldn't put it down. Can't wait to hear you play. Vanya says you are one of the best in the world."

"Oh, please. Thank you very much."

Nina was very nice, soft-spoken and humble just like Ivan Vasilyevitch. No longer in wedding splendor she was outfitted in jeans and simple shirt. After having a closer look I upgraded her age to twenty. We talked for a minute and then the newlyweds moved to a group of girls Nina's age.

"Please take your seats, the show is about to begin," came the announcement. I turned around and saw at a little distance from the tent whole platoon of knights on horses, all in armor and helmets, with swords, lances and standards, just like in the book of fairy tales. Only one maiden was with them, dressed in medieval costume. The platoon moved a little closer, locked the visors on their helmets, and the show began.

Wow! For about an hour the knights were going at it, knocking each other off the horses, fencing on foot, climbing on horsebacks again and kicking each other with lances, rushing back and forth, horses' hooves only a yard away from the stunned audience. Then they put the maiden on the way of the horses and affixed an apple on her head.

"Oh, no!"

"Oh, yes!" One of the knights galloped pass the maiden and knocked the apple off with his sword.

Jesus!

All warriors unlocked the visors, took their helmets off and started laughing, one louder than the other.

Wasn't I relieved when the show ended! I knew that the actors were very well trained and must've performed the show many times, but still, just a tiny stumble and a disaster would've been unavoidable. I think their laughter was a little uneasy too and the whole platoon with the maiden themselves were relieved, when the show ended and nobody got hurt.

I clapped my hands in appreciation and went to walk around the vineyards to clear the sound of hooves out of my ears. On the way back I saw one of the girls from the group sitting alone on a bench and enjoying the view of the valley, which outstretched at the foot of the mountain. She was not bad looking, on the rather voluptuous side and smiling at me.

"We are Nina's classmates. We are from Penza (provincial town in Russia). Is that really true that you are world famous? Nina told us, can't wait to hear you play."

"Did you read my book?"

"No, not yet, but will look for it in Moscow. I have relatives in Moscow. On the way back I will stay with them for a couple of days and then return to Penza. I gotta run. It's time to change for dinner."

The next thing I knew, the girls pulled a table and chairs from the lawn near the door to my quarters, and made a habit of gathering around it before breakfast, lunch and dinner. Their happy blabber and laughter disturbed me a little when I was practicing, but, of course I didn't say anything.

The following day my Moscow band arrived. Lyosha, Dima, Sasha and Sergei were marveling at my living space, when I invited them to get together for a repertoire discussion. The rest of the day was almost an exact repetition of the one in Reims. The only difference was tour of wine production instead of Champagne, and us playing the wedding song at the concert. The guys got it right away. After everybody blew enough choruses (form of a song on which to improvise) I sung the lyrics, but the refrain, "we wish you everything in the world, Vanya & Nina" everybody, musicians and audience, took up and kept repeating. I announced that the song was brand new, that it was our present to the newlyweds and that we would record it on our next CD. Storm of applause and resumption of the refrain followed.

When I was leaving the hall, Ivan Vassilyevitch came running.

"Valery, Valery, are you serious, you really want to record the song?"

"Sure, I may even put your and Nina's picture on the cover."

"I will pay for the recording."

"How do you want it to be recorded, in a small band, big-band, all Russian band, all American or mixed?"

"Any way you see fit is fine with me, Valery. There are dances and more drinks downstairs. Tell your guys everybody is welcome."

At first, all of the guests gathered downstairs for more drinks, hors d'oeuvres and dances, but slowly, at first older friends of Ivan Vassilyevitch, and then everybody left. By 4:00 a.m. it was only me and the girl from Penza still "dancing" in semidarkness and drunken stupor. Then we too left to take a look at my splendid apartment and ended up in my royal bed for the battle of the sexes, which continued for at least a couple of hours.

Mercy, mercy, mercy, telephone rang like a fire department truck waking me up. The girl was gone. I must've fallen a sleep during the battle.

"Valery, it's 7:00 a.m. already, you are not ready yet? It's Svetlana from the Ivan Vassilyevitch's Lyon office. I am to drive you to the Lyon airport. Quick, quick, if you miss this plane you won't make the connection in Paris, quick."

Five minutes later, showered and clean-shaven, I stepped outside of no longer my royal quarters. Traveling as a touring musician all over the world for almost thirty years was not for nothing.

Sveta was a real Russian beauty, tall, gorgeous slim figure, beautiful face, features and charming, care free smile—complete package.

"Life is easy. My husband is taking care of everything. Very often he is on the road, so it's just me and my daughter in the house. We spend a lot of time at the sea. I work only when I want to, for fun."

Sveta was telling me everything about her life in France, how she met her husband while he was on a business trip in Russia and what year was good for this wine and what year was good for that wine…

Lyon, routine check-in, "Oh, it's a trumpet! There is no need to change terminals, only a short walk to the gate 49. No rush, no hurry, plenty of time to make the connection. Have a good flight."

"Thank you."

Charles de Gaulle International Airport.

My rule is to check with the gate first, make sure there is not any kind of local time change or mistake in the booking and only then, with that peace of mind, walk around, look at the stores, check out some reading matter, gaze through picture books maybe, buy some souvenirs. Kills time superbly.

Gate 49, what?! A thick crowd of confused and disappointed people packed the hall. Some of them were gawking in disbelief at the board with a flashing announcement: Flight to New York # XXX is delayed indefinitely. The nightmare had already begun, but I, lulled by the fairytale of previous two days, was totally oblivious of it. No sirens or at least bells rang alarm in my mind; my alter ego was in the clouds, just like me, and there was nobody to remind me that in the fairy tales there were love, princes and princesses, castles, balls, masquerades, Champagne, happy endings, friends but also foes, insecurity, jealousy, vengeance, hate, wild dark woods, Baba-Yagas and ogres too.

Indefinitely is indefinitely. It could be for half an hour or an hour or even two, but one can't go into the city, that's for sure. I didn't mind, although it was only an airport, it was still in Paris, the center of civilization and culture. What difference does it make if I come home at 4:00 p.m. or 6:00 p.m.? I still had no problem making the gig the following day at the 92nd Street Y, a beautiful club on the Upper East Side.

Breakfast, window shopping, souvenirs for two hours, new announcement: "Flight to NYC is further delayed for at least two hours." Window-shopping, picture books, reading matter, a glass of gorgeous French wine, killing time superbly for two more hours; new announcement: Flight to NYC is further delayed indefinitely. Jesus! What do you do now? I sat on a chair in front of the gate and fell asleep.

I believe in reincarnation. Years before then I read a book on it with a lot of pictures of contemporary celebrities: Charles Lawton, Vivien Leigh, Presidents, famous athletes and their doubles as marble statues from the times of Greek legends and Roman Empire. They were not just looking similar; they were exactly the same people, only separated by thousands of years. Amazing, ah? Not if you believe in reincarnation.

When I woke up there was a conveyor belt in front of me and the toilet pug dog from my childhood behind it. I mean she was not just similar looking to the "toilet authority" of almost sixty years ago, no, she was exactly the same person—very small, black hair, with a round face and small nose, mad-authority-desire look on her muzzle. "Here it is Valery, the disaster is right here." No, I couldn't see it, alarm didn't go off. The fairytale totally fogged my sensitivity. The dog was already there, the stage had been already set, the nightmare was about to unfold.

I got up, picked up my horn, and still smiling to the dream (which had just ended), walked up to the belt.

"Where have you been?" The dog angrily snarled at me from behind the belt. "The boarding should've been finished by now."

I didn't say anything, just put the case on the belt leading to the screening apparatus and the conveyor-belt operator with the lust for power written all over her muzzle grabbed my Conn Connstellation and started walking away.

"Hey, what is it you are doing?"

"It goes to the cargo compartment."

"What do you mean cargo compartment? It's a musical instrument and had been booked as a hand luggage. It had been booked by this very airline as such from NYC to Paris to Lyon and back from Lyon to Paris to NYC."

"I don't care for this. I am in charge here. It goes under the plane." She barked and proceeded walking away. She didn't even try to give me any kind of documentation or a receipt or a tag, not that it would make any difference, just grabbed my horn and walked away.

All the recent crazy stories of lost or damaged instruments rushed at me. One guy I knew had his saxophone stolen from the plane, another guy had his guitar broken by the security while "inspecting" the cargo in the luggage compartment. There were rumors of criminal rings in the airports which, under the guise of authority, were stilling passengers' belongings. There was even a rumor of Al'Quaida infiltrating security forces of all major airports around the world.

I walked around the belt and took my trumpet from the paws of the "authority."

"You can't put it under the plane; it had been booked already as hand luggage as it had been booked for very many years. You must be new here; it's not within your authority to change the bookings. Musicians travel with much larger instruments all year around. You wait a week and see whole orchestras flying with saxophones and trombones and whatnot."

The dog didn't hear a word I was saying. Her eyes were bloodshot with inborn hatred. She knew only one thing; that she just got a job where no education or experience was required, except for a couple of days of training maybe. She was not good enough for the lowest pay anywhere, but here she was an authority and this passenger didn't want to recognize her supreme power at the conveyor-belt.

Whatever she communicated into the speaker phone brought her supervisor from the depths of the tunnel which led to the plane. The manager was young, taller than medium height, with kinda regular features and a little anxious expression on his face. Without even looking at the case he commanded "It goes under the plane." He sounded exactly like the conveyor-belt "authority."

"It's a musical instrument; I will show it to you."

"I don't need to see it. It goes under."

"How is it going under, when it had been booked already as hand luggage by this very airline from NYC to Paris to Lyon and back?"

"I say it goes under."

At this point one more passenger arrived. He was a small and young Indian guy with a case almost twice the size of mine. Nobody yelled at him for being late. The guy, with a, businesslike manner, opened the case partially, (just enough to reveal a sitar) and zipped it up again. The supervisor waved him to go through. I decided that misunderstanding had been resolved and made a step towards the tunnel. The supervisor pushed me with both palms of his hands on the chest and ran away. Just like a spiteful child in school, who would hit a schoolmate from behind and run away to complain to the principal, so the principal would make any kind of reprisals impossible.

What right did he have not to let me on the plane, push me—a passenger? I was lost standing with my back to the wall, which grew out of nowhere and extended to the end of the terminal, leaving only a narrow strip which separated the whole area around the gate 49 from the rest of the terminal. This was a nightmare. The next thing I saw was four policemen running full speed from the far end of the strip towards me. Without slowing down they smashed me against the wall and one of them violently pulled the case from my right hand, but couldn't get it because the fingers of my right hand clasped in a dead lock around the handle.

"This is a musical instrument. It's booked as hand luggage. I am changing planes here. I flew from Lyon." I yelled as loud as I could, so the passengers on the other side of the wall would hear me. I knew from experience living in the Soviet Union that one had to scream as loud as he could, so the police wouldn't be able to keep its actions secret.

All I heard in response was "American. Ha, ha, ha. We don't speak English," as the pushing, shoving and kicking intensified. Four of them, then a couple more joined in the fun, still trying to yank the case out of my hand and pull my left hand behind me.

"It's musical instrument. I will show it to you." I kept yelling as loud as I could and heard in response only: "American. Ha, ha, ha. We don't speak English." The scene was becoming more and more like the one from the American news I saw a couple of years before then, when four white policemen were beating the life out of dark chocolate color Randy Jones, or four black guys pulling a nameless white driver out of his truck and beating the daylight out of him; except this time it was me in the very center of it all.

All of a sudden a clear understanding of what happened to Hilton Ruis flashed through my mind. Hilton Ruis, a brilliant Jazz piano-player, was killed by New-Orleans police earlier the same year. He must've screamed back at the pack of crazy dogs in police uniform just like the ones in the "Center of Civilization." Where was I? Did I wake up and found myself back in the Soviet Union with its militia-KGB system? Or had a war movie, I have seen so many of them as a kid, turned to reality and I was in fascist Germany captured by Gestapo? I knew deep down in my heart that if I as little as cursed them out, let along pushed back any one of them, they wouldn't have any problem pulling the gun out and shooting me dead. And then, of course, they would've "found" incriminating stuff in my trumpet case and the truth would've been forever buried. Even my close friends would've been saying "I never knew that about Valery. He never even smoked pot."

No, it was a nightmare, it couldn't be real. We were in Paris, of all places of the world. It lasted probably a minute or two, but felt like an Eternity. Now a whole gang of young six feet and taller guys in police uniform were still kicking and shoving and pushing me and trying to yank my Conn Connstellation out of my right arm.

"You are making a mistake. I am a passenger. I change planes here. I came from Lyon."

"We don't speak English."

All of a sudden one of the goons succeeded in lifting my left arm behind me and expertly, deliberately breaking the ulna bone.

"Aaaaaaa…………., he broke my arm."

"Ha, ha, ha, American."

I had to let the case go and support the broken arm with my right one. I screamed as loud as I could to the passengers on the other side of the wall. "They isolated me. Somebody call U.S. Embassy. Somebody call a lawyer. Somebody call International Police."

"Ha, ha, ha, American. He wants a lawyer. Ha, ha, ha."

The more I was screaming the angrier they were getting and still pushing me and shoved me and dragged me along the floor. One of them was caring my horn, while I couldn't hold on to it any more and traveled on my back, supporting the broken arm in the air. They didn't want me to communicate with the passengers; that was obvious.

I was born and raised in Soviet Union. I knew too well that screaming was my only salvation. To cover its tracks was a specialty of a police anywhere at any time. That conviction was flashing loud and clear in my mind and there was no other way about it, nightmare or not.

"Call a doctor, call a lawyer."

"Ha, ha, ha."

"You are making a mistake my friend. I am just a passenger." I said to the clerk inside the station."

"You are not my friend."

"How is that, what did I do?"

All of the "heroes" of the attack were inside and still screaming at me, but with less confidence. The goon, who broke my arm, was sitting in front of me, big, for a Frenchman, guy, black hair, with regular but blank features. I did tell him that I would sue the department and would identify him.

It was already one hour later, and still no doctor or a lawyer or a representative from the US Embassy. Obviously the law enforcement was deciding what to do with me.

The voices of the passengers were very close, right behind the wall next to the door leading out of the station. As soon as nobody looked at me I walked out of the station and yelled as loud as my very well trained lungs allowed me. Didn't that anger Charles De Gaulle's finest? Disregarding my broken arm, they viciously shoved me back in. One of them even tried to put handcuffs on me.

"I already have my arm broken. What do you want to do now? Where is the doctor? Where is the U.S. representative?" He backed off. I knew I was on the right track. Don't let them completely isolate you. Don't be afraid. Just yell to the passengers for help at every opportunity, otherwise who knows what's going to happen.

It continued for SIX hours: No doctor, lawyer, international police or U.S. representative. Every so often they would leave me unattended and I would sneak out of the station and scream my lungs out. The uniformed gang in their madness would shove me back in. "Where is the doctor, lawyer, US representative?" For SIX hours!!!

Finally, the largest of them, in a pretty quiet tone invited me to step into the adjacent room. Then he really shocked me.

"Why did you do this?" He asked me with a very heavy accent and in a sweetest of voices possible. It would've sounded artificial even in the voice of a girl trying to convince her boyfriend that she hasn't hung with any other guy the day before. But that was a huge burly guy, trying to sweet talk me. Jesus! I couldn't help but laugh.

"What did I do? Can you please tell me?"

"You need to sign here, so we could release you to the hospital."

"Finally! It's already midnight."

I thought the nightmare was coming to the end. But no, it continued on the way out of the station and out of the Airport to the hospital. Even in the hospital, while waiting for the x-rays, they would push and shove me back if I, in my upset state of mind, would walk too far from them in the dead end corridor. It was like if they got into one mode of behavior and that was it; like if they were robots with only one program.

I don't know how long it would've continued if not for the chief doctor of the hospital. Dr. Barnard kicked the goons out of his domain and told them not to come back. I didn't know that a doctor in emergency room had superior power over police. Thank God!

From that point the nightmare turned onto the other side: everybody, from nurses to surgeons to fellow patients, loved jazz. Some were at my concerts at different times. Dr. Barnard heard me play that past summer at the Club Le Sunside on Rue Lombard in Paris. The anesthesiologist doctor turned out to be an ex girlfriend of my buddy Olevier Hutman, a brilliant piano-player, who played with me every time I was booked at Billbouquett.

Three days later, upon returning to NYC, I was met by torrential flood of phone calls. The first one came from Daniel Brown, an American journalist living in Paris.

"Valery, our station is playing your CDs all the time. Do you need a lawyer? Call Mr. Stephane Maugendre. He is a real professional and won a similar case recently against the same Charles De Gaulle police. Abuse of foreigners is extremely high in Paris and has to be stopped. In that case he proved the police's action had been absolutely unjustified in... you ready for this?... in killing two foreigners."

"Jesus!"

"He doesn't speak English very well. You need to speak with his secretary."

When I called Mr. Maugendre's office, the very pleasant voice of Frances, his secretary, told me: "We love jazz. My boss has all your CDs. Can you, please send him your latest one?"

It took me a very long time to finish this story. I certainly didn't want to meet with the "magnificent gang"—the "heroes" from the end of it. Not that they could inflict any more damage on me. No, the ball was in my hands now. It's just the whole thing is so ugly, so stupid, so unfair. People to this day ask me what happened, but the first months it was call after call from all over the world. Media around the world; several TV channels, including CBS News, carried the story. People I never knew would stop me on the street, students, journalists, audience at performances, everywhere I had to go again and again through: "I was coming from Lyon…"

I know deep down in my heart, regardless of the outcome in the French Court, that all the guilty ones will pay for their part in the crime they committed against me. It's just so. World is the balance. They broke it. But it will be restored. The dog, her supervisor, the gang, they have to meet their doom. Any kind of energy, whether good or bad, once put out there, comes back.

Yes, these are times of heightened security, but professional policeman are supposed to be able to decide within split-second time whether it's a criminal in front of him or an innocent bystander, whether to shoot or help the person out of danger. They study for that and take graduation exams. How could they possibly confuse me with a terrorist? At the time of the accident I was 63 years of age, with all gray hair and slightly built; 5'5" short.

I am sure there are real heroes on the French police force, but not this gang of goons. Those were cowards who couldn't wait to demonstrate their bravery at the expense of a helpless victim. What are they going to do when they meet with a real terrorist? I will tell you exactly what they are going to do—run away, hide, let their comrades do their duty. But, no, no, no, the balance will be restored. Somehow, somewhere they would have to meet with Marshall Michael Illarionovitch Kutuzoff and dearly pay for their stupidity. Maybe it will be in the form of a real terrorist dragging them out of their hiding place and breaking every bone in their stupid bodies. Whatever happens to them, the balance will be restored.

It is the same with the Dog. Whatever she told on the speakerphone to the supervisor and he to the police, she will have to pay for it. With that kind of insatiable lust to inflict harm on others she can't have normal life. Sooner or later whatever her common law husband will be overwhelmed with her commanding, will snap and smear her stupid snout over a stove. Or, maybe, they all will be exposed as collaborators with the Al-Quaida or some other terrorist organization and the rumor will prove to be true. A Russian proverb clearly says: "There is no smoke without a fire." After all, they achieved exactly what the terrorists want—scare passengers from flying. Every musician in the world is very concerned now about flying—me too. I am concerned with stepping into a situation, sooner or later, where no reason, no common sense matters, where only the red-eyed lust for power reigns supreme. I don't let it bother me very much and put it in the back of my mind. I believe in reincarnation and many other things. Fate is among them. Whatever is destined to happen will happen.

It's almost a year later and since then I had flown already very many times to a multitude of places around the world. Nice, France included. I will go to Paris soon too. Almost everywhere I heard at the check-in, and looking forward to hearing again and again, the customary:

"Oh, it's trumpet! You are a trumpet-player. Have a good flight."

Thank you.

5 Sept. 07

# Novokuznetsk-Moscow Express

Benny was standing next to the entrance of his building (he then lived on 101st Street and Amsterdam Avenue) on a very nice December day, dressed in a stylish, early spring or autumn season light brown coat, red scarf and black beret; garment bag in one hand, saxophone in the other.

I kinda got used to calling him Benny, but to the rest of the world he was known as Benny Golson—genius composer, arranger and tenor saxophonist of jazz, legend in his own lifetime.

He looked happy and obviously felt just as good, because he was smiling his wide warm smile in anticipation of the trip we were just about to take.

"Benny, we arrive in Moscow tomorrow. Then in the evening of the same day we will fly to Novosibirsk. I hope you haven't forgotten that it's in Siberia. No piece of your very stylish clothing will stand a chance against the cold so common for that part of the world. You need to take with you a warmer headdress and a scarf at least."

"Don't worry Valery, I will be fine. A friend of mine was in Moscow a couple of years ago also in the winter. He said it wasn't bad at all."

"Benny, Russia is an enormous country. It covers eleven time zones. The climate varies from subtropical to Eternal Freeze. It's another five-hour flight to the location of our first concert. It could be -30°C there. It is southern Siberia, but it's still Siberia."

"Valery, I'll be fine."

To me it was obvious that Benny had no idea of where he was going. Well, the car was waiting, the stretch of time before the flight was shrinking. I decided that if things got bad I would give Benny my fur hat, which was packed together with a winter scarf in my suitcase, and would wrap the scarf around my head. We would survive.

Off we went.

Weather in Moscow was not very typical for that time of year—the temperature was above the freezing mark, slush everywhere, overcast. Most of the day we spent at my childhood buddy Kleinot's house, who lived then on the way to the Sheremet'evo II International airport. Vitaly and his wife Marina gave us a royal reception. Marina outdid herself cooking up a storm of all sorts of courses. Kleinot, like a happy child, sang "Moanin" and clapped his hands over his ears, filling in the rhythm section part. Then he played for us a thirty something year old recording of young Vitally Kleinot playing tenor saxophone ala Sonny Rollins. Benny was telling us a story of recording his beautiful tunes and a story of him helping Bobbie Timmons to write "Moanin.'"

That part definitely sounded different from what I have heard from Art Blakey. According to the leader of the Messengers, when they were short of a tune to complete the recording, Bobby Timmons went to toilet and came out with "Moanin,'" which became one of the greatest hits in the whole history of jazz. I loved that version and thought it was funny and spontaneous. Benny, on the contrary, sounded like he was pulling the blanket over his side a little. Any way you look at it, the history is always interpreted by the history teller.

I definitely preferred Kleinot's kitchen for several hours to a hotel room or a restaurant table. Our cordial hosts were in seventh heaven from delight of having me and Benny Golson over their house. Kleinot's dog Patrick befriended Benny at first sight and made himself comfortable next to him. When Benny got up from the table, Patrick led the way to the bathroom, then made himself comfortable again when Benny came back and took his seat at the table. I thought that the great man of Jazz also felt himself very comfortable when Benny all of a sudden said:

"It feels like in a black folks' house in America. We too prefer to get together in the kitchen. It's warmer and more relaxed here."

Benny couldn't have paid a better compliment to my childhood buddy.

"Mr. Golson, Mr. Golson." Vitaly almost choked on the next shot of Chrystal vodka, the best vodka in Russia at the time. "Stay with us, don't go to any Siberia. We will give you the big room, you can do anything you want—practice, eat, drink anything you want. We will be your servants; you will be our family. Who needs to go to Siberia?"

At this moment, Benny probably realized what I knew already for awhile, that the latest shot in Kleinot's hand was one of very many which followed each other at regular intervals from the very beginning of the dinner.

"Oh, it's so nice of you, Vitaly, but Valery and I have to go to the airport and take the plane to Novosibirsk. I can't stay. We have to go to Novokuznetsk too and then to Saint Petersburg and only after that we will return to Moscow for a concert. I would love to stay longer, but music is first."

With that said, the dinner was over and everybody got up. At the last goodbyes Benny attempted to take Marina's hand in his and kiss it, but Patrick, with a nasty snarl and gnashing of teeth, jumped in the air. Thank god Benny's reaction was quick, otherwise the offending hand would've been off. Jesus! "What kind of loyalty is this?" I thought, but everybody else broke out laughing.

Yes, it was already time to go to Sheremet'evo I, domestic flights, and find the plane which would take us to the cold country. Today it's probably one of the most beautiful airports in the world, but then, in 1996, it was still a dirty barn, a pigsty, some kind of a marshalling yard, a monument to the Soviet Era which ended only six years before. Melted snow mixed with sawdust was everywhere inside the "terminal." Conveyor belts looked like shrunken prehistoric monsters clanging, jerking and shoving their loads with inborn hatred.

The country, which had sent man to space, didn't have funds to treat its own citizens like human beings. To live through tickets and the luggage checking process was an ordeal of its own. The lines didn't have any order to them. It was very difficult to determine who was cutting the line and who belonged to it. All sorts of discussions, arguments and even fights would erupt continuously between passengers, other passengers and/or airline clerks. Militiamen were always around, but never there when you really needed them. Almost always, regardless of the size of the luggage, the passenger had to cross the hall to stay in another disorderly line to pay for the "extra" weight. To Benny that whole scene must have looked like a surreal, nightmarish psychiatric ward.

The plane was no better either. It did look strong from the outside, but inside it was just as unfit for transporting the highest primates as the "terminal." Seat covers were all in gray-brownish stains; seats were fallen through, backseats loose. It was packed with bodies, bags, heavy cloth, suitcases, and stuffy air. Domestic flight! Five hours in it!

A man across the aisle volunteered to pack Benny's saxophone over his seat. I managed to squeeze my sheepskin coat and trumpet in the compartment over my head.

Buckle up, ready for takeoff.

Let's be optimistic.

I did bring on the plane good sandwiches for us, which I bought in the waiting room before the boarding; because to expect anything edible to be served during the flight was a little too optimistic.

Guess what? Food on the plane was good. Ha! How about that! Atmosphere on the plane was good too, that of camaraderie. Is it always like that when people are stuck, not for too long, in the same predicament?

Piece and quiet, sticky air, hot, somebody snoring in the back of the plane... "Buckle-up, we are descending in the Novosibirsk International Airport." Smooth landing, storm of applause.

Why do Russian air travelers always applaud after landing? Of course the tradition comes from the time before the automatic pilot, but it still feels strange. The pilot is not a singer or a clown. A plane is not a theatre or circus.

7:00 a.m., local time of the next day. When I came up to the exit my first thought was that of my luggage, where my winter headdress and scarf had been safely stored. It was 20° below zero Celsius! Not 30°, but 20° is not a joke either. Somehow we made it down the ice covered ladder. Benny was in shock.

"Valery, can you get me a fur hat when we get to town?"

"I'll do my best."

It was about 20 yards between the bottom of the ladder and the entrance to the "terminal"—a one-story, 20-square meter wooden structure. A small crowd of people was cheering arriving passengers. I've never seen Sergei Belichenko before, only spoke on the phone with him, but recognized him right away. There is certain look in the eyes of a person who came to meet you. If the welcoming committee is there, you always know it.

"Welcome Valery, welcome Mr.Golson."

"Sergei? Hi, we need to get Mr.Golson a fur hat."

"We'll think of something. How was the flight? Are you tired? Are you hungry? Now you are going to the hotel, so you can rest and sleep, dinner is at 1:00, rehearsal is at 3:00, concert is at 7:00. I am on drums, Novosibirsk musicians on bass and piano. All tickets are sold."

The 2,000 seat capacity Novosibirsk Philharmonic Hall was packed to the doors for "Tribute to Art Blakey:" Siberian musicians accompanying guest stars from America, Jazz Messengers Benny Golson and Valery Ponomarev—storm of applause.

We hit.

All of the tunes in the repertoire had been prepared at the rehearsal when Benny distributed the music to the rhythm section and on "Killer Joe," the Jazz Classic by Benny Golson, my mate in the front line personally played for the guys on the piano.

"Tiny Capers," our opener, sounded beautiful. A storm of applause followed without delay. Benny was about to announce the next tune and have me translate when I noticed a commotion in the back of the packed house.

A fight?

A fight in Russia can break out anywhere anytime. No, thank God. A couple of tall and very beautiful young ladies, one of them with a package in her hand, were making their way through the crowd towards the stage and making signs to wait.

Belichenko with a sly smile climbed from behind his drums and came up to me.

*In Novosibursk with Benny & the Girls*

"Val, please give me the microphone for a minute."

Sergei announced into the microphone as the two young ladies climbed the stairs leading up to the stage, "Dear audience, the City of Novosibirsk Welcoming Committee would like to present our guest from America, Mr. Benny Golson, with a souvenir from Novosibirsk. Dear ladies and gentlemen, let's together wish Mr. Golson never to have his ears frozen, and remember our City."

With those words, one of the girls took out of the bag a beautiful mink hat and gave it to stunned Benny.

"Oh my god! Thank you so very much." Benny came back to his senses pretty quick and tried the hat on.

Usually when a foreigner puts a Russian traditional fur hat on his or her head it shows right away. One can tell immediately that this stranger and the hat are from two different cultures. Not this time, the mink hat looked so very natural on Benny's head, as if he was used to wearing it all his life. A storm of applause and cheering shook the building. Even if we didn't continue playing after that, the concert would've been a complete success anyway.

After the sounds of the last encore and applause died out, Benny and I received more souvenirs. This time they were huge bottles of the best Siberian vodka wrapped in colorful gift paper. Yeah, Siberia may be very far from the Jazz Headquarters of the World, it may be a very cold place in the winter, but people's hearts were just as warm as they could be anywhere.

There was no reason to go back to the hotel, because in only a couple of hours Benny and I were scheduled to travel east by train for eight hours to the next closest city of Novokuznetsk for another concert. In the meantime we were invited to go to a café in the lobby where a whole bunch of excited guys were getting ready for a jam session in honor of the guests from America. A jam session in Siberia. Yeah.

Benny, myself, the welcoming committee, Belichenko and organizers of the concert were crowding around a table next to a huge window. From the frost on the glass and the trees and the ground outside I knew that the temperature must've dropt to 30° below. I was prepared to have my ears assaulted by uncountable choruses of Blues in F. What can you do?

A rather tall and slim guy with a babyish face came up to the piano. A short guy with a hooked nose and very closely set eyes was holding a trumpet. An alto-player of about the same height and a tenor-player, taller and older than the other horn players, lined up next to each other. The drummer and the bass player were in the back and I couldn't see them clearly. I turned to the two beautiful girls at the table, who were trying their English out on Benny.

"Sound of Voyage" startled me. How do these guys know "Voyage?" This is a new very hip tune by Kenny Barron, which just became popular among musicians in New York. Alto player took the first solo. What?

I turned to Benny. He was sitting motionless with his mouth open staring at the musicians. Then the trumpet player and the tenor player after him took chorus after chorus of beautiful lines over the intricate changes of the tune. The alto player sounded more on the Charlie Parker side. The trumpet player was more of a Freddie Hubbard disciple with very similar embouchure setting, which I always envied. The tenor player sounded exactly in the middle between Coltrane and Wayne Shorter. The kid on piano was playing with brilliant precision giving away several influences. How do you like that? We were half the world away from New York. It was already 30° below zero C and complete darkness outside, but the Siberian cats were swinging up the temperature inside to a white heat.

All the way to Novokuznetsk Benny and I were talking about Novosibirsk musicians and jazz as a very young but so strong and influential form of art. Benny liked the alto player more than the tenor player. I disagreed.

"Jazz will find its way anywhere." We both agreed on that.

"Don't take me wrong, Valery, all of the guys were great. What did the piano player say his name was?"

"Alexei Podymkin. He is 19 and a freshman in the local conservatory. Andrei Lobanov on trumpet, Vladimir Timofeyev on tenor. Sorry didn't get the alto-player's name. They were hoping we would sit in."

"Yeah, but then we would've missed the train."

Anatoly Berestov, the director of the Gelikon Jazz Club, The Venue in Novokuznetsk, was a very kind chubby man of about forty.

"I play piano too. I am not really on the same level of playing like you and Mr. Golson. But I hope you will be patient with me," Tolia told me at the rehearsal before the concert, and introduced us to the rest of the rhythm section. "Oleg Petriakov is from Novosibirsk, but Sergei Kushilkin, he plays drums, is from the Varkuta region. It's about nine hours north of here by train. Sergei goes back after the concert. He lives in a house which is built on permafrost."

I had heard of those. I even heard of the houses built on ice north of the Polar Circle Line. Yes, with the foundation dug deep into the Eternal Freeze. But to imagine a jazz musician living in the Eternal Freeze was too much even for me.

"Jazz will find its way anywhere." I told Benny and translated everything Tolia told me.

"We should start rehearsing. Concert starts at 7:00; all tickets sold," said the director of the club, and sat at the piano smiling at us an apologetic humble smile.

Yes, that was true, Anatoly was not falsely modest and told the truth about his level of playing, but he did know enough jazz standards and played them with a genuine feel for the blues, squeezing particles of a

271

blues scale everywhere he could with real emotion. How does that work for someone being so far in time and space from the cotton fields of the American south?

Benny and I just looked at each other. Musicologists, go ahead, explain this.

Packed house, excited people, storms of applause, journalists, TV cameras, beautiful welcoming committee—Sisyphus labors all over again.

Tolia was also a very generous and kind man. I had played at his club several times after that with several different guest artists. After each concert he would pay everybody in cash and throw a party. Benny's salary was "enormous" and mine "half enormous," measured by the limitations of funds available anywhere in Russia then and particularly in Siberia. Tolya never tried to cut corners or cheat. I even remember him giving more money to a vocal guest "star," who felt herself more of a star than the initial agreement outlined, and insolently demanded extra money. He gave it to the "star" wishing her to just have good memories of Siberia and the club.

After the concert, we had to take a train back to Novosibirsk, because our next engagement was in St. Petersburg and Novokuznetsk didn't have an airport big enough for a plane capable of flying for five and a half hours. Of course we could take train all the way to St. Petersburg, but that's a half-week journey.

The drummer was traveling with us westbound on the Novokuznetsk–Moscow train for a couple of hours before switching to the northbound train.

For two hours, Benny and I were showering him with questions.

"How do you function in the 60° below zero Celsius temperature?" "Where do you work?" "How do you deal with the never-ending darkness of winter?"

"Man adapts himself to anything, to any conditions. I teach music in local music school."

"Do you have cars?"

"Of course we have cars."

"What if it stalls in the middle of a night and there is no life anywhere in sight?"

"Very simple. Everybody has Vodka and salted pig's fat in the car. If, God forbid, something happens, like a flat tire or antifreeze turns into ice in the radiator, you drink a big shot of Vodka, eat a piece of pig's fat and walk till you reach an inhabited area. If you only knew how honored I am to have played with you!"

The Novokuznetsk-Moscow train slowed down.

"I have to get off here to change trains. Oh, thank you so very much, you are so generous, you really mean it?" He couldn't stop thanking us for our CDs, which we gave him and our wishes for a safe journey.

Six more hours to Novosibirsk. About four hours later, dawn lit up the sky. Benny left our compartment and went up to the window in the aisle. I stayed where I was for a while until Benny's counting aloud attracted my attention: "124, 125, 126 …….. 134, 135, 136…Valery, come, take a look at this." I joined him at the window. There was a freight train in the distance traveling east.

"I have never seen a train that long. 140, 141, 143… I counted 156 cars."

"In Russia, freight trains, for the most part, fit her expanses."

We both were ready to change means of transportation and say goodbye to the train when it stopped in Novosibirsk.

"Goodbye, train."

"Goodbye, train."

"Here they are, here they are." I heard and then saw a little crowd of happy people on the platform, which had come to meet us and take to the Airport.

"You are really lucky. There is a big warm-up in Novosibirsk area. The temperature is only 10° below freezing."

"You don't mind a little interview? We have to wait for three hours in the restaurant anyway before the plane."

Food was good. It's not that I was hungry. It was good home cooking.

Stories of my escape from USSR, of joining the Messengers. Benny's stories of helping to run the Messengers before the band's first worldwide success, recording future jazz classics, helping Bobbie Timmons write "Moanin" all followed one another until it was time to fly to the western edge of the world's once-richest and most powerful empire.

Benny wanted an aisle seat, so I ended up looking out the window for almost the duration of the flight.

Woods, rivers, woods, lakes, woods, lakes, woods, rivers, some clusters representing inhabited spots and then again woods, rivers, woods, lakes, lakes, woods, woods, rivers, clusters. All together for almost five and a half hours…

Russia! I couldn't take my eyes off Her.

David[3] Golostchokin, the Director of St. Petersburg Jazz Philharmonic Hall himself, and a couple of his assistants met us in Pulkovo International Airport.

"Valeraaaaaaaaaa… man, I haven't seen you for ages. Mister Golson! Welcome to St. Petersburg. Oh man! Can you believe it?!"

Hugs, handshaking, introductions.

"We are taking you to the Hotel Tavricheskaia. My wife is the manager there. It's one of the best in the city. It's located across the square from the Smolnyi Institution.

3        * All Russian first names have several variations denoting respect, care, familiarity etc.- David, Dod, Dodik.Valery, Valera, Valer, Valerka, etc.

Before the Revolution it was an exclusive school for young ladies from noble families. Tsar sponsored it. Get settled and come down to the lobby in an hour, we will take you to the meeting with the press, then a reception in your honor, then dinner, then a concert by our Jazz Philharmonic orchestra for you. Tomorrow—breakfast in the hotel, tour of the city, visit to Hermitage, lunch, rehearsal, snack, concert, supper, walk to the Moscow Train Station, ten minutes from the Philharmonic Hall. We have your schedule cut out for you, haven't we? All on the house."

My, oh my! Spacious quarters, shining parquet floors, expensive furniture, huge bed. Go St. Petersburg! Benny and I had identical suites.

One event on the very well cut-out schedule followed the other like on a conveyor belt, with Benny and me being center stage. Sisyphus labors, extended version.

"What do you think of Jazz in Russia?"

"What are your plans for the future?"

"What is the program going to be tomorrow?"

"Are you going to play at least something from the "Moanin'" record?"

"Do you know who is going to be in the rhythm section?"

"Did you have a chance to see our city yet?"

"I am a tour guide at the Hermitage, would you like to visit our museum?"

Next morning, after breakfast, Benny and I went back to our suites for a minute and then came down to the lobby where the Hermitage tour lady was already waiting for us.

"Hermitage, even after years of criminal waste and neglect during the first years of Soviet Era, is by far the largest museum in the World. It was open during the reign of Catherine the Great. Masterpieces by all major artists of the world had been continuously added ever since. Cezanne, Monet, El Greco, and Picasso were exhibited in Hermitage well before they became successful in their own countries. There are more priceless works of art here than in the Prado, Louvre and Metropolitan combined..."

Here comes the freight train. Her English was not bad, so there was no need for synchronized translation.

"At the beginning of World War II all of the exhibits were carefully wrapped and prepared for evacuation, but the city fell under siege when only third of the canvases was safely rolled out of St. Petersburg in special trains. The rest had been taken to the cellars beneath Hermitage, where it would have been safe from the Fascist Luftwaffe bombing raids.

"I will show you major works of every period. For that we would need to switch from floor to floor because, if a visitor spends only a minute in front of every exhibit in the museum, it would take 22 years of his or her life."

Walking from hall to hall and particularly climbing stairs up and down for two hours was good exercise. She was talking with expertise and deep knowledge of every period and every artist. But what particularly showed was how proud she was of the museum and her city.

"Now, before we finish I will take you to the painting by Rembrandt. Sometimes he used to insert jokes into his paintings."

We climbed the stairs for the last time, and entered a hall with a multitude of different size paintings all over the walls from floor to a very high ceiling. The tour lady walked to the left and pointed to a painting.

"It's called 'Young Lady Dreaming of a Male Member.'"

"Ah?"

"Yes, that's what it's called. You don't see it now, but if I show it to you, you won't be able to look at the painting and not to see the top of a penis."

Benny and I looked at the canvas this way and that way, but were not able to see anything more than a beautiful girl in a reclined position resting her head on a pillow. Yes, she did appear to be in a dreamlike state with her eyes gazing at a little cherubim flying in front of her, but that's it, nothing more. We turned to our tour guide.

"Want me to show it to you?" She said and smiled.

Benny hesitated for a moment and said yes. I looked at the girl one more time and also said yes.

Natasha circled the pillow with her baton and this time I clearly saw the "helmet." Jesus! No matter how many times I tried to look at the painting again and not to see the "helmet" I couldn't. It was dominating the frame loud and clear. I gave up.

It was time to leave the girl to her dreams and return to the Jazz Philharmonic Hall for lunch anyway, for rehearsal and the rest of the Sisyphean labors, extended version. We heartily thanked our Art Angel and took a taxi to the Jazz Headquarters of St. Petersburg.

After lunch, I had half an hour to find a foreign currency exchange joint and come back to the Hall to meet with Benny and the rhythm section guys for a rehearsal. So I put a hundred dollar bill in my pocket and went outside in pursuit of rubles.

"It's a short walk from here. Make a left after you exit the building and walk for a hundred meters or so. You will find the sign easily," Dod assured me.

Ok, let's go. Yeah, no problem, five minutes later the sign with an arrow to the left was in full view. So I made left into a yard and climbed over piles of snow to a door with a plaque saying "Foreign Currency Exchange" and a window under it. The line in front of it was only two people. One, an older woman, was actually at the window having some kind of discussion with the employee of the joint. The other one was a young lady. Good pair of legs in beat-up shoes was showing below the stem of a worn-out and shapeless coat. Even with the coat on I could tell she had a well-built behind.

"Enough already, how long can this drag on?" She said more to me, obviously looking for support than to the customer in front of us. "They are arguing for twenty minutes already." This time she fully turned to me. The features of her face were rather plain, but the sensuous and alluring smile made it look very attractive. I didn't have much time either, so we talked for a little while of how inconsiderate people could be and then switched to "Are you from St. Petersburg? What do you do?" etc.

Her name was Svetlana, she was from out of town, living with her relatives, was a student at a college majoring in advertising and organizing some kind of promotional events to support herself. And me, of course, a jazz trumpet player from New York, playing a concert the same night at the Jazz Philharmonic Hall.

"Oh, I know where that is. It's a couple of hundred meters to the right and up the street. I always wanted to go there."

At this moment, the old lady finished her business and hobbled off leaving the space in front of the window unoccupied.

"I will be quick." Sveta assured me, and stepped up. A minute later my new acquaintance cleared the way and stopped to wait for me. I made two steps to the window, put my hundred dollars into the sliding compartment and pushed it forward to the lady behind the glass window.

"Your passport please."

"What are you talking about?"

"These are the regulations. Every customer must produce a valid passport."

"What do you mean? It's only hundred dollars."

"It doesn't matter. You can't do the exchange without identification."

"I have never heard of it. Nobody asked me for identification before. Not in Moscow, not in Siberia."

"These are the regulations here. Next please." The lady said sternly from a position of power.

"Give it to me. I will exchange it for you. I have my passport." Whispered Sveta. I snuck the bill to her.

"No, I won't accept it. It's torn at the corner." Said the lady behind the glass and pushed the bill back.

"Listen, it's only a little scratch. I got it from a bank." I couldn't believe it.

"Ah, hell with her. Let's go, there is another exchange around the corner." Said Sveta impatiently and pulled me by the hand out of there.

"Everybody is the boss. Big deal, a scratch."

There was no problem at the other exchange at all, but I was already pressed for time. So Sveta walked me to the Philharmonic Hall.

"Your last name is Ponomarev?"

"How do you know?"

"It's right here on the poster. I am coming tonight." She stated confidently.

"Of course you are. I will put you on the guest list." I confirmed with an air of a "star" to whom worries of mere mortals were nothing at all.

"See you in the evening." Purred Sveta and walked resolutely away. Her agile body moved with dexterity. After a few paces she turned around with a ballerina-like jump, smiling the same alluring smile and waving her hand at me.

"Girls always know when you look at their behind." I thought, slightly embarrassed, walked three steps leading to the entrance of the Hall and pulled the massive door.

Rehearsal, snack, brightly lit and packed to the ceiling, in the back of the second level people could touch it, Jazz Philharmonic Hall, etc., etc., etc.

"No, can't call it Sisyphus labors any more." I was thinking before the concert. "That guy had to fill up the bucket with water, spill it, fill up the bucket again and so on without any deviation for an eternity."

"No Ponomarev," that was already my alter ego talking "you travel to beautiful and always different places, meeting different people, different musicians, different welcoming committees, playing and hearing different notes. No Ponomarev, in Jazz nobody plays the same solo twice. Even arrangements never sound exactly the same. Think of something else to call it."

For this concert, the executive director of the St. Petersburg Jazz Philharmonic Hall, Russian jazz legend, David Golostchokin, joined us. Dod was playing beautiful notes on piano, vibraphone, violin, saxophone and trumpet of all instruments. He learned to play jazz on all those instruments during the dark and gloomy "eternity" of the Soviet Era right behind the Iron Curtain.

Victor Epanishnikov was on drums. He put a couple of shots under the belt before the concert and played a little too noisy for my taste. Very good as usual, but banging some extra rolls.

"Val, how did I play? How would you evaluate my drumming?" inquired Victor when he, Dodik and I were standing backstage.

"Good."

"No, really."

"Good. You always play good."

"Come on Val, drop that good manners shit. Tell me, how did I play?"

"Enough already, leave him alone." Dodik interfered—"Val played with Art Blakey!"

All three of us broke out laughing.

There was a very nasty scuffle during the second set. A famous Russian movie director, with his entourage and cameras, pushed through the crowd close to the stage. They made so much noise that we had to stop playing. It didn't bother any of the crew that shooting was strictly prohibited.

"You should be thankful to me for coming here. You idiots. You stupid people." The movie director kept on screaming as the plain clothed militiamen and some volunteers from the audience were kicking him and his crew out into the street.

Forgot his name, he was more famous for his scandalous character than his movies anyway.

Benny brought his garment bag with him but my luggage remained in the hotel. I was going to pick it up after the concert and bring to the Hall before supper, so I wouldn't need to worry about it and could hang till it was time to go to the train station. As soon as I left Dod's office and came down the stairs, Sveta came up.

"Oh Val, you play so good. Everybody loved your playing. You translated everything Mr. Golson said. You speak English that well."

"I've lived in America already for 23 years."

"I liked the concert so much. How does it feel to be on the stage, in the stage lights, when everybody is looking at you, applauding?"

"It feels fantastic. Listen, I need to run to the hotel for a minute to pick up my luggage and come back here to have supper and then go to the station. Will you wait? You can go to the supper with me."

"No I can't, I will miss the last bus. Where is your hotel?"

"Across from the Winter Palace. I am taking a taxi."

"I'll go with you. I will help you to pack. The bus is not far from there either. Where are you going from here?"

"Moscow. We have one more concert tomorrow. The day after tomorrow Mr. Golson returns to the States, but I will stay in Moscow for a few days and then fly to New York too."

"Where are you staying in Moscow?"

"A friend of mine gave me his apartment for four days."

"I will come to see you in Moscow."

To sneak Sveta in the hotel was no problem.

"What a beautiful suite! I can live like this."

We kissed in front of the bed and then Sveta sat down and I remained standing.

What followed would've been labeled by some Communist Party advocate in the old Soviet Union as an immoral, antisocial, degrading act well below the dignity of a Soviet Citizen. But I can only compare it with an impatience of a dominant chord to resolve into tonic. The pull is so strong that one can not leave it unresolved. They say that Rimsky-Korsakov once was at a rehearsal, where a conductor stopped the orchestra on a dominant chord. Rimsky couldn't stand the tension of the unresolved chord in his ears and ran outside, grabbed a coach and drove home. There he ran up to the piano and slammed the notes of the tonic. Only then he could think of anything else.

Yeah, yeah, old Soviet Union, to transport people in a pigsty "terminal" is fine, but a dominant chord is below the dignity. What a moral standard!

"Valerochka, I have to run. See you in Moscow."

Everybody from the lunch party went with us to the Moscow Station to see us off and wish us a happy journey. Somebody was rolling my luggage and Benny's garment bag. A few people tried to take my trumpet out of my hand and carry it for me, but I couldn't allow it. Trumpet is sacred; I always carry it myself.

The train was beautiful. They say it was a replica of the last Czar's train. Every car was spanking shining new. The conductors for every car were all little cute girls of about 19 or 20, all in a semi-military railroad winter uniform; the summer uniforms are cute jackets and short skirts. When they were all standing on the last step of each car and waiving their signal flags before the last whistle, the train looked fantastic. Our compartment was gorgeous—very spacious, plush seats, expensive drapery, two convertible chairs. I thought I would sleep my heart out till the next morning in such a beautiful compartment, but Benny kept on talking and we ended up rapping all the way to Moscow, all eight hours of it. Well, not bad hanging with a living legend.

The trip from the western capital of St. Petersburg (St. Petersburg was the capital of Russia for over two centuries before the capital was moved back east to Moscow. Strategic move. Russians very often refer to Moscow and St. Petersburg as the two capitals.) to the eastern capital of Moscow was coming to an end.

The train slowly pulled in the station and was coming to a complete stop when I noticed that another train, tired and slow, emitting its last breath but still big and confident, pulled in on the other track coming from the opposite direction —from the east. "Benny, Benny!" I heard myself screaming, "Come, take a look at this. Do you know what's written on top of that train on the opposite track? It's the Novokuznetsk–Moscow train, the one we took to go from Novokuznetsk to Novosibirsk, to take the plane to St. Petersburg. Remember? It just arrived."

Hotel, shower, sandwiches, rehearsal, cameras, interviews, lunch, concert, applause, encores, hang, hotel.

The next day I had to go with Benny to Sheremet'evo II and help him to go through all the formalities of checking in and departing. Yeah, then it was unsafe for a foreigner to travel in Moscow by himself.

When I got back to New York, the first call came from Benny.

"Val, when do you go back to Russia?"

"Three months from now. Right before we play Tribute to Art in Paris. Actually I will be flying to Paris from Moscow. Why?"

"Bobby (Benny's wife) took my hat. That's it, she won't give it back. Can you please bring me another one just like that?"

"Sure, no problem."

"How about that train? 156 cars. Can't forget it."

Three months later I was in the dressing room of Petit Opportune, the club in Paris, and distributing Russian souvenirs before the concert. Curtis Fuller, Carl Allen, Buster Williams, Molgrew Miller, everybody got a can of red caviar and a matr'oshka. Only Benny got neither caviar nor matr'oshka, but he got a black mink hat. Boy! Wasn't he happy?

Packed house, applause, encore…

06/25/07

# BAND BUS

I am a lucky guy. Again I am working with a great band. This time it's a legendary big band which made its mark in the history and development of Jazz, and I am going on a five-hour trip to X.............. City in the state of X........ for a concert.

For the most part, New York musicians are very punctual—by 10:00 AM, time of departure, everybody who didn't travel on his own had presented himself; garment bag in one hand, instrument in the other.

"Hi Jim, hi Mike, hi Mat, hi Clint, hi Glenn, hi Phyllis, hi Arturo, hi Rick, hi Kevin, hi Yoshi, hi Todd, hi Grant, hi Joseph, hi Kristen, hi Jerome, hi Sam..."

"I will be right back, just grabbing a sandwich." "Came back late after the gig last night; didn't sleep much at all." "Have you heard this? It sounds incredible."

These are the archetypal phrases ringing in the air while New York's best socialize and crowd around before committing themselves to the confines of a tour bus, rented by a promoter of the concert.

"Hi Val, who are you subbing for?"

"I am not subbing for anybody; I am steady now."

"Oh, cool, welcome, congratulations."

"Hi Val, I just got back from Russia. We've been to five different cities, a day in each. Girls are beautiful everywhere. I hooked up with one in Krasnodar. Man, she is beautiful. She says she loves me and wants to join me in the US."

"Pete, do yourself a favor, don't believe a word she says."

"Yeah, you are right. I had heard stories already." The charmed-dreamer smile on his face turned right away into a grim mask of cold reality. I knew he hated me for a sec.

"Val, I was in Russia a year ago too. Man, as soon as I said that I play with you they started pouring vodka and toasting." That was Jim, fantastic trumpet player and the main soloist in the band; my mate in the section.

Like most of the passengers on the bus I made myself comfortable in a big seat, put headphones over my ears and turned on my iPod.

"No, no, not the Messengers, you need something with sustained chords in the string section. You can't even eat when Art Blakey is playing, how do you intend to sleep?"

That was my alter ego lecturing.

"When you right, you are right." I never leave my alter ego's lecturing unanswered.

In an hour or so I woke up. The initial couple of pieces played themselves out and now the headphones were no longer delivering sound, but working as earplugs. So I turned the iPod off and took them out of my ears.

"Cool ride."

"Yeah, I am in total agreement." Our big tourist bus was smoothly gliding along the Interstate # whatever. My alter ego decided to leave me alone.

"Hey Val, What do you think of President Putin?"

"I don't really follow Russian politics. I only keep hearing from my American friends that things are getting tough. Can't be worse than Bush, that I am sure of."

"Don't I agree with that!" Several voices eagerly joined in.

"What's with Russia now anyway? Everybody is going to Russia to play?"

Oh boy, I was center stage and my favorite subject was on.

"I had been saying this for a very long time, that once the Iron Curtain falls, Russia will produce a lot of great players and then the Jazz Headquarters of the World itself will move to Moscow, to Russia anyway." Once I got on the subject, it was hard to get off it. Several inquisitive pairs of eyes turned to me and waited for an explanation.

"It has moved already several times—from New Orleans to Chicago, from Chicago to the West Coast, from the West Coast to New York, now its time to move again." I stood my ground.

"Why are you saying, that it's time to move again?"

"Don't you see how stagnant the scene is? Regular fans complain that in every festival, every major club there are the same tired individuals featured. All these businesspeople in the 'Jazz Industry:' agents, critics, club-owners, big recording companies, had done their dirty work."

"If not for the small labels, Jazz wouldn't be even recorded anymore."

"Or small clubs, away from big venues."

"Look what this big company came up with."

"Jesus! What a creation!"

"Haven't heard uglier nonsense than that, no swing, no melody, nothing."

"And they keep pushing and pushing it."

"It's like a conspiracy against Jazz."

"Revenge of the nerds, that's what it is."

"They always stick themselves into everything to make money and end up ruining whatever they touch."

"Just like cancer metastasis. That's what they are."

"There are only a couple of organizations which work for the interest of musicians and music, the rest of them is 'making money.'"

Everybody was talking at once.

"It's the same in all forms of art."

"And sports too."

Hockey, soccer, cheating in the Olympics...

"Yeah, as soon as commercial interest gets involved the talent is out. Remember that Russian female tennis star?"

"Oh man, she is beautiful" A Unison of several voices declared.

"Not playing tennis at all, only poses for pictures on her all fours; with ass in the air."

"Man, I wouldn't be surprised if she shows up in a hard porn in a couple of years." "If they come up with enough money, she will."

"You dreaming"

"I want to see that." A multi-voiced chorus thundered in perfect unison.

"I tell you who they are. They are the same people who were at the bottom of every class in music and art school. They didn't have talent enough to play a C scale clearly, but they are moving the 'Industry' now."

"Yeah, running clubs, writing reviews, deciding who to hire, who to fire, who to promote, telling a musician what to play. How could this 'Mover of the Industry' make a right decision if he is tone deaf and a boring personality to begin with? Of course he will promote a guy with the same boring no-talent features. Or, if the guy wants to play good notes, wants to be original, wants to have fun, wants the audience to have fun along with him—no, no, no, the 'Industry' can't allow it and will coach this out of line upstart how to behave."

"Yeah, and ultimately it will cripple him, musically speaking."

"Yeah, remember that guy, remember this guy? Remember how great he was when he started. Look what he turned into – stiff, pretentious, boring and with an attitude."

"Man, I saw in Downbeat a review of a totally mediocre pretentious effort rated at 5 stars out of 5. Right next to it is a CD packed with great arrangements of standards and originals, fantastic playing by all the guys– 3 and a half stars. Man, that's too much."

"What do you expect from a critic, he is not a musician."

"I know he is not a musician most of them can't tell the difference between F and B. That's why he dropped out of music school and became a critic. He just can't make any sense."

"But what right does he have to promote his favorites and put down real talents?"

"All right then. Let's organize our own Industry - United Jazz Artists."

"Yeah, right. I don't have time to write reviews. I hardly have time to practice my instrument."

"That's right. That's where the sleazy snake crawls in. Remember the story of a sleazy snake and a blind rabbit?"

"Man, I told you, its revenge of the nerds. He has to get even with those who were at the top of the class. Maybe on a subconscious level, but that's what it is."

"You know what? It was the same in Russia. There was a 'critic' there, Boltashov (boltat, in this context means blabbermouth) his name was. At the very outset of his career he tried to play Mack The Knife on tenor, had a long and painful struggle with the first three notes of the melody and decided to do something else. So he became a critic, a big jazz personality, 'Soviet Jazz Historian,' and a talent agent. Man, he used to promote junk, you wouldn't believe. And if a guy would try to play a good note, he would hate him."

"Why are you saying that the Jazz Headquarters of The World will move to Russia then?"

"Well, that Boltashov guy used to be the Ultimate Jazz Authority during the Soviet years. They even say he was a KGB informant."

"He is out of business now, right?"

"Totally, just like the agency. Nobody wants to have business with him. His last effort was to cheat a couple of American musicians."

"So you think that Jazz in Russia has a chance to establish itself before the metastasis spreads there too."

"Something has to happen. There is too much talent there. Russia was always rich in natural resources, treasures. Human resources are also treasure."

"Man, girls are beautiful in Russia."

"It's some kind of ecological phenomenon. Everywhere you turn, there is a beautiful girl there."

"You sure you are not just horny away from home and every stump looks like a beauty to you?"

"You haven't played in Russia yet."

"No, I haven't."

"Wait until you get there. I want to hear what you say when you come back."

"Who knows, maybe you are not joking after all. Over here if it's a new star, he is always stiff and boring. Amen. How many real stars are left there and for how much longer will they be representing real jazz and true manners on the bandstand?"

"No wonder that people who judge jazz by today's stars think it's boring."

"Talent agents themselves think jazz is boring and hard to book. Can you imagine! I was in this talent jazz agent's office. With a countenance of scorn she proudly told me that she doesn't listen to jazz, and has classical music on in the background. I don't think she liked or understood any of it either, but she thought it was 'classy.'"

"I wish she told that to Art Blakey or Louis Armstrong. You know how many times I heard from fans after a gig "I didn't know jazz was so beautiful. I thought it was boring."

If you ask why they say that, you always hear the same thing in response: "I saw this or that." And a couple of names of the 'Industry's favorites' will follow. But then they'll say: "I am a Jazz fan now. Oh, please tell me where to find it."

Most of the time several people were saying, in total unison, exactly the same phrases. Then, out of respect to the next guy, they'd drop out one by one until it was only one voice left talking and the rest would be just nodding their heads in support.

"That bitch had the nerve to call the club where I had been booked to play for the New Year's celebration, and insist that the club owner hire an artist in her roster instead, on the grounds that her boring, no talent, mediocrity is better known. Now how do you like that? She and the talent agency and the big company behind them had been pushing this no good boring individual denying me the time of day and now she has the nerve to call the club, where I am already booked and insist that the owner engage the puke of their own because it's better known."

"...and you lost the gig?"

"No, the club-owner refused to make changes in the program because the puke had already played at the club and bitterly disappointed the audience."

"So, wait a second. Now you saying that there are 'Movers of Industry' who are capable of standing up for the musicians and the music."

"Yeah, sure, there are talent agents and critics and producers who truly love and understand Jazz, but how many of them are there, every second, every tenth? They are the 10%, the rest of them are sleazy snakes. And not only club owners; agents are telling musicians who to hire, who to fire. They are reigning supreme now."

"Art used to rebuff anybody who would try to tell him who to hire with "don't tell me who should play in my band."

"That was Art Blakey! How do you expect this boring generation to tell the talent agent, without whom he can't even sit in at a student jam session without looking stupid, 'Don't tell me who should play in my band,' ah?"

"Yeah, that's what happens; masters of PR for the company and the talent agency will make any nonsense look good for the event. They will use their PR techniques to convince potential customers that this or that 'Star' of theirs is a marvel, a God of Modern Jazz and that you miserable paying customers need to drop everything and run to see the 'second coming'. Don't you dare to admit that you didn't like what you saw. They don't even say 'heard,' they say 'saw.'"

"That's cheating, brainwashing; disrespecting the audience."

"Art Blakey used to say: "Don't disrespect the audience. One can't get away with it for too long."

"Yeah, after all this hype, audiences pay their money for immature junk on the band stand."

"Yeah, yeah, yeah, there is another slogan the 'movers' used to employ: 'Come listen to them now, they are the stars of tomorrow.'"

"That's a paraphrased Art Blakey's saying the Industry thought it could use. Art was talking about the Messengers, who without exception became stars and/or great players. The Industry is talking about artificially made-up names. That's a big difference. Who in their right mind would pay money to hear some guy who might learn to play in the future? Guess where those would-be stars are now? Even the talent agents who pushed them don't remember their names any more."

"Man, I saw a caricature in the Village Voice, man, I couldn't stop laughing. There were three old nuns with mandolins on the band-stand, looking more like three old church mice than glamorous beauties, obviously singing some old tired Church Hymns. Huge house was totally packed. On the front ground two people, misled by PR work for the concert, talking: "How could I not have known they were so good and famous?"

"Well, it's their work to research the market and come up with the right product."

"Oh, yeah, to come up with market research puke."

"They stick anybody they want to in concerts with real musicians, they make stars out of boring individuals, they …"

"You had said that already enough times."

"Man, did you hear this? They put a rock drummer into a major jazz artist's group for a gig at a major jazz club!!!"

"No…" in several voices.

"Man, I was there. Guess what happened?"

"I was there too."

"I missed it."

"I didn't want to go."

"What do you think had happened?"

"I know."

"Man, it was terrible. There was nothing to listen to. It was so boring and artificial. Maybe the old man didn't have it to say 'no' anymore, or, maybe he thought that close encounter with the younger kind would rejuvenate his creative vital organs. It was horrible."

"Were there any people?"

"Oh, man, it was packed to the doors at the beginning of every night, by the end a lot of people were leaving in disgust."

"So the Industry Movers did good, packed a jazz club for a week."

"Oh yeah? All those people, who were not very familiar with Jazz will be saying this new classic: "I don't like jazz. Jazz is boring. Jazz is not commercial. If that was one of the Jazz's greatest people, I don't want to spend my time and money on it. I'd rather go to karaoke bar and sing myself."

"You are not joking either, I hear this karaoke statement all the time. Yeah, the Industry Movers did make money for themselves, but look what they did for jazz. The more people they drive into clubs, the more people will be saying I saw jazz already, I want to see something else now."

"Have you ever heard of Willis Conover?"

"I think I have heard of him. He was a radio announcer or something?" Only one tentative voice responded to my question.

"That's incredible! He had done for Jazz as much as Louis Armstrong, Duke Ellington, Count Basie, Charlie Parker, Art Blakey...anybody."

"Oh yeah, yeah, yeah, I think I've heard of him. He was Jazz disc jockey in the fifties, right?"

"Check this out. He was a radio host at the Voice of America jazz program from the mid fifties through the end of his life (October 18, 1920 – May 17, 1996). The reason he is not known in the United States is that the program was broadcast by a government agency, and by some kind of law it couldn't be transmitted to the U.S., only to foreign countries; particularly to the countries behind the Iron Curtain. Millions of people in East Germany, Czechoslovakia, Poland, Bulgaria, you name it, in the Soviet Union were glued to the radio at the time of the program with the risk of being reported by neighbors to the authorities for having a 'capitalist U.S.A. radio' on. Western influence, you know. If not for that Voice of America Jazz Hour, that was the name of the program, half the world would've never known Louis Armstrong, Charlie Parker, Coltrane, The Messengers, Horace Silver, Jazztet, Duke Ellington, Ella Fitzgerald etc, etc, etc....Guess what? Listen to this. Here I am, in Washington in 1996 playing at the Willis Conover Memorial Concert. Most of the participants were stars from foreign countries, the ones who grew up on Willis' Jazz Hour together with jazz stars like Billy Taylor, Charley Bird. There was one guy in the program, who not only didn't command his instrument very well, but wasn't even a jazz musician. I asked Maria Ciliberti, a long-time colleague of Willis, what was that guy doing here.

"Well, he's playing with a group, I call them Lounge Lizards, which is a favorite of one of the talent agents for the Tribute To Willis."

"How is that possible? A tribute to Willis Conover and the guy doesn't even play jazz, but trying to play some rock?" I couldn't believe it. Listen to what she told me.

"Oh, Valery, if you only knew how hard it was for Willis all this years. They were attacking him from all sides: some using influences, some threatening to close the program. When I came back from the Soviet Union in the early 1960's and told people how popular Willis's JAZZ HOUR was over there, I found out from Willis that at that time, the bigwigs were talking about taking his program off the air with the excuse that it wasn't the VOA's job to "entertain" the listeners. Over the years, they would say to him: don't play this, don't play that, why are you playing this, play this one or that one. He never wavered. Willis used to call them the "bureaucraps". One reason these government bureaucraps opposed him is that no one could take credit for creating him or the program. Thankfully, Willis always had the support of the U.S. Information Agency directors all through the years as well as help on Capitol Hill. That's what kept the program alive, that as well as the fact that foreign service officers knew of the amazing popularity of Willis's programs overseas. And he was on contract and not a staff employee. Only a couple of years before he died they left him alone." I was in shock. 'Don't tell me who should play in my band' kept pulsating in my head.

Can you believe this - if not for Willis Conover all these boring protégés would have flooded the airwaves and I would've never heard Clifford Brown, Art Blakey, I would've never become a Jazz musician. Half the world wouldn't have a clue as per what real jazz was, would've been saying 'I don't like Jazz.' I am not the only one to tell you how much people around the world loved America and its spirit in those years. And that's largely because of Jazz. Want to hear the end of the story?

The Tribute had been transmitted on radio and TV stations all over the world, everywhere, except United States."

"Wow."

"How do you like that?"

"Jee . . .s."

"I am telling you, it's not only Jazz music, anywhere you turn – it's the same thing again. Why do you think we have a war in Iraq? It's commercial interest again. If not for their oil we would've never gone there."

"How many lives lost to rob somebody of his possessions?"

"Our government is trying to convince me that we went there to establish a Democracy. A three-thousand year old museum destroyed by the 'conquerors.' Three thousand year, or even older, manuscripts thrown in the streets. What a Democracy!"

"That's right. Why didn't we, or any of the 'Free' World, go to Africa in the Lake Victoria region and help to restore peace and establish Democracy there when two neighboring tribes, the Tutsis was one and Hutus was the other, were slaughtering each other and throwing thousands of dead bodies into the lake. Now the largest fresh water reservoir in the world is contaminated beyond any use for 200 years."

The bus was no longer gliding along a five lane super highway, but slowly crawling through the streets of the City of Z and came to a stop. Everybody got up and reached for the above-the-head compartments to retrieve their instruments and possessions.

"Have you heard that the aliens rule United States?"

"Yeah, World Government."

"They say there is a picture on the Internet of high rises on Mars."

"Yeah, yeah, with wise men of Zion on the roof, on Mars."

The doors of the bus opened and New York's best started to leave one by one.

"To Hell with all this. Let's go play music."

07/13/ 07

# Barbarians

There is a book of psalms exhibited at the little museum on the first floor of Notre Dame of Paris, safely covered by a glass enclosure. No one can touch it and the temperature inside the enclosure is kept at a certain level so the pages will never be harmed by too much heat or cold. Crowds of tourists marvel at the beautifully illustrated antique treasure. Music is written on five line staves just like musicians use today, but stems, bar lines and lengths of notes were not invented yet.

I could never imagine that the art of printing was invented before the art of notating music. Every capital letter is intricately designed in different colors. Together with the rest of the letters, the staves and little cubes (forerunners of today's notes), the spread of the book looked like one complete picture—a masterpiece indeed.

A couple of times I had seen similar books in Italian churches. Once I played a concert in front of a church in an Italian village. The occasion was an unveiling of a renaissance painting, returned to the village after restoration. Big crowds of tourists were hanging out in front of the improvised stage and gazing at the work of genius, which was affixed right above it. Backstage, where I was warming up for the concert, stood an old bookcase. On its shelves, to my great surprise, I found three books very similar to the one I had seen in Paris. Sometimes tourists were walking through, but for the most part I was there one-on-one with the bookcase and kept on warming up until the priest, who organized the concert, came by to start the event and explained to me that they were very old volumes. They had been passed on from generation to generation of parishioners, who still use them in the Church.

The next week, after returning to the States, I went to an antique show in Madison Square Garden. Instead of wrestling, boxing or basketball, this time all the space was occupied by dealers from different stores exhibiting and selling their goods, a whole ocean of antique furniture, paintings, jewelry, clothes. But the atmosphere there was not like the one in a museum, it was rather of a scrap-heap, dump of very expensive items, but still a dump (one enormous storage space). After walking around for at least a couple of hours the exhibition started to seem more like one shapeless mass of figures, forms and prices constantly quoted around me.

All of a sudden, I stood frozen, unable to move. The word "barbarians" stopped me. It was repeated by a man sitting on a chair with a razor in his hand. He was cutting a page out of a sacred book of psalms, just like the one I had seen only a couple of weeks ago. I couldn't move, as if I were in a nightmare. The man looked up at me apologetically. "You see," he said, "there is no reason to buy the whole book, because a lot of pages had been already cut out." That didn't help much. I was still in a stupor with my eyes glued to the mutilated treasure. The man got up, pushed something into the hands of a lady, dressed all in black, and walked away repeating: "We are barbarians, we are barbarians."

The lady turned to me saying, "It's five dollars a page." Then she added, "You see, I could never make as much money by selling it as the whole piece to one of the New York museums. This way—five dollars a page—I make much more." With a crooked smile, she tried to cover the expression of inborn greed on her face. God! She looked so ugly.

"For the front page it's ten," she added. She said something else and something else, but I only remember her saying into my back as I was walking away, "Come back tomorrow if you don't have money on you." I kept walking and thinking of how ugly she was and that black dress of hers. Nobody forced her to put on that garment; she herself put it on this morning because it reflected her morose soul. She didn't even know why she chose the executioner's colors. She stole the book, while being on a "hunting trip" in Europe most likely. None of the museums would ever offer her any money for a stolen volume of psalms. She was lying. She knew in the morning of that day that she would have the treasure cut in pieces and get five dollars for each one of them. What did it matter that the treasure belonged for a long, long time to parishioners of some church in a distant village in Europe. Money, money, that's what mattered. And that smile of hers, that's probably how human excrement would look if you spray it with some cheap cologne. I could so easily imagine this dealer in her black dress passing through a church in any Italian village, putting the books into a handbag and just walking away.

I left the Garden with a feeling of disgust right after I walked away from the executioner's stand. But before I had walked away, I sat down on the chair. Just like the man before me, with my own hands, I cut four pages out of the book—the best I could find in the crippled volume.

The pages are "safe" now, framed on the wall of my apartment.

07/14/07

# ACKNOWLEDGMENTS

My deepest appreciation for years and years of inspiration, musical and personal support goes to Maria Ciliberti (also for contributing to the Band Bus story), James & Rosalind Crombie (also for years of producing my concerts and doing the most brilliant proofreading job on the book), Chris Davey (also for doing a fantastic job on illustrations), Mark & Keila Feldman (also for years and years of producing my albums, sharing with me their unique experience in jazz and deep knowledge of business called "music"), Clint Glenn (also for financial support of the project, introducing me to the publisher, years of producing my concerts and spiritual guidance), Reggie Marshall (also for being the most professional music agent. His insistent encouragement, bordering on forcing, made me finally realize that I needed to start writing the book; his reading the work in progress, sometimes ad infinitum, and always offering valuable suggestions), Marie & Ron Mogul (also for never missing a single gig of mine when they are in the city), Steve Robinson (also for generously providing decisive help at my most desperate hour), Peter Rubie (also for most generous professional advice), Kristen Sergeant (also for doing fantastic job on proofreading the stories), all of my students and everybody who had ever asked me: "Is the book out yet? When is the book going to be out?" or said, "It's an incredible story. There should be a book about it. There should be a movie after it."

I've been very lucky to have friends like these. Few people can claim that luxury.

Russian proverb clearly says: "It's better to have a hundred friends than a hundred rubles."

Valery Ponomarev

11, 05, 08

Breinigsville, PA USA
14 July 2010
241740BV00001B/1/P